Case Closed

Case Closed

HOLOCAUST SURVIVORS IN POSTWAR AMERICA

BETH B. COHEN

Rutgers University Press
New Brunswick, New Jersey, and London
Published in association with the United States
Holocaust Memorial Museum

Library of Congress Cataloging-in-Publication Data

Cohen, Beth B., 1950–
   Case closed: Holocaust survivors in postwar America / Beth B. Cohen.
   p.   cm.
   Includes bibliographical references and index.
   ISBN-13: 978-0-8135-3953-9 (hardcover : alk. paper)
   1. Jews—United States—History—20th century. 2. Holocaust survivors—United
States—History—20th century. 3. Jews, European—United States—History—20th
century. 4. Refugees, Jewish—United States—History—20th century.
5. Immigrants—United States—History—20th century. I. Title.
   E184.355.C63 2007
   304.8'73008992404—dc22

                           2006011618

A British Cataloging-in-Publication record for this book is available from the British
Library.

The assertions, arguments, and conclusions contained herein are those of the author or
other contributors. They do not necessarily reflect the opinions of the United States
Holocaust Memorial Museum.

Manufactured in the United States of America

To Steve

CONTENTS

ILLUSTRATIONS

ACKNOWLEDGMENTS

It is my great pleasure to express my gratitude to the many who helped bring this project to fruition. I could not have completed this work without their assistance.

This book is about Holocaust survivors who came to the United States after 1946. My dear friends Heinz Sandelowski, *z"l* (of blessed memory), and his wife, Amalie, were two of them. They opened their home and their hearts to me. Hearing from Heinz of his early years in this country provoked me to look at the postwar era with new eyes. To them, and to each and every one who spoke with me about their first years here, I am deeply indebted. I am grateful, too, to those I never met but came to know in the archives and whose stories give life to this study.

I wish to express my enormous appreciation to Debórah Dwork: scholar, mentor, and teacher. It was she who started me on this intellectual path and it was a true privilege to be one of her first graduate students in Holocaust history at Clark University. Her attentive, enthusiastic, and expert guidance never wavered throughout our journey together. I applaud Clark University for its vision, which led to the establishment of the first PhD program in Holocaust history in the United States. To my teacher Shelly Tenenbaum, I extend my heartfelt thanks. Her expertise, generously given, and insistence on the importance of American Jewish history to my project added immeasurably to my analysis. I was lucky, indeed, to have the company, encouragement, and enduring friendship of two other graduate students while at Clark: Christine van der Zanden and Beth Lilach.

I thank many scholars of both Holocaust studies and American Jewish history, including Yehuda Bauer, Michael Berenbaum, Hana Jablonka, and Jonathan Sarna, who have encouraged me with their interest in my study. My research has been enriched because of their scholarship. I especially thank Lawrence Langer, whose work profoundly informed my own.

I am privileged that the United States Holocaust Memorial Museum awarded me a fellowship that supported my postdoctoral research. This book was made possible through a Life Reborn Fellowship for the Study of Displaced Persons at the Center for Advanced Holocaust Studies (CAHS), United States Holocaust Memorial Museum. I am grateful to Paul Shapiro, director of the CAHS, for his interest and for the atmosphere of intellectual support and exchange that the center fosters. Lisa Yavnai, director of the Visiting Scholar Programs, welcomed me warmly to the CAHS. Lisa Zaid, program assistant, was always eager to be of help. The many stimulating conversations with other visiting fellows and the CAHS staff, including Avinoam Patt, Hagit Lavsky, John Roth, Martin Dean, Aleisa Fishman, and Ann Millin, pushed me to challenge my ideas and assumptions. Martin Goldman, director of Survivor Affairs, aided me enormously. Through his introduction at the museum, I was fortunate to meet many survivors who generously agreed to speak with me.

The list of individuals who graciously participated in interviews includes Hiller Bell, Dr. Robert Berger, Martha C., Edie Druyan, Simona Frajndlich, Bluma Goldberg, Alma Goldman, Rabbi Baruch Goldstein, Morris Indik, Paul Krell, Liza Levy, Naftali Lis, Marion Nachman, Sidi and Sam Natansohn, Marion Pritchard, Hannah Rubin, Amalie and Heinz Sandelowski, *z"l*, Bernie Sayonne, Gabi Schiff, Leonard Serkess, Dr. Emanuel Tanay, Herman Taube, Rabbi Isaac Trainin, Lea Weems, Roman Weingarten, Michel Yeruchim, and Dr. Gary Zucker. Theirs are the voices that truly animate and enrich this history.

A study such as this relies on all kinds of assistance. My research was furthered by many archivists and librarians, including those at the U.S. Holocaust Memorial Museum, the YIVO Institute for Jewish Research, the American Jewish Joint Distribution Committee, and the American Jewish Historical Society. Doug Greenberg, CEO of the Shoah Foundation, was exceptionally helpful. Misha Mitsel of the American Jewish Joint Distribution Committee was always ready to assist. Michlean Amir, archivist, and Judy Cohen, photo archivist, both at the U.S. Holocaust Memorial Museum, unstintingly lent their expertise.

Dr. Sam Goldstein was the first at the New York Association for New Americans (NYANA) to meet with me, and immediately encouraged my study. I am deeply grateful to him. I am also indebted to Mark Handelman, past executive vice president, who recognized the importance of NYANA's early records to this study and permitted me to examine case files from its archives. His assistant, Elia Saldana, made me feel especially welcome during my many hours there.

At Rutgers University Press, I thank my editor, Adi Hovav, for her interest in and enthusiasm for my project and her encouragement during the final stages of completion.

I would like to take this opportunity to express my gratitude to those who provided warm hospitality as well as help with travel and interview logistics. They include my sister Carol Ostroff and family in Israel; my brother, Joseph Berkofsky, and family in New Jersey; and Anat Bar-Cohen in Washington, D.C. Cathy and Marc Lasry graciously opened their home in New York City to me. In Denver, my childhood friend Judith Brodie was not only a generous host, but also lent her psychological insights to discussions of my analysis. My sister Anita Minkin and my dear friend Toby Zaitchik both brought their vast social work experience and ideas to our many conversations.

I am forever grateful to my parents, Dian and Louis Berkofsky, for what they, by example, taught me and continue to teach me. Although she never saw the finished product, I remember the many hours during which my mother-in-law, Beverly Cohen, *z"l*, enthusiastically discussed my progress. I offer my thanks, collectively and individually, to my children: Etan and Emily, Rami and Dara, and Tamar, who inspired and cheered me on in more ways than they realize. And to Beverly and Dani, the next generation, who are a source of pure and simple joy. Finally, I want to thank my husband, Steve. His support began long before this work did, and it has continued, unhesitatingly, every step of the way. His abiding love, encouragement, and razor-sharp insight accompany me daily. Of course, I dedicate this work to him.

ABBREVIATIONS

DP(s)	Displaced Person(s)
DPA	Displaced Persons Act
DPC	Displaced Persons Commission
EJCA	European-Jewish Children's Aid
FSD	Family Service Department
GJCA	German-Jewish Children's Aid
HIAS	Hebrew Sheltering and Immigrant Aid Society
JDC	American Jewish Joint Distribution Committee
JFCS	Jewish Family and Children's Services
NCJW	National Council of Jewish Women
NRS	National Refugee Service
NYANA	New York Association for New Americans
RFD	Religious Functionaries Department
UJA	United Jewish Appeal
USHMM	United States Holocaust Memorial Museum
USNA	United Service for New Americans
VSD	Vocational Service Department

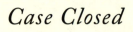

Case Closed

Introduction

————— ·≡·‡·≡· ·—

*T*he May 1950 issue of *New Neighbors*, a newsletter about Jewish refugees in the United States, contains a cheerful photograph of a young girl peering into the camera. The caption beneath it reads:

> Propitious Arrival: Happily displaying her pigtails is bright-eyed Bracha Rabinowicz, 13, who arrived in the United States from a DP camp in Germany on the day the Senate approved legislation liberalizing the Displaced Persons Act of 1948. The youngster, a native of Poland who survived the war by hiding in caves with her mother until liberation, symbolizes the new hope of the homeless men, women and children still in the DP camps abroad.[1]

Bracha Rabinowicz was one of 140,000 Jewish displaced persons (DPs) who emigrated to the United States from Europe in the years 1946–1954.[2] The pages of *New Neighbors* are filled with their snapshots. The pictures are poignant and the accompanying accounts overwhelmingly happy: refugees succeed in new professions, play on soccer teams, celebrate holidays in freedom, and are gathered in by Jewish communities around the nation. But what do these images hide? About what are they silent? What lies in the gap between these public relations portraits and the way in which Bracha, a child survivor of genocide, became part of the fabric of American life? The history belied by the celluloid is the subject of *Case Closed: Holocaust Survivors in Postwar America*.

Case Closed returns to the time before the "Holocaust" occupied a central place in American consciousness and those who had endured this event had not yet secured a place of honor and reverence as "survivors." This work gives voice to these individuals as they were then: "refugees," "DPs," "New Americans," "greeners," "units," "immigrants." And their first years here were harsh—not, as the PR images projected, unfailingly upbeat. The postwar narrative of triumph is a construct that the media promoted then and that has persisted to this day. And while it may be comforting, it effaces Holocaust survivors' struggles and impedes our understanding of the impact of genocide on the individual and on society, as a whole.

In *Case Closed* I challenge this accepted narrative by scrutinizing survivors' first years in America through the eyes of those who lived it. To do so, I synthesize a wide array of archival material, including case files of refugees recorded by agency social workers, letters and minutes from agency meetings, contemporary journal articles written by social workers and physicians, and oral testimonies. These tools add texture and depth to our understanding of the experience and throw a bright light on the survivors' perspective. The hundreds of case files I analyze give an unvarnished account of the newcomers' experiences and contrast sharply with the glowing media accounts of the day. What becomes immediately and devastatingly apparent is that these newcomers were refugees from genocide. The reason they found themselves in America made them immigrants like no other. Unlike those who flocked to the United States fifty years earlier, they did not leave the old country out of a desire to better themselves economically, nor did they save to send earnings home or to bring their families to the new country.

DP Booter: New American soccer team in Denver, Colorado. *New Neighbors* 3, no. 4 (May 1950). Collection of author.

They had no homes, no families to save for. They were the tiny remnant of a group that had been targeted for murder. Every last one of them.

Having endured, the surviving Jewish remnant desperately wanted to get out of Europe: out of the DP camps, and out of the place that had become a symbolic graveyard to them. But the world was not particularly welcoming to this small group. In Chapter 1, I begin by exploring this dilemma, the refugees' choices and the obstacles to reaching them. Palestine and the United States were their preferred destinations, for a host of reasons, ranging from ideological to practical. But entrance to both countries was limited, in the case of the former, by Britain's rigidly controlled flow of Jewish refugees and, in the case of the latter, by America's restrictive immigration laws. The American public, both Jewish and gentile, favored sending the DPs to Palestine. As it became increasingly clear that this would not happen quickly, some U.S. politicians and Jewish leaders began to advocate for admitting more DPs to America.

In December 1945, President Harry S. Truman announced a new plan, the Truman Directive, which allowed fewer than forty thousand DPs to enter the United States. With nearly one million DPs in the camps, it was a token gesture.[3] Moreover, based on existing quotas, it kept the number of Jewish DPs to a minimum. The Truman Directive facilitated immigration in one important procedural shift. It gave organizations the right to provide affidavits for DPs. Previously, only immigrants' relatives had had that right.[4] By bringing organizations into the process, Truman handed the legal and financial responsibility for the survivors squarely over to the American Jewish community. Jewish leaders accepted this challenge. They created the United Service for New Americans (USNA), a national agency, and the New York Association for New Americans (NYANA), in New York City. The former worked with local cooperating agencies (such as Jewish Family and Children's Services) around the country to resettle survivors in hundreds of communities, large and small.

In Chapter 2, I explore the subtleties of the resettlement process after the newcomers arrived in America. Because more than half the refugees settled in one city, I focus on New York. At the same time, more than 40 percent of the refugees went elsewhere, and it is important to look at their experiences, too. New York may not speak for everyone, everywhere. Thus, I analyze a range of locales, including Denver, Colorado; Cleveland, Ohio; and Columbia, South Carolina. Denver was home to some three hundred refugees, while Cleveland hosted approximately two thousand. Although just a handful of newcomers settled there, Columbia, South Carolina, emerged as an important site because of its surprising response to the refugee crisis. Each community illuminates the qualitative range of reception and resettlement experiences beyond the statistics.

The Jewish community pledged to help the refugees in their new home. In Chapter 3, I highlight the kind of assistance that the American Jewish community offered, and that which was not offered. That gap between the two is an important aspect of this story. Whether it was NYANA in New York City, or the Jewish Family and Children's Services in Cleveland or Denver, the agencies focused on those aspects of acculturation that were typical to all immigrants: employment, housing, and language. Most important was work. Within a few months of opening their doors, NYANA limited its services to newcomers to one year. Many cooperating agencies followed suit. Working against the clock, many, but not all, newcomers indeed found work by the year's end. One way or another, their files were stamped "case closed." With the closing of the file, the agency's work was done. Finding work for the newcomers became the agencies' mantra and determined the course and quality of the interaction between the refugee and caseworker. It also became the yardstick by which the agencies measured their own and the immigrants' success.

The agencies developed special programs for assisting two groups whose needs differed from the majority: the surviving remnant of European Orthodox Jewry, and orphan DPs. In Chapter 4, I address the experience of the orthodox refugees and their relationship with the Jewish, but secular, agencies that supervised their resettlement. Among the religious refugees was a discrete category of those who had professions before the war proscribed by Jewish communal life. USNA created a Religious Functionaries Department (RFD) to address the challenges that these refugees presented. The agency recognized that this group, which included rabbis, seminary students, cantors, and ritual slaughterers, was unique because of its members' specialized skills, the limited demand in America for these skills, and the newcomers' strict adherence to religious observance and lifestyle. At the same time, the organizations' goal to find jobs for them sometimes conflicted with the newcomers' desire to maintain their values and a continuity with their shattered prewar lives. A few key RFD administrators understood this. But the majority of social workers did not. As in the larger Jewish world, they had little understanding of or sympathy for the orthodox remnant who hoped to re-create the world that had been destroyed—their world.

The face-to-face confrontation with the refugees was complicated by the hosts' preconceived assumptions. Nowhere was this more striking—or more painful—than with the orphan refugees. In Chapter 5, I analyze the experiences of this group. One might imagine that orphan survivors would elicit special sympathy from the community. In a sense this was so. There was no lack of families ready to take in the orphans. Foster family and agency relationships with these young survivors, however, were complicated. American families, including the orphans' relatives, soon discovered that these were not young children. They usually were teenagers with complicated and traumatic histories. Contemporary studies indicate that foster families rejected their charges at an astonishingly high rate. What were the trajectories of these orphans' lives? How do these questions inform our assumptions about the successful acculturation of these immigrants? While there may have been more overt sympathy for orphans than for adult refugees or at least more sensitivity to their status, their experience in America was fraught with a host of tensions.

As I show in Chapter 6, finding work was important, but it was not enough for Holocaust survivors' well-being. The influence of the Holocaust on survivors was pervasive from the start. As the refugees moved forward, they harbored this trauma in their lives, deeply a part of them but invisible to the outside world. This essential difference, so critical to the survivors' existence after the Holocaust, was what made them unlike other immigrants. And this was often lost on those who were there to help them. As I show, in their pursuit of successful acculturation, the agencies ignored other pressing concerns. The manifestation of the refugees' recent trauma was painfully clear—certainly now and, presumably, at the time.

Even as the agencies pushed ahead with their goals and publicly deemed the refugees' acculturation successful, the social workers' internal reports on their clients show that survivors suffered from the effects of the Holocaust and communicated this in numerous ways. Oral histories taken after the war confirm this. Illness, often without any organic basis, abounded. However, despite the immigrants' obvious pain—recorded by the social workers themselves—the professionals rarely addressed the topic directly and discouraged their clients from dwelling on their recent past.

The newcomers usually expressed a keen desire to work, but physical ailments often interfered. Sometimes, just when it seemed that a refugee was settling into a new life, illness would strike. Convinced of the importance of work, social workers generally believed that the physical symptoms enumerated by survivors were a reaction to agency policy. Physicians supported the agencies' goals. Their usual recommendation called for employment as the best medicine.

Caseworkers had little control over the agencies' policies. At the same time, the rapidity with which their own professional and personal approach to their clients fell into line with agency goals is surprising. As I argue in Chapter 7, this is particularly confounding in light of contemporary developments in social work, which would seem to have augured well for a more diagnostic orientation toward survivors. That did not happen. The professionals' reactions to the Holocaust survivors are indeed baffling. It may not be surprising that postwar American society, focused as it was on the future, was not ready to hear about the Holocaust. But it is curious that those who were so intimately involved with survivors' care seemed so reluctant to confront the aftereffects of the Holocaust, especially when these were so obviously present in their clients.

Despite the deafness the newcomers encountered, despite the mandate they were given to forget about the past and focus on the future, the loss they had so recently experienced, indeed were still experiencing, was too great to stifle. As I demonstrate in Chapter 8, the imperative to communicate it found expression in numerous ways and shows that survivors were *not* silent. Some became members of the hometown social clubs (*landsmanschaftn*) that earlier immigrants had established, while others formed survivor-only groups. Together, survivors indeed spoke about their past and soon created the first Holocaust commemorations in the United States, as well.

The agencies' ideology of the refugees' self-sufficiency sowed the seeds for the mythology of survivors' victory from the ashes. The process of becoming new Americans was substantiation of the triumphant spirit. Contemporary publications consistently emphasized the overwhelmingly successful adaptation by the DPs into the American mainstream. This has characterized the narrative of survivors' postwar experience to this day.

But Holocaust survivors often tell a different story. They express feelings of intense isolation and loneliness during the first years in the United States and an alienation from their American co-religionists. The hundreds of agency files and oral histories in this work enhance our understanding of the caesura between these two divergent perspectives. The traumatic experiences they had endured asserted themselves in survivors' process of acculturation.

In the canon of Holocaust scholarship, historians assign a beginning and an end to the catastrophe. Hitler's ascension to power in January 1933 marked its onset and "liberation" signaled its end. What *Case Closed* shows is that trauma persists beyond chronological designations. As ardently as they had yearned for war's end, liberation did not end survivors' suffering. New agonies emerged. How could it be otherwise? In the aftermath of the Holocaust, the surviving remnant struggled to piece together an existence out of a shattered past. Many moved forward and made great strides in becoming Americanized. Some, irrevocably damaged, did not.

Case Closed: Holocaust Survivors in Postwar America does not tell a cheerful story. It demonstrates that the battles waged by survivors, despite or sometimes because of the help they received, were not over once they reached the United States. Nor is it a triumphant narrative. On the contrary: this work explores the complexity of the particular historical experience of Holocaust survivors in postwar America.

CHAPTER 1

What to Do with the DPs?

THE NEW JEWISH QUESTION

*T*he war in Europe ended in May 1945, and with its conclusion came liberation for the surviving remnant of European Jewry. *Liberation* is a particularly flawed word to describe the painful confrontation with the reality that now awaited these survivors. Exhausted in body and mind, many returned to their former homes in search of families. Some few, especially if they originated from Western Europe, were able to resume life in their countries of birth. But for the majority of Holocaust survivors from Eastern Europe there was no such possibility.[1] They found their communities erased, their homes appropriated by former neighbors. This situation was often compounded by the murderous hostility that greeted them. Pogroms erupted in Poland and Hungary. Once again, they faced disruption in their lives. Homeless, thousands moved on to the displaced persons (DP) camps in Germany, Austria, and Italy. There they considered their limited options.[2]

Desperate, one man wrote to the Yiddish daily *Forverts* from Europe:

> My name is Moses A, from the town of Zolosov, near Tarnopol. At present my wife, my two children and I are in Italy. Of our town of 1180 persons only 28 remain today. We have been through so much and are quite destitute now. It is most important that we contact our relatives in the U.S. Will you please help us to do so?[3]

Moses's relatives were indeed located, but it was more than three years before he and his family arrived in New York. Their story is not unusual. The road from Europe to the newcomers' ultimate destination in the United States was conditioned by a web of restrictive immigration laws, different agencies, conflicting ideologies, and the push and pull of families and friends.

The world was not a welcoming place for the Holocaust survivors. Where they preferred to settle is one question and where they were permitted to go is another. While the *yishuv* (the Jewish community in Palestine) wanted the refugees, terms set out in Great Britain's White Paper of 1939 limited legal entry into British-mandated Palestine to fifteen hundred visas a month.[4] America, too, had not only legislation to restrict entry into the country but also a native population that wanted to see the displaced persons go elsewhere. Often American Jewry was similarly disinclined to welcome DPs, but for different reasons. The destruction of European Jewry had made Zionists out of most American Jews and convinced them of the need for a national homeland. It was there, not in the United States, that the majority wanted the refugees to settle.

What did the survivors want? It is conventional wisdom that most wanted to go, first and foremost, to Palestine. This was not necessarily the case. Once the U.S. legislation was enacted, many survivors chose to immigrate to America. In anticipation of their arrival, the Jewish community created a new postwar refugee agency, the United Service for New Americans (USNA) in 1946. USNA worked with local Jewish agencies around the nation to coordinate the resettlement of Jewish DPs. The New York Association for New Americans (NYANA) was established in 1949 to assist the majority of newcomers who stayed in New York City.

Eventually, 140,000 Jewish DPs settled in the United States. Providing the greater context of postwar America is important for understanding the society that survivors entered as well as the environment that framed their reception. Tracing the evolution of the legislation that granted DPs admission to the United States is part of this mosaic. American Jewry's response, ideologically and practically, is another. The refugee's perspective is fundamental, too. It cannot be forgotten that this drama involved human beings. Who were the people in this tiny surviving remnant? A brief demographic analysis of this group will help give texture and humanity to the terms *refugees, DPs, newcomers, immigrants, New Americans*, and *survivors*. Furthermore, examining the characteristics that made the members of this group unique among other immigrants is critical to this story's narrative.

In 1945, President Truman dispatched Earl Harrison, American representative on the Intergovernmental Committee on Refugees, former U.S. commissioner of immigration, and University of Pennsylvania Law School dean, to investigate the situation of the DPs in Germany who were nonrepatriable.[5] Harrison was profoundly moved by the DPs' plight and called for immediate action. In what became known as the Harrison Report, he urged, "The displaced persons must be evacuated from the camps in Germany and Austria; the overwhelming majority of Jews in the displaced persons' camps want to go to Palestine."[6]

On the basis of the Harrison Report, President Truman pressed Great Britain's Prime Minister Clement Attlee to grant one hundred thousand immigration certificates to Jewish DPs in Europe. Attlee, however, had other plans. As a stalling tactic and also as a means of drawing the United States into a solution, he invited Truman to participate in an Anglo-American committee of inquiry to investigate the DP problem. The partnership was announced on 13 November 1945. The delegates had 120 days to make policy recommendations.[7]

The American people, Jews and non-Jews alike, supported Truman's request to Attlee. A Gallup poll released in January 1946 indicated, despite or perhaps because of antisemitism, that 76 percent of non-Jewish voters polled were sympathetic to permitting Jews to settle in Palestine.[8] While reasons differed, most wanted to see the refugees admitted to Palestine rather than to the United States.

American Jewry wanted more than the admission of DPs to Palestine. The vast majority ardently hoped for a Jewish state. In the wake of the Holocaust, Zionism exploded in the United States and supporters rushed to join its organizations.[9] In 1933, Zionist groups claimed approximately 65,000 members. By April 1946, the Zionist Organization of America (ZOA) saw its numbers rise to 200,000. In the same year, Hadassah, its women's organization, which supported the creation of Hadassah Hospital, in Jerusalem, saw a growth from 145,000 to 180,000 members. By 1947, the number of people belonging to Zionist institutions shot up to nearly 1 million.[10]

The organizations focused their efforts on support for the struggling Jewish settlement in Palestine. The ZOA threw itself into raising money for the Jewish National Fund (JNF) and the United Jewish Appeal (UJA). The JNF's income in 1945 was nearly 7 million dollars, which was 2 million dollars more than that of the previous year. Religious Zionist organizations such as Hapoel Hamizrachi, Mizrachi, and Women's Mizrachi expanded their educational programs about Palestine and also joined the fund-raising campaign of the JNF. The UJA approved a $100,000,000 budget for 1946, of which $43,082,000 was earmarked for the United Palestine Appeal (UPA), also a sizeable increase over the 1945 allocation.[11]

From 1946 until well after the establishment of the state of Israel, the UJA mounted a series of campaigns designed to raise funds and awareness of the DPs' situation. Appearing in both secular and Jewish newspapers around the United States, the UJA's full-page advertisements implored

Americans "for humanity's sake" to remember the Jewish DPs in Europe.[12] One such ad depicted a boy's face behind barbed wire with the caption "Shall I also die here?" It was followed by the text "Is there no place in the world where this hopeless child may be at home? Who will help him and the 250,000 other displaced Jews who survived the six million mass murders in Europe? The task is tremendous to supply the necessities of life and rehabilitation in Europe and to build a haven in Palestine."[13] Often, the campaigns included public rallies designed to encourage participation in this worthy effort.

Zionists, caught up in their cause, were not happy about the creation of the Anglo-American Committee of Inquiry. Dr. Abba Hillel Silver and Rabbi Stephen Wise, driving forces in American Zionism and co-chairs of the American Zionist Emergency Council, cabled Truman stating their opinion that the committee could serve no useful purpose. They asked him "not to countenance further commissions and inquiries at a continued cost in human life and human misery, which can only ascertain facts already well known."[14] The leaders debated whether to protest the committee's existence by refusing to appear before it. In the end, they testified, as did others, about the crucial need to lift the White Paper and allow Jewish immigration to Palestine.

While the Anglo-American Committee debated, the Senate Foreign Relations Committee approved a resolution on 12 December that supported not just the admission of one hundred thousand Jews into Palestine but also the establishment of a Jewish state. A week later, the House Foreign Affairs Committee passed the same resolution by an overwhelming majority.[15] What motivated the U.S. government to support the Harrison Report's recommendations? Clearly, some politicians felt sympathy for the idea of a Jewish homeland in the aftermath of the destruction of European Jewry. And after all, the DPs were the victims of the same enemy that the United States had so recently defeated. But it was decidedly sympathy from a distance.

The Truman administration's goal was to empty the troublesome DP camps that the United States helped to administer, while at the same time preventing a flood of immigration to America. U.S. immigration laws had remained unchanged since the early 1920s, when the country had begun to close its doors to immigrants. In 1945, America certainly did not want to lift immigration restrictions.[16] On the contrary: a number of congressmen tried (unsuccessfully) to introduce legislation in 1945 that would cut immigration quotas by 50 percent for the following ten years. The law in 1945 allowed a maximum of 150,000 quota immigrants a year but even that number was never filled.[17] In other words, the United States could have admitted more immigrants than it was demanding that Great Britain allow into Palestine. But several more years, during which the survivors continued to live in DP camps, had to elapse before that would happen.

The Harrison Report recommended the admission of DPs to Palestine. It also advocated that the United States set an example to Western European countries by admitting a small number of DPs into the United States. "The United States should, under existing immigration laws, permit reasonable numbers of such persons to come here, again particularly those who have family ties in this country," Harrison suggested.[18] To assuage the anti-immigration concern, he noted, "The number who desire emigration to the United States is not large."[19]

Truman took to heart Harrison's suggestion regarding U.S. immigration. "The immensity of the problem of displaced persons and refugees is almost beyond comprehension," he declared. "This period of unspeakable human distress is not the time for us to close or to narrow our gates."[20] And with that, he issued the Truman Directive in December 1945, which authorized preferential treatment for the admission of DPs within existing immigration laws. The point was not to encourage or allow widespread immigration to the United States but, stated Truman, "for America to set an example for the rest of the world in cooperation toward alleviating human misery."[21]

While Truman's words professed humanitarian sentiment, in reality, the directive afforded only a minimal opportunity for the Jewish DPs to gain admittance to America.[22] It allowed for the immigration each year of a maximum of 39,681 DPs into the United States from the American zones of occupation.[23] Moreover, America admitted these newcomers within the quotas of the old immigration laws, which limited the number of visas according to the immigrant's country of origin. The directive was totally blind to the demographics of the Jewish DPs. The highest quota, for example, allowed 25,957 visas for Germans. There were barely 12,000 surviving German Jews in the American zones.[24] By contrast, the directive set a quota of 6,524 for Poland, which was far below the number of Polish survivors.[25] An estimated 28,000 Jewish DPs entered America by June 1948 as a result of the new policy.[26] More than 90 percent of these were on quota.[27] While two-thirds of the visas issued under Truman's directive did go to Jews, the directive had little immediate effect on the overall DP crisis in Europe and it certainly did nothing to change extant immigration laws.[28] It did, however, set the stage for the resettlement of Jewish DPs in America.

In a way that neither the president nor the Jewish communal leaders foresaw, Truman's directive had enormous consequences for the subsequent resettlement of refugees in America. Before the directive was issued, Truman called leaders of the National Refugee Service (the predecessor of USNA) to the White House and asked for their commitment to share the expense for care of the Jewish DPs. Not only did the leaders agree, they suggested that the president grant their agency, and others like it, the authority to act as sponsors of potential immigrants. In the past, an individual, usually a relative, provided an affidavit promising that the newcomer would not become a public charge.[29] Truman accepted the Jewish leaders' offer and then announced his directive to the nation and a Congress hostile to immigration by noting that the National Refugee Service would take care of the refugees.[30]

Now specified welfare agencies could provide a "corporate affidavit" and thereby assume the responsibilities for the adjustment of newcomers. This change would have a profound impact on the agencies directing the resettlement efforts. Granting the agencies responsibility relieved the U.S. government of the major financial burden of the immigrants. Ultimately, it also absolved many American Jews from supporting their European relatives.

The Truman Directive was greeted coldly by Zionists who believed that any effort on behalf of immigration to the U.S. would weaken their cause. Many other Americans also opposed the idea of relaxing immigration restrictions. A Gallup poll in December 1945 showed that 37 percent of those interviewed felt that the number of European immigrants should be reduced to less than the number admitted before the war.[31] Nevertheless, the directive went forward.

As Truman's legislation moved ahead, so did the Anglo-American inquiry. After months of acrimonious deliberations, the committee recommended that Britain revoke its White Paper and allow one hundred thousand DPs to enter Palestine. Great Britain, however, never intended to let this happen. Instead, the partition of Palestine was proposed. That, along with the shocking pogroms in Kielce, Poland, during the summer of 1946, led to a new direction in American policy toward the DPs.[32]

The Truman administration, frustrated by the slow pace of the inquiry, had begun to think about changing the immigration laws to permit more DPs to resettle in the United States.[33] Still holding out for Attlee's cooperation, the president told the American delegates to the Committee of Inquiry that he would promise entry to fifty thousand DPs if Great Britain would let one hundred thousand into Palestine. He also communicated his intent to the House and Senate Immigration Committees. On 16 August 1946 Truman declared that he would work toward legislation that would allow DPs to immigrate to America.

Congress resisted liberalization of immigration laws that had been on the books since 1924. Hearings on the Stratton Bill, which called for the admission of one hundred thousand DPs a year for four years, began on 4 June 1947, nearly a year later. In an attempt to broaden the focus of the law on Jews alone, Truman appealed to Congress "to turn its attention to this world problem, in an effort to find ways whereby we can fulfill our responsibilities to these thousands of homeless and suffering refugees of all faiths."[34] The Senate, however, pushed through an even more restrictive bill, on 2 June 1948. The Wiley-Rivercomb Bill allowed for only fifty thousand DPs a year for two years. Clearly biased against Jewish DPs, it demanded not only that 50 percent of admitted DPs be farmers but also gave preference to those from the Baltic region. There were few farmers and few surviving Balts among the Jewish DPs; that was the area with the greatest number of Protestant DPs.[35]

The Wiley-Rivercomb Bill also stipulated a cutoff date. In order to be eligible to enter the United States, one had to have been in Germany, Austria, or Italy before 22 December 1945. This was the kiss of death for Jewish DP immigration, because the majority had entered these countries after that date.[36] The Senate passed an amended version of the bill that raised the number of people who could be admitted annually to one hundred thousand, but, accepting Nazi ideas of race, allowed *Volksdeutsche* (persons of German descent) from Eastern Europe to enter under the Austrian or German quota.[37]

More moderate legislation was introduced in April 1948. The Fellows Bill allowed the entry of one hundred thousand DPs a year for two years, extension of the cutoff date to 21 April 1947, and the apportionment of visas according to nationality and population. The House passed this bill with a minor amendment that granted entry to two thousand refugees from the new Communist regime in Czechoslovakia. A compromise was reached on 18 June 1948.

The resulting legislation, called the Displaced Persons Act, combined the worst features of the two competing bills. While it allowed for 205,000 DPs to enter America from 1 July 1948 until 30 June 1950, the cutoff date for those reaching the DP camps stayed fixed at 22 December 1945. Anyone arriving in the DP camps in the American zone after this date was ineligible to come the United States under the Displaced Persons Act. The bill reserved 30 percent of the entrance visas for agricultural workers who would continue as farmers in the United States and 40 percent for those of Baltic extraction.[38] Although he called it "flagrantly discriminatory" and a travesty of "the American tradition of fair play," President Truman signed the bill, which became law on 25 June 1948.[39] For a moment, an opportunity for more humanitarian legislation appeared possible at a special session of Congress on 26 July 1948, but the legislators chose not to act and the new bill stood unchanged.

The timing of the new legislation is significant. Just two months earlier, in May 1948, the state of Israel came into being. It would offer unrestricted immigration to the survivors. If the majority of the Jewish DPs wanted to go to Israel, perhaps, the U.S. politicians who were anti-immigration reasoned, even if the Displaced Persons Act passed, surely, between the new law's restrictions and the chance of legal immigration to Israel, few DPs would ever enter the United States. What actually happened, however, differed from the expectations not just of the politicians but of the Zionists as well.

The commonly held belief, in both popular and scholarly circles, is that the overwhelming majority of refugees ardently wished to go to Palestine and, later, Israel and did so.[40] This is certainly what the media promulgated, beginning with the Harrison Report in 1945. My research supports the statistics, but points to a different reading regarding intent. While the majority did settle in Israel, a significant number went elsewhere. Putting an exact figure on the number of survivors is problematic because of the chaos of the period and the definition of *survivor*. An estimated 350,000 survivors did make *aliyah* (immigration to Israel) by the early 1950s. Nearly 140,000 immigrated to America and several thousand went to Canada, South America, Australia, South Africa, and elsewhere.[41] Some also stayed in Europe. Further, data on final destinations are misleading because refugees sometimes moved on from their first arrival point. A not insignificant number went first to Israel and then left for the United States in the 1950s. Postwar surveys indicate that most of the refugees who immigrated to Sweden wanted to remain in Sweden, the majority of those in Austria wanted to go to America, and 50 percent in Belgium wanted to go somewhere besides Palestine.[42] These surveys indicated intent, not action, and reflect the fact that far from all survivors expressed the inclination to go to Palestine.

Even among the Zionist leadership in the DP camps the rate of aliyah was disappointing. Most left for the United States, not Palestine.[43] The desire to emigrate was often less about ideological concerns than about simply getting out of Europe. For many who were the sole survivors of their family the

Amalie and Heinz Sandelowski with baby daughter Margarete, in Germany, April 1947. Courtesy of the Sandelowski family.

question of where to go was answered by the location of relatives, usually in America.

Some refugees registered to go both to the United States and to Palestine; when the U.S. consul notified them first that they were eligible to enter America the possibility of leaving, not idealism, was the motivating factor.[44] Others felt that they had endured one war, and wanted to avoid another. Some believed that Palestine was just too dangerous, not because of war, but because of myriad difficulties. Heinz and Amalie Sandelowski speak to this point. While they were pulled ideologically toward Palestine, they registered to go to America and considered both options. As Germans, they became eligible to enter the United States under the Truman Directive. By the time they received their visas Amalie was pregnant and her health was precarious. After their daughter was born, the couple decided it would be safer to go to America rather than enter Palestine illegally.[45] They were strongly motivated, too, by the desire to leave Europe as quickly as possible. Many such factors entered into the calculus of their decisions.

The Sandelowskis were not unique. Another survivor, a twenty-six-year-old man, reasoned this way: "I am honest enough not to say that I above all others would like to go there [Israel]," he wrote on 15 July 1948 from the French zone. "I am as much afraid as anybody of getting my throat cut or killed now that I have barely escaped past killings. However, this would certainly not prevent me from going there if it would not mean having all that I have built up again and all that I try to build up come toppling down like a house of cards." Then too, he also had to "think of my fiancée who, after all she has been through, is physically absolutely unfit to stand the climate in Palestine. She has stood by me when the going was rough and the least I can do for her now is offering and securing a decent life." Besides, he added, "there is my mother completely depending on me for support whom my going to Palestine would rob of every help for a couple of years maybe."[46] For many survivors, then, the question of destination was a complex issue.

In the end, when the opportunity to come to America through the Truman Directive presented itself, many took that route. In May 1946 the first group of DPs arrived on the S.S. *Marine Flasher*. The National Refugee Service (NRS) kept its commitment to the president and took responsibility for those who arrived on their corporate affidavits. Representatives from the NRS, the Hebrew Sheltering and Immigrant Aid Society (HIAS), and the National Council of Jewish Women's (NCJW's) Service to the Foreign Born greeted the survivors at the port. They arranged for transportation to temporary shelters, meals, and clothing and medical care for those who required immediate attention.

In anticipation of increased immigration, the NRS decided to restructure itself into a new agency. The goal was both to expand services and to avoid duplication of effort. Subsequently, on 1 August 1946, it merged with NCJW's Service to the Foreign Born to create the United Service for New Americans (USNA).[47] While—intentionally—there was nothing in its name to suggest it, USNA was a strictly Jewish agency funded by the United Jewish Appeal. Its goal was to work with the American Jewish Joint Distribution Committee (JDC) in Europe and with local cooperating Jewish communal agencies around the United States, such as the Jewish Family and Children's Services in Denver, to facilitate the refugees' resettlement away from New York City. This was a significant goal. As in past times of increased immigration, there was fear among the New York Jewish community that New York would become a dumping ground for the majority of newcomers, significantly increasing antisemitic sentiment.

The tension between New York and communities around the country did not disappear. This thread weaves its way through the entire resettlement process. Similar to attitudes during earlier periods of immigration, it reflects American Jews' sense of themselves and their standing in America. The postwar period ushered in a new age of both material and social comfort for American Jewry but the community was still mindful of its minority status and the vicious antisemitism of the earlier part of the decade. Should it be a surprise that many second-generation American Jewish hosts viewed the thousands of Eastern European newcomers with a discomfort that took precedence over sympathy?

The Jewish community's commitment to helping its own, however, was deeply ingrained and so was its institutional response. It created USNA, a vast bureaucracy with a board of directors, an executive director, president, and numerous departments staffed by an army of workers. In 1946 the machinery of the new organization was poised for action.

The agency was divided into two branches of service: national and local. Its national arm included Migration Services, Location Services, the Corporate Affidavit Reporting Unit, the Naturalization and Americanization Service, the Port and Dock Department, the National Reception Center, National Settlement Services, and European Jewish Children's Aid (EJCA). Its local unit for refugees in New York and Long Island included Family Services, the Religious Functionary Division (RFD), the Vocational Adjustment Department (VSD), and the Business and Loan Services Division.[48]

USNA was a multiservice agency that supervised every aspect of resettlement, from port and dock reception to naturalization advice.

Each department had a specific function designed to streamline resettlement. The Migration Department, for example, acted as a liaison between the JDC in Europe and the local agencies around the United States. Initially, matching an individual coming into America on a corporate affidavit with an American community was made exclusively by the JDC in Europe. Once the immigrant was assigned to a U.S. community, the JDC informed USNA and Migration Services notified the cooperating community. Before the DP could leave Europe, he or she had to negotiate a maze of U.S. bureaucratic details: determination of eligibility, security clearance, public health examination, consular interview, and screening of admissibility by the Immigration and Naturalization Service. This process often lasted for months, or even years.

USNA's Migration Department worked with the overseas agency to fill the quotas submitted by local agencies. The JDC was charged with placing refugees in appropriate communities. An orthodox family desired a city with a religious infrastructure. A tailor needed a community that required his trade. This did not always happen. At times, the JDC's efforts to move refugees out of Europe as quickly as possible had deleterious effects. The Z. family, a religious couple and their children, were sent to Pocatello, Idaho. It immediately became apparent that this was a mistake, yet it would be months before they were relocated to New York.[49] These kinds of "mistakes" often created tension between the local cooperating community and the national and international agencies. They also show how little control a refugee without American relatives had over his or her destination.

While emotional reunion scenes were often showcased in the press, many DPs had no family to greet them when they disembarked in America. Amalie and Heinz Sandelowski arrived in New York in late November 1947. They were among the few Jewish refugees on the S.S. *Ernie Pyle*. Amalie remembered the first moments after she; her husband; and baby daughter, Margarete, disembarked. "We were outside on the pier with our baggage. We were very lonely because so many had friends or relatives who greeted them. We were sitting there with nobody to meet us," she recalled.[50] The job of handling such individuals fell to USNA's Port and Dock Department. Agency staff and volunteers delivered those who were going elsewhere to their connecting train while those staying in New York went to reception centers.

The stay at a reception center was temporary, but refugees could be there for weeks, even months, while they searched for housing in New York's tight postwar housing market. Whereas survivors remember the chaos of the reception centers, USNA's publicity department frequently used the centers as an opportunity to document the DPs as New Americans. In 1947, for example, USNA sponsored a Thanksgiving dinner at one shelter. Staff instructed children to dress in Thanksgiving garb. A photo captured the moment and appeared with the headline "Modern-day Pilgrims Happy" in the *New York Daily Sun*.[51] The subtitle of the article, "Beginning of Americanization of D.P.'s in Local Shelters Finds All Thankful," set the tone for the popular image of the DPs.

Newly ensconced in the reception centers, the immigrants met with caseworkers from USNA's Family Service Department (FSD). The FSD was ill prepared to handle even the small number of DPs allowed into the United Service by the Truman Directive. In its first year of existence, the FSD's relief load grew from 522 to 5,432.[52] The agency soon found that it could not keep up. At a time when immediate help was crucial, refugees

Immigrant children celebrate Thanksgiving at a reception center in New York, circa 1948. HIAS. Courtesy of the United States Holocaust Memorial Museum.

usually had to wait from five to six weeks for initial contact with USNA.[53] Disappointed, some refugees made their own plans when they felt that that could not rely on the agency.

USNA realized that it needed to respond to this challenge quickly. By the end of 1947, the staff grew to 600, 173 working for the national program and 229 aiding those in New York. This disparity reflects the greater numbers of the DPs staying in the city. The clerical staff to support this expanding bureaucracy jumped to 203. The budget ballooned as well, from approximately a third of a million dollars a month in early 1947 to almost one million dollars a month by the year's end.[54] The total budget for 1947 was $9,153,500 and with this, USNA became the second-largest voluntary social service agency in the country, topped only by the Red Cross.[55]

The FSD, which was USNA's largest division, worked exclusively with the New York clientele and eventually became the main department in New York Association for New Americans (NYANA) after NYANA's creation in 1949. Its caseworkers assessed the newcomers' needs and met with them until they were self-supporting. The social workers had tremendous control over the refugees' lives. They referred the DPs to the Vocational Service Department, to doctors, and to the Religious Functionary Department and also determined the amount and extent of relief.

The Vocational Services Department (VSD) served the heart of the agencies' goal: to help DPs find employment as quickly as possible. The department's services were extensive and included vocational counseling, a job-finding service, educational counseling to assess applicants' abilities, supervision of training plans, and evaluation of requests for special tools and expenses such as union fees.[56] While the agency perceived that this department succeeded mightily, what it purported to do and what it accomplished for the refugees were not identical.

The Religious Functionary Division was a branch of the VSD designed to help the orthodox refugee whose occupation fell into the religious-functionary category: yeshiva student, rabbi, cantor, *mohel* (performer of ritual circumcision), *schochet* (ritual slaughterer), *mashgiach* (kosher-food supervisor), teacher, and *shamos* (synagogue caretaker).[57] This was a problematic group because its values clashed with those of the agencies. Not only were the clients orthodox but they regarded scholarly study as an occupation that the Jewish community should support.

The European Jewish Children's Aid (EJCA) was a department that grew out of the German Jewish Children's Aid (GJCA), a wartime rescue agency. It worked with local agencies to place unaccompanied minors who arrived on agency assurances. The EJCA also advised those on individual sponsorship who required assistance. Although the GJCA as part of the National Refugee Service (NRS) was originally created for younger children, the EJCA's postwar clientele reflected the catastrophe that had so recently ended. The unaccompanied minors it served were primarily adolescents. Few young Jewish children had survived the war.

The postwar refugees were very different from those whom the NRS had helped in the 1930s and early 1940s. It was this distinction and not simply an increase in numbers that propelled the expansion of USNA. Edwin Rosenberg, president of the agency, commented on the dissimilarity to the audience at the 1948 annual meeting:

> A greater proportion of the Newcomers entering the United States today are dependent than was true of the earlier refugee movement. This is largely due to the fact that those now arriving here lived in camps for many years and in many instances have developed dependency characteristics since their total needs have been taken care of by others. This psychological fact requires carefully individualized service. In addition, the newcomers have handicaps due to other conditions under which they have lived these past twelve or more years. They have had little opportunity to learn trades or professions. They have had fewer cultural opportunities and on the whole speak little English. Their hardships have caused a variety of defects which require medical treatment. They are, therefore, not as readily employable and consequently a larger proportion requires help.[58]

Rosenberg's comments are significant for several reasons. His characterization of survivors as "dependent" reflected a pervasive attitude. On the one hand, it showed recognition that their wartime experiences had deeply affected survivors. On the other hand, it revealed the general perception of the experience—that being in camps had beaten people down and made them unable to think for themselves. This simplified the problem and suggested a prescriptive, external approach: to make the refugees independent. Indeed, the agencies' focus was not on individualized service, as Rosenberg recommended. Instead, the agencies pushed the newcomers to stand on their own as quickly as possible. Rosenberg's remarks are also important because they describe the survivors as they were in 1947, with obvious medical and psychological conditions that distinguished them from those refugees who came earlier. Despite this, when the number of immigrants continued to increase, the agency deemphasized health and psychological issues.

As the refugee efforts in the United States demanded more money to support the influx of newcomers, other Jewish communal agencies were also occupied with their own financial concerns. By May 1947 the United Jewish Appeal (UJA) was worried about USNA's rapid expansion. Supporting Palestine was uppermost in the minds and budget priorities of American Jewry. How could they support the Jewish state and also meet the growing demands of the refugee organizations? Then too, the Jewish leadership was aware that a DP law was under debate. Should it pass, the financial demands upon the agency would mushroom. USNA spent $11,847,000 in 1946 and 1947. Projections of estimated needs for 1948 alone were $13,664,973.[59] Already USNA's budget was nearly triple what the NRS had spent on immigrant resettlement.

On 23 May 1947 the three constituent organizations of UJA—USNA, the Joint Distribution Committee, and the United Palestine Appeal—asked the Council of Jewish Federations and Welfare Funds (CJFWF) to conduct a survey "to evaluate . . . [USNA's] policies and procedures and to appraise the effectiveness of its current operations in meeting the needs of the immigrants who are its clients."[60]

The CJFWF's survey, of November 1947, confirmed (suggesting that there were some who had doubts) that USNA was performing a worthwhile and necessary service to the immigrant community. It asserted, however, that USNA should no longer be responsible for the DPs in New York City but should focus exclusively on helping those DPs elsewhere. This conclusion addresses a problem that had been a source of tension from the beginning of the NRS's refugee program and would continue to plague the resettlement of Holocaust survivors in America: refugees staying in New York versus settling around the country. The majority of the survivors wanted to, and did, stay in New York. What they wanted for themselves and what the Jewish agencies wanted, however, were often at odds.

Over and over, USNA reiterated its goal to distribute the refugees in as geographically a diverse way as possible, even if the refugees and, for that matter, the communities wished otherwise. The importance of this had been articulated first by the NRS before the war and was underscored again in 1948 at USNA's annual meeting when Edwin Rosenberg stated, "Let us try to avoid the natural tendency of the refugees to huddle together in the port of entry, to associate only with émigré friends, to continue speaking and thinking in a foreign language . . . Let us send the refugee out, on a carefully planned program, into the smaller cities and towns throughout the United States where he will soon think of himself as American."[61] Like the NRS, USNA employed a quota system to actualize its intentions.

Communities understood this to mean that the burden of absorbing these refugees would be shouldered by many. Nevertheless, complaints among the local communities that the system was unfair were not isolated incidents. From the start, USNA struggled not only to persuade communities to accept refugees but also, at times, to enjoin localities to keep those they had taken in.

USNA was originally created with the understanding that social service agencies in New York would provide help to the DPs who settled there. This did not happen. The lack of local cooperation by the New York agencies adversely affected USNA's ability to work effectively. No communal agency in New York was willing to seriously address refugee issues. Rather than concerning itself with issues on a national level, then, USNA was primarily worried about providing relief to its burgeoning caseload. Instead of counseling agencies around the United States, USNA found itself providing relief to needy refugees in New York. Moreover, USNA expected the local cooperating agencies around the country to pick up the tab for the immigrants they had brought in on corporate affidavits. No one was pleased with this situation.

The 1947 survey resulted in the recommendation that USNA separate into two agencies. One would be an exclusively national organization. The other would be responsible for the steadily growing immigration population in New York. The conclusion of the survey captured the tensions that riddled the fledgling refugee program:

> The administrative confusions apparent in administering a national and a local program under the same administrator, the urgent necessity for clarifying the national and local aspects of the USNA program, and the need for assuring that New York City as a community assumes its proper role in planning and caring for those of the immigrants who remain in New York City, lead to the conclusion that the local services of USNA must be carefully defined and distinguished from the national functions of the USNA. To secure the full cooperation of communal services available in New York City, it is recommended that steps be taken to organize a separate corporation to assume full responsibility for service to immigrants who remain in New York City.[62]

Despite the survey's recommendations, the social service agencies in New York never became involved with the resettlement program. And despite the obvious need, it would be nearly two years until a separate New York agency, NYANA, was created.

As USNA struggled with the challenges of being both a national and local agency, the Displaced Persons Act became law in June 1948. Because of the bureaucracy involved with processing applications, however, it was late 1949 by the time a steady stream of immigrants began to enter the United States. For the agencies this was fortuitous; NYANA finally opened its doors in July 1949.

NYANA was the refugee agency that gave direct care to the greatest number of survivors, and its attitudes and policies would have profound effects on the immigrants' lives. Originally, the board of directors saw NYANA as a temporary agency. Once New York Jewish organizations absorbed refugees into their clientele, NYANA would have served its function and the agency would close. But the other New York agencies never committed themselves to the effort. It was left to NYANA almost exclusively to work with the refugees. That, too, had ramifications for the newcomers. NYANA did not shut its doors. It exists today, still funded by UJA, but with a very different group of clients from the Holocaust survivors it once served. USNA, however, merged with the Hebrew Sheltering and Immigrant Aid Society (HIAS) in 1954 to become the United HIAS Service.

Caring for immigrants, of course, was not new to the American Jewish community. HIAS was founded early in the 1900s to help the millions of Jews who emigrated from Russia and Poland to America at the turn of the twentieth century. The NRS was created in 1939 to serve the German and Austrian émigrés of that period. But this refugee population that arrived after World War II was significantly different from that which came earlier.

A NYANA study, *Demographic Characteristics of the Recent Jewish Immigrant*, published in 1950, underscores the unique nature of the recent refugees. The study was based on 17,938 NYANA clients.[63] From comparisons to other, albeit smaller, samples, it is safe to say that these demographics mirror the general refugee community. Most of these immigrants, unlike German-Jewish émigrés of the previous decade, were of Eastern European descent, primarily Polish born. They had mixed job skills, and they often required training, to enable them to fit into the postwar job market. Younger newcomers who might have been thirteen or fourteen years of age when the war started had few skills. Older people had outmoded ones. Few spoke English. One of the distinguishing characteristics of the newcomer, reported the study, was youth: 44.6 percent of the NYANA caseload was between twenty and forty years old and the median age was twenty-nine, considerably younger than the U.S. population's average age of fifty. This had far-reaching effects. In 1949, for example, NYANA adopted its "20–40" policy, requiring that all able-bodied clients in this age group be self-sufficient by the first anniversary of their arrival in the United States.

The report cautioned that youth does not mean children. While 4,500 individuals, or 27 percent of the caseload, were under sixteen years of age, there were only 1,156 between the ages of seven and sixteen, which, stated the report, was "a grim reminder of the wholesale slaughter of Jewish children during the Nazi occupation of Europe. A happier fact," the report added, "is the large number of children born since the end of the war."[64]

While this number seems, at first glance, to confirm research about the triumphant post-Holocaust baby boom, a closer inspection suggests that the baby boom peaked in the DP camps. The average family size in this sample was 2.3. Yet the study insists that the birthrate among NYANA clients remained high; forty-five babies per thousand as compared to seventeen per thousand among the general U.S. population. Again, this statistic must be analyzed with a nuanced eye; the main DP population group was composed of people in their child-bearing years, from twenty to forty years old, much younger, as already noted, than the general U.S. population.

The data describe family size and indicate that almost 30 percent of the NYANA caseload belonged to a three-member family. Again, a more penetrating look is necessary. While roughly 89 percent (of that 30 percent) constituted a nuclear family, in 11 percent all three members were either of one generation or in two generations but not two parents and a child. "In substantial measure," the survey reads, "these are family units which were constituted after the war and in many instances are composed of surviving spouses of previous marriages and a young child." In nearly one-quarter of the two-member families, which represented 21 percent of the caseload, each member was of different generation. An additional 10 percent of two-member families were not couples but two adult males, two adult females, or one of each, perhaps siblings. All in all, one-third of two member families departed from the "norm." The data indicate something else: the largest group in the distribution of caseload by family was the one-person family, which made up 35 percent of all families. In these cases, men outnumbered women in the ratio of six to four.[65]

Another fact emerges from these data. More men than women survived the Holocaust. Although the survey does not indicate numbers, the pattern echoes that of other sample survivor populations, including teenagers. While the study does not address the reasons for this, historical accounts suggest more than one possibility. After the start of the war, Jews perceived that men were at greater risk, and families sometimes encouraged husbands and sons to escape to the Soviet Union, where they spent the war years under brutal, but not genocidal, conditions. Another consideration is that men and women were separated upon arrival in concentration camps. Women and young children were kept together and, after selection, usually murdered together. NYANA did not delve into explanations. On the contrary, the organization was careful to put a positive note on the demographics. It called the slightly greater number of male survivors "altogether a happy situation, and the reverse of what is found in the United States population as a whole where women predominate to a slight extent."[66]

The NYANA study observed that the average DP was young and had "made great strides toward reconstituting normal family life."[67] This reinforced the agencies' treatment of the immigrants. To the agencies this bespoke resilience: a will to live and begin again. What they did not see was how brightly these demographics mirrored what the immigrants had endured during the Holocaust and what they lived with after it. They show a rupture of Jewish life vast and deep: a plethora of thirty-year-old widowers, couples joined together to replace murdered wives and children, youngsters never reaching adolescence, young adults facing life alone. They speak, if we listen closely, about families shattered rather than about those reconstituted, cautioning us to remember the black thread of the Holocaust that continued to weave its way through the immigrants' lives even as they moved forward.

What these refugees experienced should have also been noticeable to the American public, Jewish and gentile, if it paid any attention at all to the media of the times. Newspapers and book publishers began to print survivors' stories even as the war still raged. *Warsaw Ghetto: A Diary* by Mary Berg was one of the earliest survivor accounts to appear in the United States. Because her mother was an American citizen, the family survived and arrived in New York in March 1944.[68] The diary was serialized first in the Yiddish daily the *Forverts* and then released as a book in February 1945 before the end of the war. Upon its publication, *Warsaw Ghetto: A Diary* was immediately reviewed, glowingly, in numerous high-profile newspapers and magazines including the *Saturday Review of Literature*, the *New York Times*, the *New Yorker*, and the *Chicago Sunday Tribune*. Journalists also wrote about Mary Berg in Jewish venues, including the *Jewish Advocate* of Boston and *Jewish Social Studies*. A newsletter put out by Hadassah, the American Zionist women's organization, featured an interview with the diarist and offered a form for those interested in mail-ordering the book, which became a Book-of-the-Month Club selection. The interview, in Hadassah's March–April 1945 issue, went into considerable detail about the features of ghetto life, including the cafés, the "beaches," and the deportations.[69]

Although the common perception is that the Holocaust was absent from the public eye until the Eichmann trial in 1963, many other reports about European Jewry followed on Mary Berg's heels. Human interest stories were common. One item in the *New York Times* featured a twenty-eight-year-old Jewish woman who arrived in New York in July 1947. She had survived a labor camp; her husband, mother, and sister were murdered in Auschwitz.[70] The article described the refugee's fruitless search for a relative who had been in the United States for more than ten years. Two days later following its publication, the newspaper claimed success in aiding the reunion between the young woman and her American kin; until the previous month, the two had lived just a few blocks from each other in Brooklyn.[71] Another article described the marriage of two survivors at the Marseilles Hotel, the USNA reception center in Manhattan. The bride was the sole survivor of a family of nine. The groom's entire family had also been killed save for one brother with whom he had escaped from a train destined for Auschwitz.[72] Still another story told of a blind refugee and his goals in America. "I want to go to an institute for the blind and take up my trade again to support myself . . . and I want to get an American haircut and buy an American suit so I won't look different from anyone else," he stated.[73] These stories appeared with regularity. While they did not generally make the front page, they were there, nonetheless.

The DPs' quests for citizenship, rapid adjustment, and success at finding work were recurring themes, aimed, no doubt, at convincing an American public that not only was there good potential among the DPs, but also they did not undermine American-born workers. But some articles—including those covering the Nuremberg trials—mentioned forced separation in ghettos, slave labor, concentration camps, and mass murder. Enough so that by 1953, stories about concentration camp survivors were apparently old hat. An article in the *Washington Post* about a recently arrived DP referred to the young woman's description of her experiences as the "oft-told tale of the concentration camp, the misery, and the liberation, the coming to America to begin a new life."[74]

It was not only in the newspapers that portraits of Holocaust survivors appeared. The New York City radio station WNYC broadcast the arrival of ships bringing DPs to New York. A father and son were brought together for the first time since the war and their emotional reunion was reported over the New York airwaves. The Los Angeles station KGFJ used celebrities such as Henry Fonda to raise local awareness about DPs.[75]

In what was perhaps its first appearance in the popular culture of television, the Holocaust was alluded to in the much-beloved weekly television program *The Goldbergs*, a sitcom about an American Jewish family in New York. In a September 1949 episode, Molly, the show's heroine, emotionally announces that the Goldbergs have heard from their European family requesting a photograph and a letter. "We just received a letter from relations we didn't hear from since before the war," Molly proclaims.[76] True, the survivors were off screen and background to the episode's plot, but their presence was noted. While the exact nature of the letter that the European relatives ask for is not spelled out, it certainly suggests the possibility of an affidavit. This remains unstated and is not clarified then or in future episodes. Still, it's a timely reference since 1949 heralded an influx of refugees after the Displaced Persons Act of 1948.

The film industry was not immune, either. In 1949 a Polish film about Auschwitz made its debut in American theaters. Using Polish survivors, *The Last Stop* chronicled the experiences of women in Auschwitz. It was shown to packed houses in numerous cities, including Boston; Washington, DC; and New York. What people read cannot be ascertained. How many people watched *The Goldbergs* or went to the cinema that year cannot be documented. They were not yet called Holocaust survivors, but without a doubt the Holocaust and those who had endured it were assuredly appearing in the public eye. Anyone who was interested would have found ample opportunity to learn about the surviving remnant of European Jewry.

For the DPs who wanted to come to America, it was a long road before they were able to do so. But by the time the legislation was in place to admit the DPs, the Jewish community had organized a national agency specifically designed to receive and resettle the newcomers around the country. What happened once they reached the United States by the thousands? For many, as we shall now see, this brought a new set of challenges and obstacles that neither the newcomers nor their hosts anticipated.

CHAPTER 2

Welcome to America!

THE NEWCOMERS ARRIVE

The S.S. *General Black* pulled into New York on 31 October 1948. On board were 813 DPs, the first admitted under the new DP Act. "Welcome to America," read a banner atop a military boat that brought government officials to greet the newcomers. A *Washington Post* journalist captured the event's festive mood: "These latter-day pilgrims, first of 205,000 coming here in the next two years, crowded the ship's rail, shouted, whistled, and waved their handkerchiefs wildly as they passed the Statue of Liberty." Attorney General Tom Campbell Clark brought greetings from President Truman to "the pilgrims of 1948" and announced that the newcomers had "proved their 'worthiness' to become residents of the United States—'the greatest of all blessings on earth.'" One new arrival declared, "We are born today the second time in our lives. We are," the thirty-four-year-old Russian native told the crowd, "today liberated from every misery of existence in Europe and we thank you very much."[1]

Shortly after arrival of the first DPs, Joseph Beck, executive director of USNA, sent a memo to his national field staff alerting them to an imminent increase in immigration. On the basis of reports received from the American Jewish Joint Distribution Committee, Beck wrote, "it appears that a substantial number of Jews will be eligible for immigration into the United States under the Displaced Persons Act."[2] Both the legislation and the Jewish refugee organizations were in place. America was ready for the DPs.

Jewish leaders expected between 20,000 and 30,000 Jews to enter the United States on the DPA of 1948. In fact, the number of Jewish immigrants in 1948 and 1949 totaled more than 50,000.[3] By the end of 1954, this figure climbed to 140,000. With the help of Jewish agencies and American relatives, the survivors ultimately settled in forty-six states. This number

The S.S. *General Black* brings the first DPs under the Displaced Persons Act of 1948, October 1948. National Archives and Records Administration. Courtesy of the United States Holocaust Memorial Museum.

suggests widespread community participation, but numbers only tell a partial and limited story. Where the refugees settled, who wanted them, and how they were received upon arrival are questions that address the nuances of reception and illuminate the qualitative aspect of this experience belied by both the glowing stories in the media and the agencies' statistics.

New York City was the port of entry into the United States for most refugees, and it was there that the majority wanted to stay—and did. Still, the combined efforts of the Jewish organizations and individual sponsors sent approximately 40 percent elsewhere, to cities and towns throughout the country. What brought some to major urban centers and others to far-flung towns in remote locations? The answer to this reflects many competing interests on the national, local, and personal level.

Because of the fear among American Jews that DPs concentrated in urban centers (especially New York) would provoke antisemitism, USNA preferred to send refugees to other destinations: from Oakland, California, to Providence, Rhode Island, and from Sheboygan, Wisconsin, to Columbia,

South Carolina. At the same time, communities needed to be convinced that taking in refugees was the right thing to do. Then there were the refugees' American relatives, who played a vital role in bringing family members here. Finally, there were the Holocaust survivors themselves, who had wishes but often little voice about their U.S. destination.

The refugees' destination was predetermined before they left Europe. In order to obtain a visa to come to the United States, every immigrant needed a sponsor willing to provide an affidavit, which promised that the newcomer would not become a public charge. In postwar America, where the memory of the depression and its devastating unemployment was still fresh, the virulent antisemitism of the 1940s lingered, and nativist sentiment persisted, this promise was no mere formality. The government demanded this commitment and the Jewish community, both individually and collectively, pledged to honor it. More than a requirement, it is also a metaphor for the relationship between the DPs and their hosts, and it is fundamental to understanding the complexities of resettlement.

An immigrant could receive the coveted affidavit in three ways: an individual affidavit (for a named relative); an agency or corporate affidavit (such as from USNA for a specific individual); or, least common, an employer affidavit (unnamed). Sponsoring a refugee carried, on paper, four requirements whereby sponsors—individual or corporate—guaranteed each eligible DP the following:

1. Assurance of suitable employment at not less than the prevailing rate of wages for like activity in the community where employed without displacing some other person from employment.
2. Assurance of safe and sanitary housing for the persons and members of his family who will accompany him and who propose to live with him without displacing some other person from such housing.
3. Assurance that the displaced person and members of his family who accompany him and propose to live with him shall not become public charges.
4. Assurance that the displaced person and members of his family will be properly received at the port of entry in the United States and transportation and en route expenses from such port to the place of destination shall be provided.[4]

Each stipulation was carefully worded to remind the reader that these may be displaced persons but they were *not* to displace any American in any way whatsoever. The Displaced Persons Act of 1948 differed from the Truman Directive because it mandated that each person must have a job and assurance of housing before leaving Europe. The responsibility for taking care of the refugee clearly rested on the shoulders of those who provided the assurances. Once the refugee was firmly on American soil, however, the response by both individual and community sponsors ranged from participation to rejection.

The refugee agencies hoped that DPs with American connections would be able to secure individual affidavits and leave corporate assurances for those without American relatives. This desire was motivated by both practical and humanitarian considerations. Individual sponsorship carried an implicit financial commitment by the relatives, as well as the assumption that families care best for their own.

Because the majority of American Jews (and therefore, the largest pool of sponsors) resided in New York City, a significant refugee population settled there. But many of these New York sponsors failed to keep their commitments once newcomers arrived, which contradicted USNA's resettlement plans. As much as they preferred individual sponsorship, the agencies, and . many New Yorkers, also wanted refugees resettled in other locations.

Some refugees did not care. Some preferred to leave the hustle and bustle of New York City behind. But many did care. Approximately 60 percent settled there largely through relatives' sponsorship. Martha C., a nineteen-year-old Auschwitz survivor from Czechoslovakia, and her New York relatives found each other after the war. Her aunt and uncle provided the necessary affidavit and she arrived to live with them in New York City.[5] For Martha, the issue was clear cut. She never thought of going anywhere else. This exemplified the route for many refugees with individual affidavits. And while sponsors in New York furnished 77 percent of all individual affidavits this did not necessarily reflect the qualitative kind of support that the refugee needed or wanted.[6] Certainly, few relatives kept their financial commitment. That nearly 90 percent of survivors on relatives' affidavits turned to NYANA attests to that.[7]

Mrs. K. was among the 90 percent who requested help. She and her husband chose to immigrate to the United States over Palestine because the pull of family was so strong. Her husband's uncle sponsored them and they fully expected their uncle to take Mr. K. into his thriving business. When this did not happen, the couple turned to the New York agency. "Yes," the agency would help, Mrs. K. recalled in 1998, fifty years after her arrival, "if she would agree to be resettled outside of New York." Both out of dire need and disappointment over their uncle's lack of help, she agreed without hesitation.[8]

Mrs. K. was among the minority that considered leaving New York. USNA fought a losing battle in its attempts to convince its clients to go elsewhere. At an USNA meeting in 1950, staff presented problems that had arisen at their reception center, the Hotel Marseilles. The shelter had provided an opportunity for refugees to congregate together and had unwittingly fostered contact with earlier immigrants who "infected" the newer arrivals with resistance to leaving the city.[9] Rabbi Isaac Trainin, director of USNA's, and later NYANA's, Religious Functionary Department, affirmed that "everybody wanted to stay in New York" when he sought employment for religious functionaries outside New York City.[10]

It is no surprise that many survivors felt strongly about remaining in New York. In 1948 the Jewish population of the United States was 5,000,000 of which 2,000,000 lived in New York City out of a general population of approximately 7,455,000.[11] New York was the center of American Jewish life. A range of educational, cultural, social, and religious institutions reflected this. New York had Jewish neighborhoods with the infrastructure necessary to those who wanted it. There was a substantial Yiddish culture, both secular and religious: press, schools, theater, and radio programs. New York was also home to the majority of the country's *landsmanschaftn* (hometown social groups), which provided an important social network for survivors.

The tension between the immigrants' desire to stay within the New York Jewish community and that community's wish to have the refugees elsewhere echoed that of earlier Jewish immigration. The creation of the Hebrew Sheltering and Immigrant Aid Society (HIAS) in 1909 grew, in part, out of the established community's ambivalence about the high numbers of Jews emigrating from Eastern Europe to the United States; it felt a moral obligation to help its unfortunate brethren, but the largely German community also wanted to control the "undesirable" element they feared might descend in great numbers on New York.[12] Indeed, the prominent American Jewish leader Jacob Schiff strongly believed in distribution of immigrants around the country. Beginning in the first decade of the twentieth century, his Galveston Plan sent groups of Eastern European Jewish immigrants to Texas.[13]

These familiar tensions between new immigrants and the establishment, between New York and other locations, clearly reverberated through the postwar resettlement program. This problem was not new. And the American hosts, despite the Holocaust, were no more positively inclined than they had been at the start of the twentieth century.

In NYANA's view, "Both in total numbers and in 'hard core' characteristics, New York City will have received by the end of 1951 a heavy and disproportionate share of Jewish immigration to the United States." The agency worried how it would manage. "No other community has had to cope even remotely on a comparable scale with as many tens of thousands of newly arrived immigrants, or with so many handicapped, aged and other persons, all of whom constitute the hard core part of the immigrant population."[14] In short, not only did NYANA feel that it had received more than its fair share of DPs, but it had also become a dumping ground for problem cases.

The DPs' desire to remain in New York was contrary to the mandate of the Displaced Persons Act: the avoidance of a large concentration of refugees in major urban areas. USNA had hoped to circumvent this by matching a refugee with a community while the immigrant was still in Europe. In that way the refugee would have no choice about his or her U.S. destination. Their plan was foiled when many refugees simply refused to budge from New York after their arrival. Some newcomers started out elsewhere but returned to New York because of the pull of the survivor community there. Later NYANA insisted that communities rejecting certain refugees also compounded the problem.

Still, USNA pushed ahead with its goal for widespread resettlement by using community assurances exclusively for locales other than New York. If it could not control the disproportionate numbers settling in New York on relatives' sponsorship, then at least it could use community assurances to send as many refugees as possible away from the city. New York, then, would have no community quota, because of its large number of refugees on individual sponsorship. The local cooperating communities, outside New York, would have to assume responsibility by providing the bulk of the corporate affidavits.

The Truman administration shared USNA's plan to place refugees in communities outside New York City. One of the main goals of the Displaced Persons Commission (DPC), the first federal immigrant agency established by the Displaced Persons Act of 1948, was the widespread distribution of refugees around the nation.[15] The DPC worked with affidavit-granting organizations such as USNA to resettle DPs in a way that was fair and equitable—to the American hosts. In order for this to system to work, communities had to agree to accept a certain quota of DPs by providing assurances for them.

The use of corporate affidavits to settle DPs outside New York may have been a goal shared by USNA, the DPC, and NYANA, but certainly not one shared by refugees or many cities and towns around the country. It was difficult to convince communities not only to accept refugees but, in some instances, also to retain them. From the start this was an uphill battle.

A first step was to educate the Jewish community. To that end, USNA executive director Joseph Beck sent a letter to Jewish organizations urging them to inform their communities about "one of the most pressing problems confronting the world today—particularly the Jewish world." He encouraged Jewish leaders to host USNA's speakers on the DP problem because he was certain that "your membership will be eager to hear the dramatic story of what United Service is doing to help these ill-fated men, women and children rebuild their lives and become self-reliant citizens who can make a significant contribution to the progress of our own country."[16]

Beck seemed pleased by communities' interest. He reported to his field staff in November 1948 that the response to requests for quotas had "generally been excellent."[17] The numbers show a less salutary response. As of 15 October 1948, USNA had heard from 243 communities, of which 156 committed themselves to meet their quota. In the same report to the staff, Beck emphasized that fieldworkers must solidify USNA's role by making sure that cooperating communities had the resources for settling DPs. In addition, it was the field representative's job to follow up with communities in order to secure their quota commitments and to ensure that the community recognized its financial responsibility for DPs on agency assurance until they became self-maintaining.

In May 1949, Beck warned that USNA now faced a "crucial period. We have recently reached the point where we no longer have enough assurances on a current basis to permit the continued immigration of the large numbers who are eligible to come here."[18] USNA tried many avenues to encourage local communities to participate. A small article in the May 1949 issue of *New Neighbors* reflected this effort. "Have you received your copy of USNA's Speakers Roster Brochure?" it asked. "You may want to keep it handy for the time you wish to schedule a speaker to give an up-to-date picture on the most exciting resettlement program ever conducted in this country."[19]

Despite USNA's push, the gap between that agency's hope and the local communities' response is made painfully clear in an interagency letter written in July 1949. Al Meyers, an USNA field representative, wrote to the head of its Oklahoma cooperating agency, "I agree with you as I have had to agree with every other community that this resettlement program is one big headache, and an even bigger local responsibility." Nevertheless, Mr. Meyers went on to remind the official that "it is a responsibility that every community must share equitably."[20]

The goal of maximum and equitable participation, however, continued to thwart USNA's intentions. William Rosenwald, honorary president of USNA, sounded the alarm in November 1949. Meeting with 150 Jewish leaders at an USNA regional conference, he expressed concern that "unless American communities act with the greatest haste and determination tens of thousands of homeless men, women and children now in displaced persons' camps in Europe and eligible for admission in the United States next year would miss the opportunity to enter this country." He urged American Jewish communities to "share the responsibility of helping these people come to this country."[21]

Records show that communities eventually provided the requisite number of assurances, and the resettlement program fanned out to include almost every state.[22] These figures, however, do not reveal the effort that went into garnering and ensuring community participation, nor do they illuminate the quality of the reception or the attitude of the community to the newcomers once they came face to face with each other. The hosts' response was often exacerbated by the reality of assisting Holocaust survivors once they had arrived in their respective communities.

The Berneman family bound for Denver, 24 January 1949. HIAS. Courtesy of the United States Holocaust Memorial Museum

When a community agreed to accept a quota of DPs, it did not necessarily bespeak an unwavering commitment to the refugees. Rather, the resettlement program was fraught with ambivalence. Clearly the number of refugees sent to a location hardly reflects the tensions that existed once the DP finally lived there, or the numbers that left or were forced to leave by a community that could not or would not care for a newcomer.

Denver is a case in point. In 1948, there were 16,000 Jews in Denver out of a total population of 322,000.[23] Its Jewish infrastructure was rich for such a relatively small community. Eight synagogues flourished, as did the Allied Jewish Federation, the Jewish Community Center, kosher slaughterhouses, and a national Jewish hospital for respiratory diseases. The local Jewish Family and Children's Services (JFCS) cooperated with USNA in the resettlement program. Denver agreed to accept twelve refugees a month for at least two years. All in all, about three hundred DPs settled in Denver.[24]

Despite Denver's apparent commitment to help, the agency had its reservations, and its executive director, Dr. Alfred Neumann, expressed them often. An Austrian Jewish émigré, Dr. Neumann felt that Denver received more than its fair share of difficult cases. "A series of incidents have arisen lately which we would like to bring to your attention," he wrote to Arthur Greenleigh in January 1951, "because we feel that the continual flow of hard core cases, or the referral of families with many children poses a grave problem in our resettlement program." He went on to describe several cases and stated his conviction "that Denver has become a favorite spot for hard core applicants."[25] Dr. Neumann also wrote to Miss Beatrice Behrman, USNA's director of resettlement, apprising her of a difficult situation in nearby Cheyenne. "A delegation of the Cheyenne community arrived yesterday with Mr. G [a survivor], who is trying to leave their community since they could not handle him there any longer," he told her. A Cheyenne doctor diagnosed Mr. G.'s current illness "as a form of a mental disturbance which caused great anxiety amongst the Cheyenne people interested in resettlement," Dr. Neumann reported. He also noted that "two of the three units settled in Cheyenne are in Denver, and a third one left for Detroit." Finally, he suggested, "unless there is absolute clarity on their part as well as on USNA's part regarding Cheyenne, Cheyenne's capacity maybe [sic] considered a waste of time, money, and effort on the resettlement map."[26]

The belief that Denver was a dumping ground for difficult refugees provoked the Denver New Americans Committee into a debate about whether to continue "our resettlement program on the basis of the cases sent to us."[27]

Continue it did, although Dr. Neumann threatened numerous times to cancel or impose a moratorium on their refugee program.

Dr. Neumann's attitude affected scores of survivors. The example of A.G. represents just one of many. A.G. was a twenty-one-year-old Romanian-born man who arrived in New York in 1949.[28] NYANA sent him to the National Jewish Hospital in Denver after he became ill in Waterbury, Connecticut, in April 1951. According to his file, he "pleaded urgently to be permitted to remain in Denver explaining how lonely he feels living by himself in Waterbury."[29] NYANA asked the JFCS in Denver if it would accept the young man on its quota in exchange for a refugee who was going back to New York.

NYANA and the National Jewish Hospital agreed that the Ex-Patients' Home (EPH) would provide proper rehabilitation for A.G. Dr. Neumann, however, concurred with the JFCS's casework supervisor Ralph Ross's recommendation that "placement at the EPH, because of its institutional character, would vitiate the case work goal of helping A to emancipate and become emotionally and socially autonomous."[30] Mr. Ross responded to Beatrice Behrman, "After giving this plan the most careful thought and sharing our thinking fully with the National Jewish Hospital, we had come to the conclusion that it is unworkable from the casework point-of-view." Mr. Ross reasoned that "Mr. G.'s problem is at this point not so much one of physical rehabilitation as it is one of emotional re-education which would have to be approached by helping this deeply deprived and dependent young man towards increasing autonomy in the mastery of his environment."[31] JFCS could not assume responsibility for A.G., Mr. Ross told Miss Behrman. Why assume the prohibitive cost of accepting him, he argued, if it would provide him with the wrong type of treatment?

USNA's Miss Behrman was not pleased that JFCS refused to accept A.G. "I would like to point out," she responded on 18 September 1951, "that we are rather concerned that the family agency in Denver, in rejecting this case, negates the plan made by the hospital for the best rehabilitation of this young man. There are so few family casework services available throughout the country and we regret that the Denver Jewish Family and Children's Services is limited in its ability to take on a situation requiring a constructive casework job because of its present budget limitations." Miss Behrman warned Mr. Ross that A.G.'s opportunities "for working through his problems in New York City, as presented by the Director of Social Service of the National Jewish Hospital of Denver, are very limited and I would say that the prognosis is not good." Nevertheless, the staff in Denver remained unmoved. "Case Closed 9/30/51" was the conclusion noted in the file shortly thereafter.[32]

Some of Dr. Neumann's grievances seem understandable. After all, JFCS was a small staff of four people and the agency had to attend to the needs of its local nonsurvivor population also. Unlike NYANA, whose sole function was to service DPs, JFCS had other clients. At the same time, JFCS was strengthened by a group of volunteers who helped meet the refugees, locate housing, and transport the newcomers. One can sympathize, initially, with Dr. Neumann's agitation over the flurry of nine unexpected arrivals, for example, but his refusal to accept four of them seems heartless.[33] His concerns simply do not matter weighed against the needs of the survivor refugees.

In his view, Denver could not do more. As Dr. Neumann insisted to Beatrice Behrman, USNA's director of resettlement, "We are willing to go all the way out in the resettlement program." Furthermore, he said, "Our records speak for itself." According to USNA's figures, he said, "Denver services an unusual number of cases, more than any other American community, on a per capita basis."[34]

Denver was not the only community that accepted refugees but felt aggrieved by USNA's lack of understanding. For some communities, the idea of helping was fraught with what they felt to be legitimate complications. From 1949 until the early 1950s, Emil Saloman, the executive director of the Tulsa, Oklahoma, Jewish Federation argued with USNA that Tulsa Jews were too few and the employment opportunities too limited to absorb the number of refugees that USNA requested of them. Saloman's language implies a different sentiment, however. When USNA asked Tulsa to accept an additional ten refugees beyond the twenty-four that the city expected for 1949, Mr. Saloman replied, "Following a protracted, joint meeting of our Executive Committee and Welfare Committee, yesterday, it was decided that we dare not increase our DP Unit quota beyond the twenty-four Units agreed upon when you were in Tulsa. I have already notified Mr. Edwin Rosenberg to that effect."[35] Paucity of employment opportunity was not the only problem, however. Rather, it was Mr. Saloman's fear that survivors would not be able to work well, as in the case of the first DP to come to Tulsa who, after three months, asked to join his sister in New York. This man "failed utterly" in his first job as a tailor's assistant, Mr. Salomon reported. Perhaps USNA might send him from Tulsa to New York?[36]

Mr. Saloman clearly wished to disengage the Tulsa Jewish Federation from USNA and looked for every excuse to report the failure of the program in his city. His use of the term *unit* for a Holocaust survivor is one expression of institutional distancing. At the same time, in virtually every agency, from the USNA executive board down, the word *unit* was used when these organizations referred to the new immigrants on their quotas. The word was used mainly at the administrative level in interagency communications, suggesting that it referred to a designation of status, that is, *family unit*. Even so, as in the case of Mr. Salomon or Dr. Neumann, it facilitated a distance between the agency and the refugee, reflecting an attitude of a bureaucracy dealing with a commodity rather than a community caring for its own.

Mr. Saloman had many concerns. He voiced these matters in a letter to Edwin Rosenberg, president of USNA, in May 1949, emphasizing "the difficulties facing a small Jewish community, such as ours, when called upon to accept responsibility for a considerable number of these Units."[37] His letter was in response to a USNA National Conference on Employment Services for Jewish DPs. Unable to attend, he wanted to inform USNA's president that he believed that "present DP Settlement plans are posing a serious dilemma." Again, he emphasized the difficulty of placing newcomers with few skills in the Tulsa job market. "This utter lack of experience in some useful occupation, plus inability to read and write English, then becomes a serious handicap for persons for whom employment is sought in a non-industrial community," Saloman stressed.[38]

Tulsa, however, did not renege on its commitments. It accepted twenty-four New Americans and developed a volunteer staff to assist the refugees in their new home. Still, Mr. Saloman's communications to USNA continued to reflect the leader's unhappiness with the program and displeasure with the newcomers. A year after the first immigrants arrived in Tulsa he wrote again to Arthur Greenleigh. "Our own experience has clearly proved," he noted to USNA's executive director, "that satisfactory adjustment is well-nigh impossible when these people are being forced to live apart from their kinfolk, as their experiences abroad have made them most adept at passive resistance. The latest such Unit arrived here last week," he concluded, "and it should not be long before we may have to ask for transfer."[39] Mr. Saloman's ire is not totally misplaced. After all, most refugees indeed expressed the desire to be near relatives. Nevertheless, his example illustrates the way that attitude interfered with the noble intentions of the refugee program.

USNA asked one Jewish group in Philipsburg, Pennsylvania, to absorb three refugee families. A representative wrote to USNA that his organization needed more information before deciding "whether we can assume this great responsibility." After stating that his community was 99 percent non-Jewish, the man posed several qualified questions so that "before making any commitments, we would like to be assured whether or not we can apply ourselves to your most urgent request." The letter stated a preference for tailors and families with four or fewer members. In addition, the group's spokesman wondered about potential refugees' means of self-support and their political affiliations. He spelled out that "communist belief will not be tolerated."[40] Surely the community needed to know what type of work a newcomer might perform and how he or she would support him- or herself. At the same time, its lack of compassion toward Jews who survived the Holocaust and needed its support emerges clearly. Just as other attitudes influenced Tulsa's response, practical rather than humanitarian concerns dictated that of Philipsburg. Whether this masked a less charitable attitude toward refugees remains a matter of speculation. It is a response, however, that reverberates in the agency files.

Not all communities had reservations. Columbia, South Carolina, is an example of a small town that seemed to have responded to the refugee crisis with alacrity. The May 1949 issue of *New Neighbors* featured a story titled "A Primer in Resettlement for Small Communities," which was meant to inspire other towns. It announced: "To the Jewish Community of Columbia, South Carolina, the Displaced Persons Act of 1948 was a challenge that whetted its civic pride. Aware of the fact that the resettlement program was in great measure dependent upon the smaller communities, Columbia, with only 250 Jewish families in a population of 100,000, organized swiftly to provide a new life for Jewish DPs."[41]

Columbia appears to have been a community willing and eager to become involved. The *New Neighbors* article outlined how the people of Columbia responded to USNA's appeal for help. Representatives from the synagogues, Zionist organizations, the University of South Carolina Hillel, the Hebrew Benevolent Society, and B'nai Brith joined forces to form an executive committee, which mobilized the resources of the 250-family community. The article also described the enthusiasm that had spilled over to the gentile population of ninety thousand. Along with planning hot meals and providing furnished apartments; English lessons; jobs; babysitting; and medical, dental, legal and psychological services, the committees enlisted help from local hairdressers who agreed to provide a free "American up-to-date hair-do to each female newcomer."[42]

This was not merely *New Neighbors*'s public relations; the field reports of the USNA representative's visits to Columbia substantiate the story.[43] Why was Columbia so ready to help when others, like Tulsa, did so reluctantly? Perhaps it was because the number of affidavits that the community agreed to provide was less than ten. Undoubtedly, it was easier to manage such a small number trickling in over two years. More important was the role of local advocacy: an ambitious young Columbia couple, Mr. and Mrs. Bank, spearheaded the effort. They saw it as their mission to bring refugees to South Carolina and took a personal interest in them. This is a distinct departure from the New York and Denver agencies' strict policy against professionals fraternizing with clients. In a letter to USNA in 1950, Dena Bank wrote: "One of our DPs had his first birthday in America last week. He's single—25 years old—and without any relatives anywhere. We had a real party at our house for him—with candles, cake, ice cream etc. He was so very grateful—we really enjoyed the party."[44]

The secretary of the Columbia refugee committee, Mrs. Hannah Rubin, took a similarly warm and personal approach. In an interview a half century later she recalled her contact with a refugee family. Mrs. Rubin assumed responsibility for the first DPs, the M. family, she said. "They became independent very soon. Within two years they were functioning on their own," she noted, echoing the way in which so many in the American community judged the refugees' success.[45]

Mrs. Rubin remembered how the housing market affected their program. Faced with the imminent arrival of their sister, one of the refugee families living in a one-room apartment sought a larger accommodation. The search went unrewarded until two Jewish businessmen suggested a solution. Owners of a fast-food establishment with an unused shack, they offered the small building to the family. Hannah Rubin and the refugees cleaned and painted their new home. The newcomers settled into the town, worked hard, and became economically well off and respected members of the community.[46]

Mrs. Rubin's involvement with the M. family was personal. In fact, the relationship continues to this day. She "was really glad to help them," she explained; she "felt very close to the family." She summed up the experience by saying, "It was a real pleasure to be able to do it."[47] From Hannah Rubin's perspective, the Columbia program was a success on many levels. She is proud of her direct help to the immigrant family and of their rapid adjustment to life in America.

Looking at the Columbia example from the perspective of the refugee family reveals a more ambiguous story. The young sister (now Mrs. G.) who joined the M. family in 1949 recalled that "people were very nice. There was nothing more they could have done," which suggests that despite the community's efforts, the reality fell short of the DPs' needs.[48] Thinking about the kind of help she received, she remembered how people "brought them old clothes. We had to smile and say thank you," while others "didn't care to know about us." The hierarchical nature of the relationship predominated. "You're not human, not equal, you're a 'greener.' " She believed this changed in the 1960s, "when we didn't need anything from them."[49]

The difference between the two women's reminiscences captures the clash between the hosts and the immigrants, even in a "successful" experiment such as Columbia. Mrs. Rubin spoke about the pleasure she took from helping the families, while Mrs. G. remembered the pain of feeling a sense of diminished worth and her struggle to live after the Holocaust. In another interview, Mrs. G. spoke about her postwar depression and a suicide attempt a few years after her arrival in Columbia.[50] On one level, Mrs. G. had gone forward with life; she was married and the mother of three children. At the same time, her wartime memories tortured her. This dual reality reminds us, once again, that Holocaust survivors were not typical immigrants.

It is clear why USNA held Columbia up as a model for other small communities. But its spirit failed to inspire others, even in towns in the same area. A member of USNA's field staff reported that Columbia's response was "particularly outstanding in relation to the very poor response of the surrounding communities of equal or larger size."[51] Absent from the records is mention of what happened to those DPs whom USNA sent to Columbia. Mrs. G. and her family stayed and built up a prosperous business, which she still operates today. Two of the young men on Columbia's quota, however, returned to New York because of the pull of its large refugee community.[52]

Although USNA tried to take control of the immigrants' destination, there were those who would not allow the agency to determine their fate. Some simply refused to leave New York. Others who settled elsewhere also made choices if they felt that their destination was not an appropriate match. Numerous files are marked "unauthorized," indicating those DPs who left the place where USNA had sent them in search of a more agreeable home.

Mr. J. was an "unauthorized" refugee. A thirty-year-old Polish man, he had survived a concentration camp in which his wife had been killed. Mr. J. was sent to Omaha, Nebraska, but immediately asked that city's refugee committee for a transfer to Denver. The committee told him "to take it easy" and to wait to speak to their social worker. He promptly left on his own to be with his Denver relatives, who were "the only ones he has left in this world."[53] The newcomer appeared with his relatives at the JFCS offices requesting help. What could JFCS do to help him remain in that city, he wondered? The social worker was sympathetic but firm. "I told Mr. J. first that he really must have felt pretty lonely and that I could understand very well how much better it would be for him to be together with his relatives," she recorded in Mr. J.'s file. She then went on to explain their DP program, "which meant that we were responsible for people for resettlement here and that he was not on our quota." She then informed him that "he actually came here unauthorized."[54] Mr. J. was fortunate. His relatives were just as anxious to have him remain in Denver as he was. They agreed to support him until he found work. The agency could and did offer its employment services. A few weeks later, through his relatives' contacts, Mr. J. began work as an apprentice at a mattress company.

Many other refugees arrived in Denver "unauthorized" from all parts of the country. The reasons varied. Some, like the K. family, felt that the business opportunities there were superior to those in New York City, which indicates that there was movement away from that city, too.[55] Others, such as the C. family, were rejected by Tulsa and sent to Texas, which the C. family left because of the climate and the paucity of Yiddish-speaking Jews.[56] The F. family left Buffalo for Denver because of its reputedly healthful air.[57] Still others, like Mr. J., sought their relatives.

Although the DPs' motivations differed, the agency's reaction was almost universally the same. Unless one individual could take the place of another on its quota, the agency refused to dispense financial help. It did, however, offer vocational services. And sometimes this was enough to get a newcomer established in a first job. The agency's attitude toward unauthorized refugees was clear. Dr. Neumann summed up his feelings unequivocally in a letter to Miss Einbinder, settlement consultant at USNA. "If there is any meaning at all to a national resettlement service, it must be done in a planful, responsible manner," he wrote. "For this reason," he stated in closing, "we cannot accept self-settlers, such as Mr. and Mrs. K, as much as we may appreciate their capabilities and resourcefulness."[58]

Communities' refusal to accept "unauthorized" refugees did not stop newcomers from seeking new homes. Apparently, relocating was a fairly widespread phenomenon. When Congress amended the Displaced Persons Act in 1950 it included a Good Faith oath.[59] This required the refugee to proceed to the community of destination and stay there. The intent of this amendment was twofold: to keep the DPs in their community of destination and to avoid significant numbers of DPs in large urban areas.[60]

What happened when the refugees' American relatives, rather than communities, were the sponsors? The response was mixed—very mixed. Sponsorship brought together family members who were blood relatives but had never met and who often had vastly different expectations of one another and their new relationship. Often individual sponsors felt obliged to provide the affidavit that was the DP's ticket out of Europe, but it is clear that they never intended to make a commitment beyond this. Indeed, once the refugees arrived, despite written promises of help, situations arose that led to the NYANA files being riddled with such entries as "[the sponsor was] a distant relative who was in no position to help as she was a worker herself"[61] or "relatives could not meet the obligation they had agreed to."[62] In one situation, the caseworker recorded that the sponsor "had kept Mr. H. for three weeks and has paid for [visits to] her family physician but she cannot go further. Mr. H. is her relation not her husband's. She personally has no funds at her disposal and her husband feels that he had done more than he was under obligation to do."[63]

According to one survivor, Mr. B., his aunt shunned him not because of money but for other reasons. When asked in a videotaped interview in 1984 about his arrival in Cleveland in 1948, a flash of discomfort flickers across Mr. B.'s face.[64] Although his aunt, a widow, sponsored him, the young man paid his own travel expenses and reached Cleveland with two dollars in his pocket. "I have to be honest with you," he admits slowly, "she had some girl she wanted me to marry and she was unhappy that I came with my fiancé." His aunt's disappointment overshadowed everything else. She withheld additional help from her nephew.

Many cases indicate that the sponsor was a total stranger who never even met—or indeed, intended to meet—the individual he or she helped to bring to the United States. One refugee received an affidavit from a man who had provided at least forty other affidavits.[65] Some were relatives who had no interest in helping their European family. They did not meet the refugees at the dock and refused to meet with them at agency offices.

Even though more than 70 percent of the DPs destined for New York arrived on individual, not agency, assurances, many eventually turned to NYANA for help. The most common pattern appears to be the sponsor who offered limited help to start but then did not continue. Sometimes this was because of stretched financial resources; at other times the affiant grew tired of the burden of being needed by the newcomer. There were some survivors who were strongly against taking help. Then, as in the case of Mr. H., there were familial tensions when the spouse of the sponsor felt put upon by the newcomer. It is also possible that once word got out in the community that agency relief money was available, the DPs, either independently or through pressure from their sponsors, approached NYANA for aid.

Some refugees believed that their American relatives had legitimate reason for withdrawing their financial commitments. One client stated that his cousin "has been unemployed for some weeks and is receiving unemployment insurance."[66] Another sponsor who accompanied the newcomer to his meeting at NYANA was upset when he told the caseworker that "he was proud to have his relatives here . . . but he really could not do anything and as proof of this he showed us various receipts from a loan he had been granted."[67]

Other newcomers appreciated the limited help their relatives offered, but really did not expect or want assistance beyond an initial gesture. Mr. K. speaks to that. His relatives gave him two hundred dollars and a new suit when he reached New York. This was enough to help him find work. To this day he feels grateful to them.[68] Some people truly did not want assistance from either agencies or relatives. "You see," said Mrs. G., "we really wanted to make it on our own. We didn't want any handouts."[69]

Financial aid was one thing, emotional support another. The newcomers needed to feel that finally they were not alone in the world; that someone, especially *mishpocha* (family), cared. Therefore, when moral support went undelivered the rift could be irreparable. One NYANA caseworker noted that her client "didn't want to have anything to do with this man [his sponsor] and how much he and his wife resented him for not even inviting him for a seder, something which they had been longing to attend for years, which they didn't have after they lost their parents."[70] The longing for family was too often one-sided. Those far from the horror of Europe had limited imagination about what this need meant, while those who had passed through it were desperate for family connections.

The night Mrs. S. arrived in New York in 1946 is still a painful memory more than fifty years later. Her cousin greeted her at the dock and brought her home. Their arrival there coincided with the airing on television of *The Milton Berle Show*. It was "very, very, very popular, everybody was watching," she recalls. "It was such an excitement like who knows what was going on. And I came the first night and instead of talking to us, she left us and went to watch Milton Berle."[71]

Celia is still bitter when she recalls her first day in America from a distance of more than a half century. Their sponsor, her husband's uncle, was supposed to meet his new family at the boat. No uncle appeared. Nor did any of his five married children. With thirteen dollars to their name, the family took a cab to the uncle's address in Brooklyn. Upon reaching the home, they found it dark. A neighbor told them that a day earlier "the K's left for

Florida, they're not home." Celia greeted this news with bewilderment. "They know we are arriving the next day, they get a cable, none of the children are waiting for us. The uncle picks himself up with his wife and leaves for Florida . . . That [her husband] is his nephew, his brother's son."[72] "I was devastated," she said. She could not fathom this attitude. After all, she pressed on, "they were not ignorant, they know what happened—they know the family was killed. They are not anxious to see, they are not interested to— see somebody an—and—cheer up those people, to know we are here for you, I'm glad you survived?"[73]

There are those whom the American family did not disappoint. Martha C. remembers that her aunt and maternal uncle were very good to her and her younger sister when they came to the United States in 1947. The two girls, aged fourteen and nineteen years old, had survived Auschwitz. Their parents and six siblings had not. Their aunt and uncle were older people with a large home and grown children. They had room for their nieces and the means to support them. "Education was everything to them," commented Martha. "They bought me books and I went to night school at Erasmus [Hall] High in Brooklyn where the class was full of survivors," she recalled. "My aunt took me shopping and bought me new clothes," remembered Martha, "because she said that my clothes weren't right and she wanted us to be Americanized."[74]

Martha's aunt encouraged her to socialize at places like the Ninety-second Street YMHA where she would meet other Jewish Americans. Martha remembers feeling some pressure, yet she agreed. At the "Y" she met her future husband, an American-born, Jewish young man. Martha felt accepted by her husband's family and speaks lovingly of them. She knew many other refugees, however, for whom the encounter with American relatives was not satisfying. To this day, she is close to her cousins, her aunt, and her uncle's children. Looking back, Martha concluded, "We were very lucky."[75]

Fritzie recalls her aunt and uncle with much devotion. "If she was my mother," she comments, "I couldn't love her more and she couldn't have been better to me." "I came to a loving family . . . a family that opened their arms to me and did the best they knew how," she states and adds, "I really was one of the lucky ones."[76]

Rachel S. echoes similar sentiments. When other DPs heard of those who had family in the United States, she remembered they remarked, "Oh, they are lucky, they are going to relatives and they will be so good and. . . . I didn't say anything because I didn't know my relatives . . . I'd—couldn't say if they will be good to me or not good to me . . . I couldn't say. How would I know? I never knew them and they . . . didn't know me either." As it turns out, she, too, believes she was one of the fortunate ones. "My relatives," she states emphatically, "were very, very, very good to me." But she was in contact with others who immigrated at the same time whose experiences differed sharply from her own. Her friends confided in her quite simply that "the relatives weren't good."[77]

Every refugee who entered the United States on individual affidavits needed signed statements from family members promising unwavering support, but according to the agencies' records, the help that was actually extended to European family members fell short of their promises, both materially and emotionally. Yes, there are those who recall the relationship with their newfound relatives with warmth and gratitude. But a recurring theme among them is also the sentiment that they were among the lucky minority in contrast to other newcomers. They reiterate the belief that deeply positive mutual feelings between the survivors and American Jewish relatives were rare. The pattern that emerges from both the case files and oral histories supports this contention. It reflects a range from limited help to outright indifference to active rejection. After all, 90 percent of the immigrants who came to New York through family sponsorship turned to NYANA for assistance. That is hardly a happily-ever-after story.

It would be reassuring to conclude that because a vast organizational structure existed that sent refugees to nearly every state in the country that the American Jewish community met the challenge of resettlement with open arms. Unfortunately, it was not so. Numbers camouflage the qualitative response. The spectrum of reception by the Jewish community was wide. There were the Emil Salomans; the sponsors who reneged; and the Banks of Columbia, South Carolina. There were those who opened their homes and those who turned their backs, with all the degrees of acceptance and rejection between the two. And the survivors' responses varied as well. There were those who accepted their destinations and those who did not and moved on. Quotas, sponsors, and affidavits permitted the refugee to obtain a visa to America. But a human being, a Holocaust survivor, stood behind that commitment. More often than not, humanitarian goals were obscured by the realities of a quota immigration program and the challenges presented once these particular immigrants came face to face with their hosts.

CHAPTER 3

Case Closed

FROM AGENCY SUPPORT TO SELF-SUFFICIENCY

The American Jewish community provided affidavits that brought 140,000 refugees to the United States. But sponsorship did not stop there. The Jewish refugee agencies also set forth an ambitious agenda to see the DPs through the complicated process of acculturation. The February 1950 issue of *New Neighbors* summed up the goals of the United Service for New Americans (USNA) program:

> United Service does not consider its task completed after it has received a Jewish DP at one of our ports of entry and moved him to the local community to which he had been destined. That is merely one phase of our job. We must then work with the local Jewish communities to help them meet the many problems which each newcomer presents during his initial months in our country. The problems vary with each person and we must be prepared to extend the guidance and make available the facilities which will bring about the immediate solutions to these problems.[1]

This was an enormous and complex task. Did the agencies achieve what they set out to do? Jewish leaders certainly believed that they were extraordinarily successful in reaching their goals and expressed praise for their programs widely. In 1950, USNA president Edwin Rosenberg lauded American Jewish communities for making possible "an era of magnificent accomplishment."[2] And indeed, in many ways, the Jewish institutional response to the New Americans was far reaching and radical. Never before had cooperating communities been called upon to participate in this manner: to accept refugees into their midst, offer financial aid, locate housing, find jobs, provide social casework services, extend medical care, advise on immigration laws. It is not surprising that USNA considered itself to be at the forefront of progressive, humanitarian immigrant care—and, in many ways it was, at least on paper.

Survivors, however, experienced the process very differently. The intent of the agencies' approach may have been innovative and well meaning, even in light of their recognizing that survivors "had suffered the unspeakable brutalities of Hitler's death camps."[3] What was delivered, however, often fell short of newcomers' expectations and left them wanting. When the hosts were confronted with these New Americans, the essential fact that they were unlike any preceding immigrants often eluded those who were committed to helping them.

The Jewish agencies insisted that they were addressing many facets of the DPs' adjustment. In actuality, the focus was on finding work and getting the refugees off of relief. The belief that employment was the first necessary step in the road to becoming productive Americans was widely accepted and deemed both practical and effective. As Arnold Askin, NYANA president, announced at its second annual meeting in 1951, "I think it is significant, as a measure of the speed with which the immigrant can become part of the mainstream of our economic and cultural life, to point out that of the 38,000 people who have received NYANA's help during the past two years, 31,000 have become fully independent, self-sustaining members of the community."[4]

Mr. Askin and his constituents basked in the glow of both NYANA's and the refugees' apparent success in becoming acculturated. Mr. Askin's remarks are telling, however, both because of what he chose to emphasize and what was left unsaid. His statement certainly describes NYANA's perceived accomplishments. But Mr. Askin did not mention that speedy acculturation also furthered other agency goals. It minimized the DPs' financial and emotional dependence on NYANA and guaranteed that no refugee would become a public charge. Also unsaid was the New York agency's policy that limited financial help to one year. Once a newcomer was self-maintaining—and the sooner the better—the file ended with the words "Case Closed," marking the end of the agency's relationship with the client.

NYANA was not alone in placing work above all other goals. Nor was it alone in emphasizing that this tack was best for the newcomer. The majority of agencies stressed independence and self-sufficiency through employment. This became the focus of their assistance to the refugees and the standard by which they deemed acculturation to be successful or not. In turn, this was the message that was communicated in the media and that fueled the myth of the survivors' triumphant postwar return to life. But the

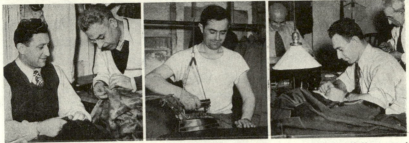

New Americans at work in Pittsfield, Massachusetts. *New Neighbors* 3, no. 3 (March 1950). Collection of author.

caseloads of the agencies' social workers, which bulged with unemployed and ill refugees, and survivors' oral histories tell a different story.

In a press release of June 1949 announcing the formation of NYANA, the major purposes of the agency were clearly defined:

A. To give voluntary financial aid, support and assistance and to furnish advice, information and guidance primarily to Jewish immigrants who reside in the city of New York and its immediate vicinity.

   These services shall be provided only as long as necessary after arrival of the immigrant in this country, but the aid is intended for persons who have been in the country less than five years, after which they become normal members of the community.

B. To provide these services in a manner which will most speedily effect the integration and adjustment of the immigrant in the American community.

C. To assist the immigrants so that they may become self-maintaining as soon as possible.[5]

Moreover, NYANA was created as a temporary emergency agency with the expectation that other public and private welfare agencies in New York City would absorb refugees into their clientele.

NYANA originally planned to help those who had been in the United States for up to five years. Within the first several months of operation, however, a much more exacting policy was established. With the arrival of more than 20,571 DPs in New York during 1949, NYANA was suddenly faced with an emergency of unexpected proportions.[6] How could the agency possibly afford to extend help to thousands of people for the first five years of their stay in the United States in order to keep their commitment that no immigrant would become a public charge?

A timely statement from the Displaced Persons Commission (DPC) in October 1949 had a profound effect on the New York agency's service to the refugees. In its Policy Letter number 7, the DPC informed voluntary agencies that one admitted under the Displaced Persons Act was legally able to receive financial help from public agencies within five years of arrival without becoming a public charge.[7] Without delay NYANA's board of directors voted to limit financial help to DPs for a maximum of twelve months. This new plan, which became known as "8–4," was put into action on 16 February 1950.[8] The NYANA social workers were candid with their clients. As one wrote in her report in March 1950 just a few weeks after the adoption of the new policy, "I could agree with [Mr. G.] that it was not easy at present to make a beginning in this country but I had to tell him that we could not make it easy for him and there were certain things that nobody could take away from him. We were here to help but could do so in a limited way."[9]

NYANA agency workers began to approach their client management in an abbreviated manner. They also initiated the closure of cases of those DPs who had been in the country for more than a year and were not in jeopardy of being deported. The stated goal was to continue closing cases "until all cases which have been in this country for one year or more (except jeopardy cases) will have received their last relief check from NYANA; thereafter, cases will be closed as clients achieve one year residence in the country."[10] This report indicated that such action would save the UJA 2.5 million dollars in its allotment to NYANA. Out of this, 1 million dollars "will result from stepping up the tempo and volume of such closings, as requested by the UJA [United Jewish Appeal] Allocations Committee."[11] In keeping with the goals of 8–4, NYANA also began to enforce the so-called 20–40 policy, which dictated that every able-bodied man and woman between the ages of twenty and forty were expected to contribute to their own or their family's self-maintenance.[12]

Since 44.6 percent of all Holocaust survivors were in this age bracket, the enactment of 20–40 had a pervasive effect on both men and women DPs.[13] It is clear that many, though by no means all, refugees did indeed express the desire to find work as quickly as possible. The tremendous pressure, especially by NYANA, to achieve this, however, affected the refugees' enormously. Even though the number of immigrants arriving in New York peaked at 20,571 in 1949 and dropped in 1950 and 1951, NYANA continued to feel the residual effects of the first wave of arrivals.[14] From 1950 on, getting the refugee working and off relief became the primary goal and the standard by which the agencies judged their success. This had a direct impact on the nature of the help that the agency offered in numerous ways.

After the implementation of 8–4, the agency stepped up its pace and usually urged the newcomer to take the first available job. Social workers were often impatient with those who had career goals that deviated from this formula. Consider the history of Mr. and Mrs. P., who arrived in New York in April 1951, the very same month that Mr. Askin addressed his group. Mr. and Mrs. P. were a young couple (twenty-four and twenty-three, respectively) with a baby daughter born in Germany in 1949. Mr. P. described himself as a watchmaker, although the caseworker comments that "he is a nice looking and nicely appearing young man but he doesn't know much about watch-making since it was just a training course at ORT [World Organization for Rehabilitation through Training Union] that he took."[15] Nevertheless, Mr. P. seemed determined to use this skill, and as was the customary protocol, his caseworker referred him to NYANA's Vocational Service Department (VSD) to discuss his options with a counselor. Several weeks later, the caseworker spoke with the VSD counselor, who said that Mr. P. "was still resisting any kind of employment because of his interest in his own trade." At the next meeting with Mr. P., which was only six weeks after the P. family's arrival in the United States (during which time they were also searching for housing), his caseworker reported:

> As indicated, he seemed to be focused only on [a] job as watchmaker. I discussed with him the focus and goal of the agency. Mr. P felt that he had a right to some time to explore employment in his field. I agreed to this relating to the amount of time he had already had and wondering how much more time he thought he ought to have. As a result of this discussion it came evident that Mr. P was not as slow-moving as he tried to impress. He had done a great deal of exploration in his own field. However, he was not yet satisfied that possibilities were not available.[16]

They finally agreed that Mr. P. would look intensively for another ten days, and if he could not find work in his field he would make himself available to the VSD for general placement in any given job.

At the next designated meeting, Mr. P. confessed that he had not been able to make his intensive job search, because his wife was ill and had to attend the clinic often, which forced him to be at home with their baby. The worker responded that "it was his responsibility in the way he wanted to use himself but I see him as the employable member of the family and that we could not accept his giving this responsibility over to the agency."[17] When Mr. P. requested additional time, the worker denied his request and said that she would not authorize his current relief check until Mr. P. made himself available for employment through the VSD. When Mr. P. again indicated that he hoped to get a job in his chosen profession, the agency worker reminded him that he was responsible for his own actions—meaning that he would only be eligible for a relief check if he followed the agency's policy. Mr. P. eventually found a job without VSD help. During the course of his first year in the country, however, he was laid off several times and reapplied twice for relief. Ultimately, Mr. P. abandoned hopes of becoming a watchmaker. Through his own efforts, he secured work as a shipping clerk.

Just as the 8–4 policy was going into effect, Mr. and Mrs. G. arrived in New York. The husband and wife, thirty-six and twenty-four, respectively, came to NYANA in February 1950. Their caseworker was particularly aggressive in speeding their independence from the agency. At their third meeting, on 20 March, they disagreed with their worker over whether they should begin looking for work while they were still at the Hebrew Sheltering and Immigrant Aid Society (HIAS) shelter or, as they preferred, to wait for a friend's apartment to become available and secure a home base before seeking employment. The caseworker remarked that "they were holding up getting settled in the community if they stayed at the hotel and I wondered if they would really find the kind of living quarters they wanted and whether this was not just fear of moving out and beginning to live on their own." The couple was upset about her reaction, but she emphasized, "It was something our agency could not accept. We were here to help people move and the first step was for them to find an apartment."[18]

The caseworker had little time or patience for the pair. "I could not spend so many interviews with them while they were still in the hotel and I gave them a time limit of two weeks and said that if by this time they had not found living quarters, I would close the case," she reported. There were rooms available, she said, and that while the time limit might be threatening, it was within Mr. G.'s reach to relocate. In fact, Mr. G. called several days later with the news that they had found a furnished room. The worker asked him how he had been using his time in job hunting. He responded that he was already looking and felt optimistic about finding something through friends. One week later, Mr. G. was back to further discuss his work plans. His wife could not join him because she was ill but the caseworker pointed out that another appointment would be arranged to see if she could help out with the "family self-maintenance." The conversation then revolved around Mr. G.'s efforts. He reported that he was "seeking all kinds of employment at present. He [was] finding difficulty in obtaining employment."[19]

On June 14, 1950, Mr. G. returned to NYANA and stated that both he and his wife were still looking for work. They had failed so far both through their own efforts and through the VSD. Out of desperation, Mr. G. had taken an "on-the-job-training" position at a friend's factory. The caseworker responded that "this would have to be evaluated by our VSD unit, first of all. Second of all, I could not see Mr. G. seeking other employment if he was busy learning in training. This cost agency money in terms of our supporting him in the meantime and we did not even know whether this was a good plan." By the end of July Mr. G. was earning seventy-five cents an hour at his friend's factory. His efforts at self-maintenance, however, were short lived. Less than a month after he started receiving a salary, he became ill with boils. At the same time, his wife was receiving medical treatment and was unable to work. When Mr. G. finally was well enough to resume working, he was temporarily laid off because business was slow; he was promised reemployment in December. Although Mr. G. wanted to return to his former job, the NYANA caseworker felt that he should work with VSD and take any available position. This turned out to be a moot point as the VSD had nothing available to offer him. In the closing entry of Mr. G.'s file, the caseworker wrote:

> Mr. and Mrs. G., 37 and 25 years respectively arrived in this country on individual assurance on February 19, 1950. Mrs. G because of a health problem seemed unable to work and emphasis was on helping Mr. G to find employment. Mr. G. found it difficult to use our VSD department [*sic*] in a constructive way. There also seems to be some question as to how he was applying himself to finding work in general. A time limit was set with family with the understanding that assistance will be discontinued as of 12/31/50. We have not heard anything further from client and case is to be closed.[20]

The example of Mr. and Mrs. G. embodies NYANA's emphasis on work for both men and women. Moreover, it illustrates the economic climate, which worked against the refugees' struggle to meet NYANA's time limit.[21] Finally, it reveals the role of persistent and pervasive personal difficulties, such as illness, which the twelve-month limit did not address. USNA and its constituent agencies may have believed in individualized care, but the treatment they delivered when it came down to the day-to-day exchanges with thousands of refugees was driven, more than anything else, by the push to get the newcomers into the workforce.

The record of another couple, Dr. and Mrs. G., offers a further illustration of NYANA's attitude toward helping New Americans in their chosen professions.[22] In this well-educated family, the man was a physician and the woman was an engineer, both European trained. After the war, Dr. G. worked for Oeuvre de Secours aux Enfants and as a doctor in various *yeshivot* (Jewish seminaries) in Paris, receiving a subsidy from the American Jewish Joint Distribution Committee (JDC). This gave them a minimal salary and allowed Mrs. G. to tend to her sick parents. After their arrival in the United States in 1953, they requested help from the agency. They asked for support (in terms of a loan, if necessary) for Dr. G. for a year, to study English and prepare for the New York State licensing exam, and for Mrs. G. for three months, to learn enough English to secure a job as a mechanical engineer. NYANA refused.

The agency agreed to support Dr. G. for three months, although its policy changed during this interval, making any help (including maintenance) for physicians on a loan basis only. The agency would not agree to help Mrs. G., insisting that she seek employment to make up the shortfall in their family budget. When NYANA remained obdurate, Mrs. G. found work as a stock clerk in a factory. Dr. G. did obtain his license to practice medicine in the state of New York. While it could be argued that this couple had their own resources to support Mrs. G.'s career goals within a fairly short amount of time, it is also true that the couple was a low-risk investment. There was every indication that, had the agency agreed to their request for a loan to both for their first year, the pair would have had the means to repay the agency. NYANA's message to Dr. and Mrs. G. was mixed. On the one hand, the couple was told that they must take responsibility for themselves, like any other newcomers. On the other hand, because Dr. G. was a physician, they were required to repay any funds NYANA gave them, including maintenance expenses.

Dr. and Mrs. G. also highlight the case of a couple in which both partners were professionals and not only the husband, but both husband and wife, wished to continue working in their respective fields. The social worker took a dim view of this and recorded that "Mrs. G may be a rather disturbed woman who wants for herself the same conditions of help as for her husband."[23] Clearly, this she would not obtain. Yes, NYANA would give Dr. G. some limited initial help, but not his wife, even if it meant that she take a position as a stock clerk. Dr. and Mrs. G were not typical of most of the newcomers. However, among those immigrant couples who had one professional partner, it was not uncommon for both to be professionals. In such cases, the agency would only support one and that was the husband.

The issue of status was complex. Many newcomers accepted the idea that they would have to start over; this belief was held particularly by those who were younger and had not yet firmly established themselves professionally in Europe, or those who were unskilled and saw the possibility for gaining a skill here in America. But for those who had a professional identity such as Dr. and Mrs. G., the transition was complicated by the crosscurrents of their status and agency policy.

These families' histories exemplify both the attitude of the agency toward what it saw as the clients' responsibility regarding employment, and the role of the agency in actually helping its clients secure a job. It is clear from the file of Mr. P., whose case was typical of that of many semiskilled or unskilled workers, that NYANA did not see its mission, except in the most limited way, to be to encourage its clients to pursue work either of interest to them, or in which they had previous training or experience. Furthermore, it left much of the job hunting up to the clients themselves. Despite the fact that one of the VSD's roles was to place immigrants in jobs, it appears to have been fairly ineffectual in that function.

In January 1951, NYANA's VSD had 2,741 active files at the beginning of the month and 1,797 at the end of it.[24] These numbers do not reflect the VSD's efficiency. The VSD did make 1,221 referrals. The actual number of jobs found with the department's assistance that month was 48 out of a total of 423 jobs secured. The ratio had been even more dramatic in January 1950, when there were 4,355 active files and only 20 jobs were found with VSD assistance![25]

It is interesting to note that in August 1949, just one month after NYANA opened its doors, 164 jobs were located against an active file of 4,226. Although this is less than 4 percent, it is still more positive than the January 1950 statistic, which was less than 1 percent. Perhaps some of this can be accounted for by the fact that as more and more immigrants settled in New York, they became a networking source for those who followed. As indicated by the numbers from January 1951, as time went on, the number of VSD job placements against active files stayed well under 10 percent.[26] This is striking given the agency's emphasis on employment.

If the president of NYANA could claim at the annual meeting in 1951 that thirty-one thousand out of thirty-eight thousand new immigrants were gainfully employed, how did refugees such as Mr. P. find a job? NYANA's VSD—lackluster as it turned out to be—was created to help the DPs. To that end, it counseled clients while also promoting the immigrant workers to potential American employers.

A 1950 VSD report stated the goals of its vocational counselors: "Immigrants with their job handicaps constitute the 'raw material' that vocational services must fashion into a saleable product."[27] Because many immigrants were unskilled, spoke little English, had trades that were not transferable to America, and did not always look the part of a proper job applicant, the VSD had much reshaping on its hands. NYANA also turned to businessmen in the Jewish community for help. The December 1950 issue of *Inside NYANA*, an internal newsletter for NYANA board members, described this effort, proclaiming that "approximately 20 NYANA clients were placed in jobs last week as the result of cooperation between the Amalgamated Joint Board and a number of employers in the men's clothing industry."[28] The article went on to note that:

> Factory representatives of the Joint Board helped to orient the new-comers in the practices of American industry and also invoked among the employers a willingness to give unskilled people an opportunity to learn in their factories. This is only a beginning; a very substantial number of job placements is expected through the continuation of this cooperative relationship. . . . This same technique it is hoped can be applied in virtually every segment of the needle trades.[29]

The VSD sponsored its so-called United Job Finding Campaign, in the hopes of matching these newcomers with suitable work. "From Relief Rolls to Pay Rolls" (a report on the campaign to NYANA's board) profiled a sampling of potentially employable immigrants. One, a thirty-year-old mother of a three-year-old, was forced to work because her husband was hospitalized. The report noted, "From 1936 to 1939, in Europe, she worked as a nurse's assistant. During the war, both in a concentration camp and the Ghetto, she did unskilled manual work."[30] In this instance, the agency promoted the refugee's time as slave laborer during the Holocaust as bona fide work experience in order to make her a more attractive candidate on the job market.

With almost three-quarters of the DPs considered difficult to place, NYANA forged ahead with its policies. It used advertisements on radio programs, solicited the support of the Rabbinical Council of Greater New York, and enlisted the help of the Yiddish press in its campaign. This enabled the agency to place fifteen hundred refugees in jobs. Despite this initially optimistic response, less than a year later NYANA was forced to admit to its board that ever-increasing numbers of problematic clients had tipped the scales in favor of the "hard-to-place." The report revealed that "the proportion of actual hard-to-place immigrants in the VSD's caseload had risen to an all time high of 55% compared with 49.2% in December 1950." Added to this 55 percent was another 17 percent made up of immigrants who required intensive help, for example, middle-aged women who had never worked, or young people with seminary backgrounds, or intellectuals, or other white-collar workers in their fifties. The report concluded by stating that about 72 percent of all immigrants registered with the VSD fell into the hard-to-place category.[31]

NYANA continued to struggle with this dilemma. A number of other communities, however, found more novel solutions to easing the transition for new arrivals who might not be able to adapt easily. In Seattle, Washington, the local chapter of the National Council of Jewish Women (NCJW) organized a thrift shop for those "not readily employable in the labor market because of language, physical, or emotional handicaps."[32] With a five-thousand-dollar down payment from the Federated Fund, the NCJW appointed a former social worker as manager and set up shop with an initial nine DP employees. They worked there on a full-time basis repairing and selling furniture, clothing, jewelry, and household items, which had been donated from the Jewish community. Furniture that went unsold was turned over to the Seattle Jewish Family and Children's Services (JFCS) to be distributed among the newcomers. This seems like a winning formula: one that helped the DPs through the initial troublesome transition, assisted those who needed additional care, and was a productive workplace, as well. It was not the only community to formulate a plan that seemed to have an inherent sensitivity to the survivors' needs and abilities. In San Francisco, the Committee for Service to Émigrés established the San Francisco Utility Workshop "to provide work opportunities and a social-recreational outlet for elderly unemployable refugees who had few social contacts and were either completely dependent on our agency or dependent, in part, on children."[33] One wonders why this model was not emulated in New York City, with the latter's high number of hard-to-place newcomers.

One of the refugees' first steps with the VSD in New York was participation in a group orientation session. Often conducted in Yiddish, it familiarized the newcomers with the American way of work, from wages and working conditions, to the types of jobs available, to unions and licensing requirements. The immigrant then worked individually with a counselor to devise a plan to find work as quickly as possible. For those with specialized training, such as physicians and religious functionaries, there were additional programs. As the majority of the newcomers were relatively unskilled, like Mr. and Mrs. G., NYANA expected them to take any job. Many did so on their own, through contacts with their *landslayt* (those originating from the same hometown), the Yiddish press, word of mouth, and the English newspapers.

Descriptions found in *Typical Beginning Jobs for Immigrants*, a Yiddish handout, enumerated the types of jobs for which refugees were qualified. It did not mince matters:

> The majority of immigrants arriving at the present time lack the skills
> for jobs paying above minimum levels. Moreover, even in cases where
> they possess skills, these skills are usually below the level required in
> American industry. They therefore, usually need additional training
> either on the job or in training classes. They also have to learn English
> and become accustomed to American methods of production before
> they can be considered on a par with native-born workers.[34]

As part of planning for the individual, then, the VSD (in conjunction with the caseworker) had the authority to refer people to training courses at vocational institutions such as the ORT (World Organization for Rehabilitation through Training Union) school. Mr. B., a forty-one-year-old man who arrived in New York in 1949, had no illusions about finding a job as a businessman, which he had been in Europe.[35] He simply hoped to find a position where he might receive some type of training in order to gain a skill. He tried unsuccessfully to find work for several months, relying primarily on a friend who owned a factory and had promised to give him on-the-job training as a machine operator. When the promises came to naught and his wife became pregnant, he redoubled his efforts and worked out a plan with the agency by which a course in power machine operating would be subsidized through ORT, which offered training and job placement.

Mr. B. began the course, but it was interrupted when his wife became quite ill. She gave birth prematurely and he stayed at home to care for their three-year-old child. While this delayed the completion of training, his caseworker pointed out that "placement for his trade and skill in the garment trade was very slow at this time, so actually Mr. B was not missing out on any jobs."[36] Again, we see the personal factors that often wreaked havoc with the newcomers' goals and the agencies' expectations. We see, too, the larger economic context in which the immigrant struggled. Earnings in the apparel industry were down 81 percent during the first part of 1949 as compared to 1948.[37] A refugee searching for work in the garment industry felt this keenly. Although Mr. B. eventually did complete his course, it was through a relative's recommendation, not ORT's, that he finally received a job earning a minimal wage.

A newcomer did not automatically receive a subsidy for a training program. Many individuals' requests were denied because the agency simply did not see the point if a job was available or if the agency felt that the refugee was using training to put off gainful employment. Sometimes, the newcomer found a job with no pay but, instead, a promise of "on-the-job training." Such was the case with Mr. N., a thirty-two-year-old man who arrived in New York with his thirty-year-old wife and two-year-old child in the summer of 1949.[38] His attempts to find work are typical of many immigrants' experiences. Although the family reached America in early June, it was not until they had moved from the HIAS shelter into their own flat in October that Mr. N felt ready to start his employment search. After submitting numerous applications as a presser, he returned to NYANA most enthusiastically, with a letter from a potential employer:

To Whom It May Concern:

Mr. N has asked me to teach him to sew ladies dresses. We will give him an opportunity to learn. The length of time necessary for him to learn to make a dress, and therefore earn some money, we do not know. But we will try to help him as much as possible.

Mr. Finklestein [pseudonym]

Mr. N. was extremely pleased about this potential opportunity. His NYANA caseworker reported that "although he knew absolutely nothing about sewing he has already learned to make a straight seam after just one day in the place." The agency worker tried to protect the newcomer and pointed out that she believed that it was against the law to work for nothing. Mr. N. countered that one of the first things that had happened was that he had broken a needle, which had put an entire machine out of commission for a while: he could not possibly ask Mr. Finklestein for a salary after that. He added that he had no idea why Mr. Finklestein decided to help somebody who walked in off the street, but "evidently Mr. Finkelstein must have liked him or felt that he wanted to do something for a refugee and so was giving him this opportunity."[39]

This kind of opportunity was a tricky situation for both the newcomer and the agency. The agency had to make the decision whether it would continue to support the immigrant in this informal training program or whether it would insist that he or she take a paying job. The newcomer had to decide whether to invest the time, given the one-year countdown, without a definite commitment for a job at the end of the training period and the potential for being exploited by the boss. For the latter, as in Mr. N.'s case, the time factor was less of a risk in NYANA's early months before the establishment of a time limit on agency relief.

Mr. N.'s caseworker and his VSD worker discussed the matter. Mr. N. was cooperative; he was willing to go along with their recommendation and withdraw from what he saw as potentially valuable training if the VSD objected. But the caseworker conferred with the VSD worker. Although the latter felt, at first, that it was not ordinarily a good plan for a man to spend two or three weeks learning a trade without getting any pay for it, she indicated that "at the present time things are not too good in the employment field and inasmuch as the letter indicated that Mr. F was willing to help Mr. N as much as possible and also indicates that he will get a job there, she has no objection."[40]

Again, the slow employment market influenced the newcomer's course of action. Had it been brisk, as it subsequently was, the agency would have been more reluctant to approve such a plan. Unfortunately for Mr. N., the situation deteriorated even further. Barely two weeks after Mr. Finklestein wrote his letter, his dress company temporarily closed down. Although he had said that he would start to pay Mr. N. when business picked up, by the end of December Mr. N. turned to the VSD for an appointment because he had begun to feel that the training program was hopeless. He was right. In a conversation with the caseworker, Mr. Finklestein confided that "he had hired Mr. N. only because he wanted to help a refugee, and he was quite disappointed that Mr. N did not learn faster than he did." Nevertheless, his desire to help a refugee was less important than business. The report continued: "There was no point in Mr. N's continuing in his place since there will be no job for him and he feels that if he taught Mr. N. anything so that he can get a job elsewhere, he has done as much as can be expected. . . . He would make every attempt to get Mr. N a job elsewhere and if he hears of anything he would be only too glad to get in touch with him." While Mr. Finklestein spoke warmly of Mr. N., his help ended there. Mr. N. did not appear to have harbored any ill will toward Mr. Finklestein. He continued to "work" in his shop, practicing on the machines, until he finally located a job. Again, through his own resourcefulness, he placed an ad in one of the Yiddish newspapers "stating that he was a refugee and would accept any kind of work."[41] Much to his surprise, he received a response from a star of the Yiddish theater, who helped him secure employment in a cap factory.

While the example of Mr. N. ostensibly illustrates an act of kindness on Mr. Finklestein's and the Yiddish actor's part, the caseworker's suspicions imply that the refugees could be the unsuspecting targets of exploitative factory owners. Numerous files in the NYANA archives support this supposition that bosses took advantage of these workers with offers of on-the-job training that never led to salaried positions, sometimes holding this carrot out for months. Holocaust survivors, like immigrants before them, were sometimes the naive victims of unscrupulous predators.

NYANA dealt with an annual caseload of twenty thousand people in 1949.[42] In contrast, with a settled Jewish community of fourteen thousand, Denver felt challenged by the approximately twelve refugees (or refugee families) that it accepted on monthly quota from 1949 to 1951. Context is important here. Newcomers represented 60 percent of the JFCS total caseload, which is significant for a small agency. Then too, the Denver JFCS did not adopt NYANA's one-year time limit for relief. While most of the NYANA files end after one year with "case closed," Denver's time limit was ambiguous and allowed for a bit more flexibility in supporting its DP clientele. True, it was most unusual for Denver clients to actually receive financial help for more than one year initially, but many of the Denver case files were reopened after this period.

NYANA was created specifically for New Americans and therefore its entire clientele were refugees. In Denver, the newcomers received the same services as local clients. JFCS had a vocational counselor on staff to help direct individuals to specific jobs. As in New York, high early numbers set the agenda. An analysis of the growth in the agency's caseload from 1 October 1951 through 30 September 1952 showed that the numbers visiting the Vocational Guidance Department (VGD) ranged from a high of 69 people in November 1951 to a low of 13 in August 1952. The higher numbers had influenced the VGD to develop an innovative program. Mr. Cohen, the department head, announced at a board meeting that "the special employment technique used recently had been better than anyone had hoped for."[43] This technique, which echoed attempts in New York to establish relationships with Jewish businessmen in the community, was a "big brother" program adopted by the thirty-member employment committee in which each "was given responsibility for job-finding for one case only." The report continues, "This plan has worked quite successfully for both the hard-to-place and 'normal' cases. Whereas last month there were fifteen unemployed as of now there are only five persons who are in the 'unemployed but employable' category, receiving help from the agency."[44]

While most refugees arrived in New York City on individual affidavits, the majority of the DPs who settled in Denver were on community assurances. This was a selective process in the sense that the JDC and USNA were supposed to work with the local cooperating agency to match suitable refugees to the appropriate community. It seems that one of the bargains the JDC and USNA struck with the local cooperating agencies was giving the latter a voice in the occupations of the refugees whom they would accept on quota. To facilitate this, every cooperating agency received a list of jobs typically filled by refugees. Some of the 170 occupations noted as most common among DPs included baker, butcher, clerk, dressmaker, electrician, factory worker, household worker, laborer, saddler, seamstress, tanner, and tailor.[45] But communities did not always have employment opportunities in these fields. In order to inform USNA that it could not accept one man on its quota because his skill as a textile worker was not in demand, Denver's executive director of JFCS, Dr. Alfred Neumann, listed twenty-two skilled occupations that could be useful in Denver. These included auto mechanic, chocolate maker, dairy products worker, chemist, gardener, and saddler. This list appears to have been prompted by the agency's efforts to maximize the Denver quota match between immigrant and host community. From Dr. Neumann's many letters to USNA, however, it seems clear that he used his list as a way to control who came to Denver. In a query by USNA in December 1949 about whether Denver would accept a man who was a knitter, Dr. Neumann responded:

> First, there is no employment possibility open for a knitter in our community. We have received one unit of this type some months ago, and this gentleman is still unemployed and very much a problem. Second, will you kindly check with the enclosed list of major occupations as to what type of resettlement units are desirable in Denver and the region which Denver supplies with resettlement units. Third, I am aware it is difficult to change the community, but I believe we save time, energy, money, community relations if we send the right units to the right communities.[46]

This letter is significant for a number of reasons. First, it indicates that JFCS had leverage regarding who it would accept in its communities and acted upon this authority when it saw fit. Second, the letter suggests that the head of the Denver agency was wary of problems. The first knitter to go to Denver set a precedent as a "problem." Thereafter, the agency sought identical matches between future newcomers and listed professions. The chilliness communicated in the letter, in part by the frequent use of the word *unit*, and in part by the emphasis on saving "time, energy, and money," indicates the agency's focus on what is best for JFCS, rather than for the newcomers. Finally, when the USNA Migration Services worker responded to Dr. Neumann suggesting that the DP in question would be willing to work as an unskilled laborer, Dr. Neumann remained discouraging. Insisting that newcomers are better off if they can use their vocational skills, he wrote back to USNA, "It has also been our experience that units coming to America conceive a very unrealistic picture of what America holds for them. If the above unit meets with any success in establishing themselves as American citizens and becoming a well-integrated part of the community in which they resettle, it will only be possible by resettling them in a community where previous learned skills can be utilized."[47]

If at first glance it might appear that Dr. Neumann was genuinely concerned with placing the newcomer in the most advantageous situation, his last sentence reveals his true motives. He simply did not want them. "In addition to this," he wrote, "housing for a family with two children is almost impossible to find." When read in the context of numerous exchanges over the years between Executive Director Dr. Neumann and USNA headquarters, it is clear that these early letters set the parameters for accepting future newcomers and chronicled Dr. Neumann's ongoing argument that Denver was a dumping ground for problem cases. More than three years later, in July 1953, when USNA requested that Denver accept a seamstress, he answered that he was concerned about employment possibilities for this woman in Denver and suggested that "this client could only be served in a larger community where there is a needle trade"[48]—notwithstanding the fact that cap maker, cutter, presser, electric-sewing-machine operator, tailor, and upholsterer were skilled occupations specifically listed earlier. Dr. Neumann was evidently adept at using work and skill as a way to control the resettlement process in his community.

Given Dr. Neumann's strong position, one would assume that he would support his clients using previously learned skills. JFCS, however, shared NYANA's concern that immigrants should get to work as quickly as possible. Thus, although there was no 8–4 policy in Denver, JFCS's philosophy was based on the same principle that becoming self-maintaining was the gold standard of success.

Mrs. F.'s history not only speaks to the issue of skills and support, but also illustrates the problems an older woman faced in her new environment.

Mrs. F. arrived in Denver, alone, in the summer of 1951. Her husband and daughter had been killed in Europe and she had no one in America. She told the caseworker at their first meeting that "she has learned to be a cosmetician and wishes to pursue this work here." She was "dressed all in black, wearing silk gloves and a large picture hat" and although she maintained that she had come from a cultured, well-educated background, her caseworkers noted that they believed this was a fantasy and that she was prone to self-aggrandizement.[49] At the first meeting she was directed to begin English lessons, which would be followed by a search for work.

Less than a month after her arrival, Mrs. F. told her case worker that "she had investigated at the Opportunity School and found they were giving a course, beginning in September for beuticians [*sic*] and cosmeticians, and she would like to take this course." The worker responded that she believed that this was a nine-month course and she doubted that the agency would support her. Mrs. F. countered that she had inquired at beauty shops about licensing and "no one will allow her to sit around a place." When asked if she would go into another field if cosmetic work were not available, Mrs. F. responded that "she had trained for this and this is what she wanted to do. . . . There will have to be a way for her to get the training that she needs." The JFCS worker "explained to Mrs. F that the Agency has certain limitations, that when an individual is ready for employment and we do find a job that will not interfere with their physical or emotional health, the agency did hope that the individual would consider such employment." To which Mrs. F. replied that "she wanted cosmetician work only."[50]

Nevertheless, Mrs. F. was expected to work and she did. But "jobs such as waitress at JCRS [Jewish Consumptive Relief Society], working in a factory, practical nurse, lasted for a short while. The complaints about them were less in terms of hard work; rather she complained in terms of the menial position that she was forced to occupy, where the people she had to work with were more stupid and more coarse than those she had hired for menial services in her better days." So wrote a worker in his summary of her adjustment through September 1952.[51]

Eventually, without the agency's knowledge, Mrs. F. borrowed money from an acquaintance and enrolled in a licensing course at a local beauty school. Although the agency believed that she was unrealistic about her goals, it continued to dole out minimal financial help ($22.20 a week) until she could support herself at her chosen profession, which occurred in September 1953. This is a remarkable example of a woman whose desire to pursue her prewar career did not fade despite the agency's lack of enthusiasm and her own considerable emotional and physical troubles. While the agency, indeed, hoped that she might find a job, her caseworkers doubted both her stability and her ability to achieve her particular goals. Then, too, both the agency in general and her caseworker in particular failed to recognize the power of status as a fuel to move newcomers forward. Mrs. F. perceived herself as a woman of status because of her prewar circumstances. Her desire to achieve a similar sense of prestige in America spurned her on even though the agency did not quite hold the beauty profession in such high esteem or seem to recognize the motivations that drove Mrs. F. to push ahead.

After Mrs. F.'s untimely death in 1955, just four years after her arrival in Denver, the agency succeeded in claiming part of her very modest estate in order to recoup some of the financial assistance that it had provided. The agency's claim to be entitled to Mrs. F.'s money points to a central difference distinguishing JFCS from NYANA: the former hoped that its clients would pay back their debts. As a caseworker explained:

> I translated the liability sheet to Mr. S. When we came to the paragraph which says that everybody is expected to pay back the money we lend them so that we can have other people come over, Mr. S became very serious. He said that this is something he was terribly worried about since he did not want to take any charity. I explained to Mr. S that what we gave him was not charity but that we lend him the money.[52]

This was entirely out of step with accepted practice, and moreover, the explanation that the refugee's repayment of his debt allowed other DPs to come to Denver was blatantly untrue. In addition to the token one-hundred-dollar bonus from USNA for every DP who came in on an agency assurance, JFCS received an allocation from Denver's Jewish Federation to support its resettlement program.

Mr. and Mrs. J. and their baby daughter (thirty-two, twenty-five, and two years old, respectively) arrived in Denver in 1950.[53] Their experiences are emblematic of many newcomers: an initial burst of energy for their new environment and a focus, with the JFCS's help, on work, followed by a slow but steady unraveling of their efforts. In the beginning, the agency gave the family limited financial support (their relatives—including a refugee family—were subsidizing the family's housing costs) while Mr. J., a barber by profession, studied to obtain his Colorado license so that he could join the barbers union and begin working. Mr. J. was determined to pass the examination as quickly as possible. All his waking hours in the two weeks prior to the test date were spent studying. The agency showed its encouragement of Mr. J.'s efforts by stating that it "would not send Mr. J on a job, but give him that period for studying." When Mr. J. asked for ten dollars for the barber's license application, the agency gave it to him as a loan to be paid back once he began working. Although Mr. J. was fearful about the exam, he passed it on his first try and found himself a barber's job immediately. The couple felt confident about their future and the caseworker reported:

> Mrs. J thanked me then for all the help I had given to them and it was her feelings [*sic*] that things really had been working out satisfactorily for them. I shared this with her and told her that it was really they who had accomplished so much in this short of time. I gave Mrs. J her relief check and told her that although she would not come anymore for relief, she should feel free to call on me whenever she wanted to. Mrs. J felt happy to know that and thanked me again for all I had done.[54]

This, however, was not the end of the J. family's story. As shown in Chapter 6, just when it seemed that Mr. J. was making a rapid and smooth adjustment, he became ill and eventually required psychiatric treatment.

The refugees' first steps in America were fraught with difficulties, often following a trajectory that went out of control and required services from the agency for which there were few precedents. That, in turn, demanded interaction between the local and national agencies, as illustrated by the example of Mr. B., a "typical" DP; male, Polish, thirty-two years old, relatively unskilled, destined for New York on a community affidavit.[55] After arriving in New York, Mr. B. was sent to Denver because of its special medical facilities for tuberculosis (TB) patients. As he was about to be discharged from the Jewish Consumptive Relief Society, in stable condition, he learned about a watch repair training course sponsored by the Colorado State Vocational Rehabilitation Board (SVRB). He wanted to stay in Denver, rather than return to New York City, in order to learn this new profession. Although the SVRB in Denver recommended that he try to find a job in his own (unspecified) field, he believed that the watch repair field was more promising. He needed to find an agency that would support him for the almost two years of training this required. JFCS was adamant in refusing this because Mr. B. was part of the New York, not Denver, quota. This was an ongoing point of contention between JFCS and USNA. Dr. Neumann "considered the incidence of TB as a special injustice heaped on Denver with malice" and wanted to enforce a policy of nonacceptance of ex-patients in Denver.[56] Without the agency's financial help, Mr. B. doggedly pursued this plan and learned that he could receive room and board at the Ex-Patients' Home, for discharged TB patients, during his watch repair course.

Mr. B. began to train in June 1952 and returned to JFCS the following month for advice about employment during the summer break. The JFCS worker referred him to several other agencies that handled temporary employment and his case was closed; it had been three months since he first came to the agency for advice. While the future seemed somewhat uncertain, Mr. B. was pleased to be working toward a goal and had hopes that his plans would come to fruition. But less than three months later the case was reopened and remained so, on and off, for nearly five years as he continued to struggle with adjustment issues.

The histories examined here illustrate the mechanisms by, and the degree to, which the expectations and the needs of the newcomers and their sponsors meshed. In the course of this interaction, other difficulties often emerged, which required a different kind of help. Self-maintenance did not necessarily mean "adjustment." For many survivors of the Holocaust who came to America, unbidden problems surfaced, as both the hosts and the newcomers pushed forward. The goal of self-maintenance did not address the emotional needs of the refugees. In a letter to his social worker at JFCS, a young man expressed his feelings about his new life in Denver. After describing his satisfaction with his office job and his progress in English, he continued:

> This is one side of the medal. The other side is not hot. Am very disgusted and from day to day am getting worse. Very nervous. I feel some kind of nostalgy [*sic*]. Not for my country. The word "my country" doesn't exist to me. I miss my lost family, my friends and the system of living. I can't get adjusted here regardless of my attempts. I really drive myself very hard in order to get Americanized but this is useless. My trying has no success as yet and I don't think that will ever have. There is a wall of customs, characters and attitudes. I do not have anything in common with my surrounders [*sic*]. They will never understand me even if I speak a better English than they do. It's a terrible problem to me. Furthermore, I don't seem to see a sense in life and little by little I lose the courage to live and that worries me. We all can take only so much and I am only a human.[57]

What the agencies expected from their clients and the nature of the help that the former extended to the DPs is fundamental to this story. How factors such as the refugees' skills, status, age, and gender affected the objectives of a particular agency is also important. What transcended an agency's objectives, however, is the Holocaust. The process of acculturation was played out in its shadow. That essential piece of the story was relegated to the background, while agency goals came to the fore. That the agencies aided the newcomers cannot be disputed. But the nature of the help and its effectiveness must be assessed in the context of who the refugees were.

The newcomers' voices in the agency files make it clear that it would be false to conclude that self-maintenance equaled adjustment. Hardly. The road was bumpy and fraught with dangers to which the caregivers were all too blind. Moreover, it was less a fresh beginning than a piecing together of a path that had been irrevocably shattered in Europe. In the agencies' rush to close the refugees' cases, this was forgotten.

CHAPTER 4

"*Bearded Refugees*"

THE RECEPTION OF RELIGIOUS NEWCOMERS

---

*T*he photograph of the family of ten that appeared in the *New York Times* in April 1949 is astonishing. Even more so is the accompanying story. "DP Rabbi, Family Dock, Full of Joy, Father of 8 Can See New Life Here after Wanderings and Imprisonment," the headline declares.[1] The article details how Rabbi Goldman, his wife, and seven children evaded the Nazis in Hungary. One son was killed and another born in Germany after the war. They came to the United States under the auspices of USNA and were to be resettled in the Midwest. The reporter was curious about the man's plans for the future. "I don't know what I want to do," said the forty-two-year-old newcomer, who had been a rabbi since the age of twenty-one. "Maybe teach Hebrew; maybe become rabbi of some synagogue where I could do some good," he reflected. But he did not want to speak about his future, he insisted, rather "about America—this greatest land of refuge in the world, this wonderful nation that has taken us in and given us a chance to begin living once more."[2]

Five years later, on a late summer day in 1954, Judge Rosenbaum of Denver, Colorado, found one Rabbi F. wandering around Union Station, not knowing where to go or what to do. He brought the man to the offices of JFCS and left him with a caseworker. The rabbi asked for financial assistance to carry him through until he reached New York and help in finding kosher lodgings because he could not travel on the Sabbath. The caseworker wrote in her report:

> Rabbi F was a Roumanian by birth and Orthodox in practice. He was finding it difficult to establish himself in this country and earn a living because of the different nature of religious functionary work in the United States. Rabbi F showed us a newspaper clippings [*sic*] from a New York paper, indicating that his wife had died aboard ship en

A religious family arrives in New York, circa 1948–1953. HIAS. Courtesy of the United States Holocaust Memorial Museum.

route to this country. . . . The infant and his four year old daughter are in a Children's Institution in Brooklyn, New York, where the rabbi lives. . . . He was en route from L.A. back to New York when he came to our office to seek assistance. The clippings indicated that he had been a man of influence in his small hometown in Europe where he led a congregation. He keenly felt the difference in his position now as well as anxiety around making a livelihood. One could also sense difficulty in acculturating to American life and accepting patterns of religious activity other than what he himself is accustomed to. He looked older than his 48 years, and he was garbed in traditional Orthodox clothing and wore a beard.[3]

The descriptions of Rabbi Goldman and Rabbi F. capture both the promise and the dislocation that many survivors experienced in their early days here. We do not know what became of either one. These brief glimpses of their lives are all we have. Like all DPs, religious refugees struggled to find their place in America. The Holocaust demolished their previous lives and tossed them into an alien world. As happy as Rabbi Goldman was to be in the United States, he, like Rabbi F., would soon have to confront his future and the demands of the Jewish, but secular, agency and of the greater society as well.

After the war, orthodox organizations such as rabbinic seminaries and the Vaad Hatzala (the wartime orthodox rescue committee) joined together to bring religious survivors to America.[4] Shortly thereafter, other institutions approached USNA for financial support for this group.[5] USNA (and eventually NYANA) and its cooperating agencies agreed to help shoulder this responsibility. At the end of 1947, a Religious Functionary Department (RFD) was created at USNA to respond to the specific vocational needs of certain orthodox Jews. The RFD's goal was to assist those Jews identified as religious functionaries (RF) in finding appropriate work.[6] USNA, NYANA, and local cooperating agencies also aided religiously observant refugees who were not religious functionaries, but part of the agencies' general caseload.

USNA attempted to find a way to satisfy both its own and its orthodox clients' needs, but sympathy toward these newcomers was mixed. Added to the already complex adjustment process was the fact that for strictly orthodox refugees their religious values defined who they were and how they wanted to live. This was often at cross-purposes with the agencies that emphasized employment and self-sufficiency above all. The organizations did help the orthodox refugees, but the aid often exacerbated the challenges facing these newcomers.

The orthodox refugee group as a whole was not homogenous. It spanned a spectrum that ranged from Hasidic *rebbes* and their followers to yeshiva (men's seminary) students to working-class Sabbath observers. Their appearance varied, too. Some men dressed in the Hasidic tradition with beards and side curls; others were more Western in appearance. Women might wear wigs or kerchiefs.

Their wartime experiences were as varied as their dress. One seminary, the Mirrer Yeshiva, had survived in Shanghai, China. One of two institutions that fled to China and remained intact, the Mirrer Yeshiva immigrated, en masse, to America after the war. A few illustrious rabbis had escaped Europe before or even during the war and had transplanted their institutions in the United States. Rabbi Aaron Kotler arrived in the United States and founded the Beit Midrash Gevoha (a replica of the yeshiva he headed in Kletsk) in Lakewood, New Jersey. Yeshivath Chachmey Lublin, for example, was wiped out during the first years of the Holocaust but reestablished in 1941 in Detroit. Rabbi Bloch of the Telshe Yeshiva of Lithuania came to Cleveland via Shanghai in 1941. The sixth Lubavitch rebbe, Joseph Schneerson, arrived in 1940 and established his Chabad community in Brooklyn. Other remnants of celebrated Eastern European yeshivas survived the ghettos and camps, eluded the enemy by hiding, or even operated as partisans. They now looked to America as the locus of Jewish learning and would ultimately infuse American orthodox Judaism with new vigor. The majority were not elite scholars but, nevertheless, had lived religious lives in their prewar communities. And they assumed they would do the same in America.

There were orthodox refugees whose greatest wish was to re-create, through new orthodox institutions and communities, a life similar to the one that was destroyed. For some, this was a way of honoring the vanished world, by continuing what had been lost. For others, being orthodox was simply being who they were. It would not have occurred to them to be otherwise. Still others were trained in professions that were an integral part of the orthodox communal life of their prewar communities. These were the religious functionaries: rabbis, cantors, teachers, yeshiva students, ritual slaughterers (*schoctim*), supervisors of kosher food (*mashgichim*), and those who performed ritual circumcisions (*mohelim*). Many others did not work in Jewish professions but assumed that employment would not compromise their religious practice.

The context in which they now had to live was vastly different from the one they had known. Europe, even with the changes that the twentieth century had brought to Jewish practice, had been the center of Jewish learning and life. True, there were orthodox communities in many large U.S. cities, but they paled in comparison to what had been destroyed. In the late 1940s a growing number of American Jews identified with Conservative and Reform Judaism and even centrist Orthodox American Jews embraced some secular American values. Yeshiva College, the first Orthodox Jewish university established in New York in 1928, was shaped by the idea that it was essential to offer secular and rabbinical courses of study.[7] How would USNA, a secular agency, help the various threads of this remnant of European orthodox Jewry in a way that was compatible with agency goals? Indeed, its very mission to help newcomers acculturate often conflicted with orthodox values and echoed greater tensions between the parochial and secular Jewish world.

Isaac Trainin, a young, enthusiastic orthodox rabbi with legal experience who was both American born and Yiddish speaking, was hired as director of USNA's nascent RFD. "I was told that I would deal with religious functionaries coming in: rabbis, cantors, *schoctim*, *mohelim* . . . you name it," he recalled. "In the beginning of 1946, many of them were coming over, especially from Shanghai, the Mirrer Yeshiva, 500 or 600, and many of them claimed to be rabbis that weren't really rabbis, I mean they were learned men [without official rabbinic ordination] . . . and I had to try to train them or retrain them and place them."[8]

Rabbi Trainin appealed to religious leaders in the community. He approached Rabbi Belkin, president of Yeshiva University, and Rabbi Dr. Louis Finklestein, president of the Jewish Theological Seminary, and explained his problem. The two men were sympathetic and immediately set up a series of courses at their institutions. One, in homiletics, was designed to familiarize European rabbis with American-style sermons. Another was intended to retrain men for employment as Hebrew schoolteachers, positions that were becoming increasingly popular on the American landscape.[9] An article in the *New York Times* described one seminar "that forty-two teachers and rabbis from displaced persons camps in Europe were attending at Yeshiva University."[10] The journalist noted that the seven-month USNA-sponsored course was "aimed primarily in American teaching methods and procedures, but will place stress also on American history and proficiency in English." The context was certainly worlds away from the students' previous lives, but Rabbi Trainin's efforts kept the men in Jewish education and addressed "the shortage of instructors for Jewish schools throughout the country."[11]

The head of the RFD had others, however, who did not qualify for retraining as American teachers. "I was faced with young men in their late twenties and thirties," Rabbi Trainin recollected. "They certainly were rabbis. How are you going to place them? So, what I suggested was that some of them learn to be a *schochet* or a *mohel*," he recalled.[12] Teaching the refugees skills that would make them more employable was desirable from the agency's perspective, but the response from some students and their rabbis was not always favorable. When the head of the prestigious Mirrer Yeshiva learned that the RFD wanted his students to learn to become ritual slaughterers, he confronted Rabbi Trainin. The head rabbi of the Mirrer Yeshiva expected that USNA would support the seminarians in the tradition of the European *kollel* (that is, the students would study full time at the community's expense). As Trainin remembered, "He started to bang on my desk . . . and he gave it to me." Rabbi Trainin stood his ground, bolstered by the fact that USNA was supporting the men. He established contact with a kosher slaughterhouse in New Jersey and gave each student $250 worth of knives with which to begin training. "And then we would place them," he continued, "and we had no problem placing *schoctim* . . . all over the country. We placed them in L.A., in Dallas, a few places in Florida, in Kansas City . . . and they were making good money."[13]

This example illustrates the not infrequent cross-purposes of the agency's goals with those of the yeshivas. While many rabbis and students had the expectation that the community (namely, USNA, NYANA, and other agencies) would support their studies, agencies wanted the students to become self-supporting. True, the employment was often within the orthodox world, but it garnered far less status than Torah study and it represented a rupture, rather than continuity, with the past.

Some who came through the doors of the RFD did, indeed, maintain the status of their former lives before the Holocaust, but that was reserved for a privileged few. Rabbi Trainin pointed out that "there were some very, very outstanding scholars who we trained, and we placed them as principals in Montreal [and] all over [this] country. We placed quite a number of them. They did very well."[14] Command of English, in addition to prewar stature, helped some to assume these roles. Those who had escaped to Shanghai learned English there, and this made them seem more American and thus more marketable than others who had not learned the language.

At times, however, some nearly slipped through the RFD's cracks. "A young man came into see me, crying," recounted Rabbi Trainin. "They [the Vocational Service Department] placed him in a job as a clerk. . . . [H]e was a graduate of the Budapest Reform Seminary . . . a shipping clerk! . . . I hit the ceiling. . . . I went in to see the top man at USNA . . . and I raised hell. . . . So," continued Rabbi Trainin, "he agreed with me and he brought in the social worker, 'How could you have done a thing like that?' Well, she did. . . . I don't know if it was done in other cases. . . . [T]his fellow was smart enough to speak to a local Reform rabbi, Rabbi Julius Marks, at Temple Emanuel, who told him to speak to his friend Ike Trainin." Rabbi Trainin immediately "called Hebrew Union College and he [the young rabbi] spent six months there. We supported him—to learn all the techniques of a Reform rabbi, of course homiletics, etc., etc. and then I got him a job in Claremont, New Hampshire. . . . [I]t was the end of 1948, a nice Reform temple."[15] Perhaps because the young refugee's training was at a Reform seminary, the agency did not initially refer him to the RFD. Fortunately, he was able to speak up. Because he did, along with Rabbi Trainin's forceful advocacy, his future took a turn for the better. The two kept in touch for many years and Rabbi Trainin was able to follow the young rabbi's career as it flourished in New Hampshire.

Age, as well as youth, could influence one's future. The *Jewish Morning Journal*, an orthodox Yiddish daily, published an article on 1 July 1949 titled "Regarding Refugee Rabbis." The author excoriated USNA for its treatment of aged rabbis who could not adjust to the demands of the American rabbinate and claimed that "lately these respectable rabbis are being badgered by the officials of the United Service."[16] The journalist, Mendel Hausman, wrote that USNA asked these rabbis to take jobs as sextons or even dishwashers. These men were not Torah luminaries, but they had lived as rabbis in their homes in Europe and had expected the same after the Holocaust. USNA's policy demanded that they work, yet few American Jewish communities had need for this aging group.

While the RFD, then, was ostensibly created to help orthodox refugees seeking suitable vocational placements, it shared its parent organization's perspective that finding work as quickly as possible was of supreme importance. This aim, however, was even more elusive with this particular population. In June 1948, the department had 1,400 open cases representing 2,661 people, who differed in a number of ways from refugees in USNA's other casework departments. According to an USNA report on the RFD, more than nine-tenths of its caseload were on relief and almost 43 percent had been on relief for a year or more.[17] This speaks to one of the most striking differences between the RFD group and other refugees: initially, more than half of these newcomers had temporary visa status, which precluded employment.

Many had temporary visas because they were yeshiva students. Rabbinical academies in Detroit, Baltimore, Chicago, and Cleveland were among those responsible for bringing students to America; indeed, they saw it as their mission to do so. For example, on behalf of one former student, Rabbi Rosenberg, dean of the Yesivath Chachmey Lublin, wrote to the American consul in Shanghai. "I would like to bring him over to the United States and have him continue his theological education in our Theological Seminary Yeshivath Chachmey Lublin which has been transplanted from Lublin, Poland. This boy will devote his full time to study in our Seminary." The dean went on to declare, "Our Seminary will provide him with room and board and all other expenses for a full five years from date which he arrives in America."[18]

Rabbi Rosenberg duly persuaded the consul, and the twenty-seven-year-old was sent to Detroit. Twenty-nine others followed him to that city and the seminary agreed to also support them for five years. Yet within a few months the yeshiva applied to its local Jewish Federation and Resettlement Service for a grant to help provide for the new seminarians. After the federation had twice denied the yeshiva's grant applications on the basis that the seminary was a national, not local, institution, Harold Silver, executive director of Detroit's Resettlement Service, turned to USNA for advice. "You can appreciate the difficult spot in which this places us from a financial and community point of view," he wrote to Joseph Beck, executive director of USNA. "No one will quarrel with the Yeshiva's success in bringing the thirty Polish refugees from Shanghai outside quota, much as we might deplore their failure to plan ahead or to consult with us before this," he continued. He explained the dilemma for the local cooperating agency: "Refusal to help them will, doubtless lead the Yeshiva to campaign for extra funds on a basis that will have great appeal, but will, at the same time, prove very embarrassing to Federation and to Resettlement Service. The Yeshiva would actually be caring for a larger relief load than the official communal agency." Moreover, he added, "giving the Yeshiva the required assistance would place an unexpected and very heavy burden on our resources and would seriously curtail our capacity to accept new refugees for settlement."[19]

Mr. Silver concluded his letter by informing Mr. Beck that the yeshiva had also applied for student visas for an additional group of thirty boys, thirteen to seventeen years old, to permit them to study at the Detroit seminary. One wonders what the American Jewish community of Detroit was thinking. While Mr. Silver paid lip service to the rabbi's success in bringing this refugee group quickly to America, he clearly did not throw his support behind the effort. Was it really because helping them would have meant less help for others? If so, why were these boys less worthy of help than future groups? Perhaps Mr. Silver did not appreciate Rabbi Rothenberg's approach to bringing the students to the seminary and his apparent attitude that getting the boys to America was paramount and figuring out how to pay for it later was secondary. It may have been something not stated: that it was not the responsibility of the local communal agency to help this orthodox group in the custom of the European *kollel* (in which the Jewish community supported full-time Torah study by a select group of adult males). One point seems clear. Mr. Silver was more concerned about his agency's standing within the local community than he was about the welfare of these yeshiva students. Indeed, as will be seen shortly, less than a year later USNA moved to minimize its aid for these refugees.

Agendas clashed in Cleveland, Ohio, too. Beginning in 1946, when the rabbis at the Telshe Yeshiva initiated discussions with the Jewish Family Service Association (JFSA) about planning for the arrival of the yeshiva's survivors, there were ongoing arguments over the absorption of the newcomers.[20] These disagreements echoed those in Detroit and other communities where yeshivas were regrouping. The yeshivas' leaders believed that bringing the European remnant back to their yeshivas was a holy mission.

This took precedence over everything, including the secular communities' way of operating.

The question remained: Who would shoulder the primary burden of the religious refugees? The executive committee of USNA called a special meeting on 30 June 1947, shortly after the DPs began to arrive in the United States, to discuss a number of concerns around general relief to immigrants. The following action was taken for yeshiva groups and students:

1. For the entire Yeshiva Group reduce the relief grants in accordance with steps taken under "Maintenance Grants" for other clients.
2. Notify all the established Yeshivas which have signed affidavits for persons that a time limit will be set for continued support during which they are to plan to secure their own financing.
3. Notify all the Yeshivas that we will assume no responsibility for future groups coming to this country. Those without a place to go on arrival will be sent to the New York Jewish Transient Shelter operated by HIAS.[21]

Even though USNA, and later NYANA, then, were involved with helping religious newcomers, the agencies clearly felt that other organizations, especially those religious institutions that had sponsored refugees, should assume their share of the responsibility. An advisor on religious functionaries at USNA claimed that "religious groups in the community as well as other sections of the Jewish community considered the giving of contracts, not legal obligations but a means of helping *to rescue* Jews in Europe."[22]

USNA and NYANA, however, felt that rescue was all well and good but they should not be the sole supporters once the immigrants arrived. In 1949, a discussion ensued between Charles Jordan of the American Jewish Joint Distribution Committee in Paris and the executive level of USNA.[23] The two organizations debated whether to require yeshiva students to sign a statement that they would not request USNA assistance. This was never effected, but when the Displaced Persons Act was reinterpreted to allow students to work, NYANA insisted that every such client seek employment. For those students who came to the United States after 1 January 1949 and were not able to work, NYANA terminated relief one month from the day that the student arrived.[24] Thus, when Mr. and Mrs. F., a twenty-two- and twenty-three-year-old couple from Romania on student visas, appealed to NYANA in 1950, they were told that the agency no longer helped students. The social worker wrote that this distressed the young couple, who "found it very difficult to accept the statement that we give no financial help to students at this time. They kept pointing out that they were a young couple without relatives or real connections in this country." The caseworker was unmoved, even though the young man "kept pleading that he just wanted our help until he could find employment." To this the caseworker replied that "the policy was specific, and that we could give no assistance to persons on temporary visas."[25]

The relationship between the agencies and the orthodox refugees in their care was indeed complex. Sponsored by yeshivas, many orthodox young men entered the United States on temporary visas although they knew that they intended to remain in the country permanently, because quota visas were more difficult to obtain. Some, such as one group of thirty-five families, were in the United States on transit visas on their way to Israel but were waiting indefinitely in New York because "housing and living conditions in Israel [were] very bad. Later, however, they [planned] to go to Israel." Dr. Isaac Lewin, representative of the Agudas World Organization (the Union of Orthodox Rabbis), presented their case to NYANA's Religious Functionary Committee. "The situation of some 35 families, comprising approximately 140 individuals, is tragic because they have been living on a starvation basis, begging from friends and relatives, because USNA, and now NYANA, have refused to give them assistance," he argued. He went on to plead that "the Committee recommend to the Board that assistance be granted to this group, pending their future movement to Israel," which, he added, "had recently been discouraged by their representative in Israel because of the difficult situation there."[26]

Mr. Telsey, the NYANA committee chair, indicated that NYANA's main purpose was to help those who could begin to work and become self-maintaining as quickly as possible, and that NYANA did not have the funds to help others. Dr. Lewin then wondered whether NYANA was suggesting that these men secure positions as rabbis in the United States, thus enabling them to obtain permanent visas. When Mr. Telsey countered that this would still require financial help from NYANA, Dr. Lewin "appealed to the Committee to make their decision purely on the basis of the human factors involved and not on the basis of what he described as any technical or legal basis." Dr. Lewin's pleas fell on deaf ears. He departed from the meeting and the committee discussed the matter. The committee's minutes reveal the outcome:

AGREED:

That NYANA follow the policy established by USNA in reference to the cases brought to the United States by the Agudas World

Organization. The policy provides that assistance will only be granted in those cases where the individuals agree to move on to Israel immediately. Emergent medical needs, however, can be given on an individual basis.[27]

Mr. Telsey's point about helping those who could become self-maintaining illuminates one facet of this problem. On the one hand, the RFD was designed to help find jobs for the religious functionaries; on the other, USNA and NYANA did not see it as their role to support those who would not work at gainful employment. Some of the orthodox refugees felt that maintaining their status as rabbis or students was their only choice and the only path for which they were equipped. Some felt that this was a sacred obligation in the Holocaust's wake. Moreover, as indicated earlier, many were initially precluded from working because they were in the United States on temporary visas.

Religious functionaries who did arrive on quota—either through individual or corporate affidavits—were expected to find work as quickly as possible and were also subject to the agency's 8–4 policy.[28] Again, their hopes and the agency's demands did not always mesh. Sometimes, as Rabbi Trainin indicated, the RFD did indeed match the refugee with a suitable job. At other times, as in the instance of the Reform rabbi mentioned earlier, there were problems, which were resolved. There were those, however, who either did not have the confidence, the necessary connections, or the training to obtain their goal of becoming a rabbi in America.

When what the immigrant hoped for and what the agency's policy dictated diverged, it was the latter that usually won out. Rabbi E.'s experience illustrates this point. When he appeared at the USNA office in 1949, his caseworker described him as "a young man, tall, broad shouldered. He wore very long curls that came down over his shoulders. He had an unkempt beard."[29] Rabbi E. discussed "his past experience in relation to employment." He explained that he had been a student all his life and had received *smiche* (rabbinic ordination) right before the war broke out. He had been in a concentration camp during the war and had served, afterward, as an assistant rabbi in a DP camp in Germany. His caseworker felt that he had very limited experience and that he should only spend a short amount of time looking for work as a rabbi. Rabbi E. resisted this idea and expressed the hope that he could find work, if not as a rabbi, then as a teacher or *mashgiach* (kashrut supervisor). The RFD counselor, however, noting Rabbi E.'s lack of qualifications, discouraged him. Perhaps more to the point, his caseworker felt that the young rabbi, in his desire to find work as a religious functionary, "had no intention of pursuing any course, which might lead him towards becoming independent of this agency." Gradually, the rabbi was persuaded to look for employment if, he told the social worker, "the work is of such a nature that he will not have to compromise with his own principles or give way in any way in his religious habits." The worker reminded him that "there were others with similar religious habits as his own, who were finding their way here in America and securing lucrative employment without compromising with their principles and faith in any way."[30] Eventually, Rabbi E. found a job as a presser in a neckwear factory but was laid off after a few months. In keeping with the agency's 8–4 policy, the E. family was referred to the Department of Welfare and their case at NYANA was closed. In this instance, not only did the Jewish agency discourage the young rabbi from working as a religious functionary, they also refused to support him financially when he could not maintain himself and his family. Perhaps things would have been different if Rabbi E. had had the kind of connections enjoyed by the Reform rabbi mentioned earlier. Possibly he did not have the right credentials. The Holocaust had robbed him of the life he had imagined for himself. And the community help he found after the Holocaust fell short of what he needed to live the kind of life he had had before the war.

Religious immigrants sometimes sought agency support for the completion of studies that had been interrupted. Such was the case with Mr. R., twenty-five years old, who had studied to become a rabbi in Prague.[31] His father had been a well-known rabbi in Czechoslovakia and Mr. R. had trained before and after the war to follow in his father's footsteps. Because of a bureaucratic mix-up, the RFD initially would not accept him. NYANA's Vocational Service Department (VSD) would also not support him for the two to six months that he needed to complete his rabbinical training. The social worker informed Mr. R. that he would have to work with VSD's counselor to find suitable employment. How did he feel about giving up everything he had worked for throughout his life? "This was very difficult for Mr. R to accept," wrote his caseworker. "It was quite evident that he could make no brake [*sic*] with his past experiences in relation to his social status, and feeling that it would continue in this country."[32] Mr. R. persisted in his goal to be a rabbi and also in his desire to be transferred to the RFD. Finally, after ten months, he was transferred to that department.

While the RFD acknowledged the desire of another refugee, Mr. E., to become a rabbi, the goal was, his caseworker reminded him, "to assist him in becoming self-supporting." Like the VSD, the RFD felt that, if the husband could not move toward self-maintenance, then the wife should consider employment. Again, this often was at variance with the life that refugees had formerly known. As Mrs. E. confided to the caseworker, "It is unthinkable for a Rabbi's wife to work and he never expected that she would have to work."[33] While the worker expressed sympathy, she wondered if Mrs. E. thought she really had a choice in this matter. Again, we see how values and desire for continuity were often at odds with what the agency presumed. Through his own perseverance, Mr. E. eventually found work as a *shamus* (synagogue caretaker) in a Brooklyn synagogue.

In some instances, the newcomers entertained the idea of a religious-functionary profession because they felt ill equipped to enter the American job market. Mr. J. had worked as a furniture salesman in Czechoslovakia before World War II. His poor knowledge of English, "bearded" appearance, and lack of readily transferable skills influenced him to turn to what he felt he knew best.[34] When he discussed employment possibilities with his case-worker, he told her that although he had no formal training, "he would like to find work as a *mashgiach* or a *shamos* or a religious teacher" because his interests were in this area. Furthermore, "he usually goes to synagogue morn-ing and evening as well as noon and that he would need special time on Fridays and other days." Despite caution from NYANA about the difficul-ties in finding such work, Mr. J. continued to search for a religious func-tionary position. He was not successful. Instead of using his first year in a way that the agency saw as productive, he remained committed to the idea of some type of religious job. The case was closed. Since neither Mr. nor Mrs. J. had worked during their first year, they were in possible jeopardy as public charges and in danger of potential deportation.[35]

By contrast, there were those who, despite former professions as reli-gious functionaries, had no interest in such jobs once they arrived. They were much more interested in obtaining other kinds of employment. Usually these clients were referred to the regular VSD. This also presented problems for USNA, since at times the agency was caught between honoring a prearranged contract that had secured the visa and the newcomers' rejection of the posi-tion upon his or her arrival. The agencies were reluctant to set a negative precedent that not only affected their standing in the community, but also could affect employment possibilities for future refugees.

Orthodox beliefs and appearance could be a handicap for those who were willing to accept most any type of job in the secular world. NYANA's regular VSD, not the RFD, counseled these religious immigrants. As part of its United Job Finding Campaign, Jewish leaders sent letters to potential employers in the business community. These immigrants "are able, competent men and women . . . only waiting for a chance to work," they claimed. "Those who are Sabbath observers are prepared to go more than half-way to compensate for observance of a ritual which is so vital a part of their lives."[36] How exactly these Sabbath observers would compensate for their beliefs was not explained.

NYANA decided to elicit support from the observant business community in New York. To address this pressing issue "a special meeting of orthodox businessmen was held in the office of Mr. Samuel Kramer, and initial steps are being taken to help solve this most difficult problem of placing the ultra-orthodox and bearded men in gainful employment."[37] This group, along with those for whom physical problems interfered with employment, was labeled "hard-core." The Job Finding Campaign Report profiled a number of "typical" hard-to-place newcomers such as Mr. B.:

> A young man who is a strict observer of the Sabbath and wears a skull cap. He is 20 years of age, single, clean shaven and neat. He had no work experience in Europe and arrived in the U.S. in December 1946 at the age of 16. He attended Yeshiva and evening high school. He studied typing and bookkeeping and can at present type 40 words per minute. He is good at figures and record keeping. From October 1949 to January 1950 he worked as a clerk in a Yeshiva. Due to mistreatment during the war, Mr. B. suffered amputation of all the toes on both feet. This is not readily observable since he walks without a cane. However, he must have work which enables him to sit most of the time. Mr. B is willing to accept any type of work for which he is suited and which will enable him to observe the Sabbath. He is intelligent, cooperative and responsible and would be a valuable asset to any organization.[38]

In other such profiles, the candidate's observance of the Sabbath is also stated in the first or second sentence, along with a physical description indicating whether the man wears a beard. Although the phrase "he makes an excellent appearance" was largely reserved for the nonorthodox, some positive reference to the refugee's appearance such as *neat* or *presentable* was invariably included in an effort to make the potential employee as attractive as possible despite his obvious handicap. The emphasis was on the practical. It was placed squarely on the vocational skills of the newcomer rather than on any reward gained from helping a refugee.

Those on the executive level of the agency sought to find jobs for these newcomers. Locally, they stimulated interest in the New York orthodox business community. Rabbi Trainin of the RFD worked in New York and also traveled tirelessly around the country seeking opportunities for his clients. These efforts were significant.

From the start, however, the general sentiment at the administrative level of USNA and, later, NYANA was that dealing with this group was a tremendous challenge that they had not wanted. USNA felt pressured by orthodox groups and the Council of Jewish Federations and Welfare Funds to deal with these refugees. The agencies accepted this challenge begrudgingly and responded accordingly. As the number of religious newcomers requiring help grew, USNA and NYANA kept their RFD operating but sought ways to decrease services to these clients.

An unsympathetic attitude trickled down to many of the social workers who worked directly with these clients. They had little patience when they perceived that religious values undermined agency goals. Mrs. L., a NYANA social worker, recalled, "We had to start a special unit [RFD] for rabbinical students and rabbis because they were *so* demanding and *so* difficult and, I must say, there was a lot of feeling against them." Why? Because "they demanded so much of our time and they would *not* go to work and if you said to the students, look you are entitled to work twenty hours a week [on student visas] and it will not be held against you—you can make money— they would say 'we have to study.' "[39]

The refugees' attitude clashed with the agency's policy on employment and rankled Mrs. L., prompting her, as she reported, to ask one yeshiva student, " 'So, what's going to happen to you?' " upon which "he looked at me and held out his hands and he said, '*Gott vilt hilfn*' (God will help). That was their attitude," she commented and added, "they were really very difficult."[40] One caseworker struggled to find something positive about her client, reporting that his clothing "seemed in good shape but un-pressed and dirty. He wore the formal chassidic dress with long beard and *payes* (sidelocks). In this worker's opinion, his manner was ingratiating and he smiled frequently, showing an excellent set of teeth."[41] In another example, the caseworker thought that the immigrant, a Mr. G., belonged in the religious-functionary division because he was a "Yeshivah type, wearing the curl pinned up." In fact, this young man was willing to consider any kind of job provided he would not have to work on the Sabbath. This same agency worker was dismissive of Mr. G.'s fear about being in an English class with women. She "tried to explain to him that in America such things made no difference and that if he could come to accept the idea of sitting in a class and learning with women he could then be placed [in a class]."[42]

Such statements reveal the lack of understanding and respect for the newcomer's beliefs and behavior. Not only were they seen as representing customs that the refugee could relinquish at will should they conflict with an American way of doing things, they were sometimes perceived as lack of ambition. Such was the case of Mr. R., who, as we saw earlier, wanted to be a religious functionary. His caseworker believed that this wish had more to do with Mr. R.'s disinterest in becoming self-maintaining than with his deeply held convictions.[43]

Most orthodox refugees felt that maintaining a religious life was synonymous with remaining in New York City. Indeed, Rabbi Trainin, director of the RFD at both USNA and NYANA, commented, "Everybody wanted to stay in New York." Persuading refugees to settle outside New York was one battle. Convincing orthodox communities throughout the United States to accept religious-functionary refugees was another. "It was not easy," he recollected. "I didn't find any hostility but I didn't have any great help either. It depends on which orthodox community," he recalled. "I would say that the reception was not exactly very . . . I was kind of disappointed . . . I spent two weeks in the L.A. area," he continued, "and the only thing I was able to find at that time was a community outside of L.A. needed a rabbi. They were willing to take a refugee rabbi but he had to be 'Anglo-Saxon looking,' quoting them. . . . I just walked out on them."[44] The ultraorthodox appearance of some religious functionaries was a sore point with many communities outside New York City. Ultimately, Rabbi Trainin estimates that the majority of religious functionaries, perhaps as many as 75 percent, or one thousand families, did settle outside New York City.

There were those who settled outside New York voluntarily. Mr. Lis was not a religious functionary but he was orthodox.[45] A Polish survivor of Mauthausen and Dachau, he arrived in the United States in 1949 at the age of twenty-seven. A childhood friend was working as a tailor in Hartford, Connecticut, and convinced his boss to provide an affidavit. "I never held a needle in my hand," Mr. Lis admitted in 2002, but he had grabbed the opportunity to come to the United States. He considered staying in New York, but felt it would be easier to adjust to a smaller city and continued by train to Hartford. There was no job for him, however, and he soon began looking for work. Mr. Lis had no relatives to approach and yet did not want to turn to the local Jewish agency, which he knew was helping refugees. Like many others, he stated, "I was independent. I didn't want to beg."

Mr. L quickly found an opening working for a *landsman*.[46] It was a menial job but the pay was good. At ninety cents an hour, it was thirty cents above minimum wage, but he would be required to work on Saturdays, the Jewish Sabbath. "I don't work on Saturdays," Mr. Lis recalled telling the man. "What do you think . . . you're still in Slobodka? Everyone here works on Saturdays," the man replied. "I didn't take the job," stated Mr. Lis. He settled down and began attending services at a local orthodox synagogue every Saturday as he had done in Poland. It was a lonely life he remembers, made even more so by the fact that none of the other congregants ever invited him for a Sabbath or holiday meal. "No one asked, 'Where are you for Shabbos? Where are you eating? Never,'" he emphasized.[47] What accounts for this ungenerous response? "We were looked down on," Mr. Lis explained, especially "those like myself who had nobody." As survivors did in other communities he found a social life with other refugees. He worked hard to support himself and make a life. Eventually he married and prospered. He takes pride in his family, his current financial security, and the fact that he learned English and finished high school at night while working in a printing concern by day. Mr. Lis is not rancorous about his beginnings in Hartford, but, he asserts, "it was a very difficult life, a very difficult life."[48]

Rabbi Baruch Goldstein had a different reception. A survivor of Auschwitz, Buchenwald, and a death march, he arrived in New York City in 1947, sponsored by a yeshiva. He had grown up in a deeply religious home in Poland and describes his prewar self as a "yeshiva bocher" (seminary student).[49] Baruch remained true to his beliefs in the ghetto. He recalled Talmudic discussions with a fellow inmate in Auschwitz. After the war, when he was confronted with the murder of his family and the magnitude of the Holocaust's destruction, his faith crumbled. He was indifferent to the world. In a DP camp in Italy, he recalls observing a group of men praying in a High Holiday service and thinking, "This has nothing to do with me." Through Baruch's aunt in California, a young woman, Rifka, heard about the young DP's plight and implored her brother, a rabbi in Pittsburgh, to intervene. Sometime later, Baruch received a visa to come to the United States under a yeshiva's auspices. He was conflicted. He had an aunt and uncle in America but he was preparing to go to Palestine. The pull of family overrode his plans. In 1948, he came to New York and enrolled at the yeshiva, attending classes and going through the motions of his daily prayers. He lived with his uncle, but after his cousin returned from the army, the refugee felt he could ask for his uncle's help no longer. He turned to NYANA briefly but was intimidated by the social worker's questioning. At the same time, a friendship was growing between him and Rifka, a Hunter College graduate who was working as a nursery school teacher in Manhattan. Rifka's family had arrived from Europe in 1941 and settled in Worcester, Massachusetts. Her father was an illustrious rabbi from Zhitomer, Poland. The young woman knew that Baruch was not a believer. Baruch insists that it was precisely for that reason that she invited him to come to Worcester for the Passover holiday. He accepted with trepidation. The family's holiday celebration triggered an intense feeling of nostalgia in the survivor for his lost childhood home. "It was exactly the Pesach [Passover] I had known," he recalled.[50] The visit transformed the young man in more ways than one. Baruch returned to Judaism with renewed belief and soon became engaged to the rabbi's daughter. Rabbi Goldstein spent his life in America immersed in Jewish education. He struggled in his early years both spiritually and psychologically, and he believes intensely that his wife's love and her family's similarity to his own helped restore him. He now speaks and writes about faith after the Holocaust.

Some survivors' paths, then, independent of agency planning, took them outside the metropolitan New York area. At the same time, USNA did its best to ensure that orthodox survivors were sent around the country, especially away from New York. As a result, USNA also found it necessary to institute an informal rotation system so that individual communities did not feel that they were receiving an undue number of difficult cases. Number one on the list of those defined as "difficult" were "Chasidic in dress and appearance."[51] On the surface, the concern of communities—especially those that did not have an established orthodox sector—that it was counterproductive to receive a religious newcomer seems reasonable. But the archival records reveal that the American communities' response focused on these practicalities, perhaps, to obscure other sentiments. There are numerous comments in the Denver files, for example, that reflect local feeling that they were getting more than their fair share of difficult or "hard-core" cases.

In a letter to USNA, Dr. Alfred Neumann, the JFCS executive director, wrote that Denver's New Americans Committee was considering "refusal to accept for resettlement orthodox clients or religious functionaries." He asked USNA "to very carefully check the units which are earmarked for Denver, so that we, for a change, get units which are employable and placeable. This will ease our burden."[52] Dr. Neumann wrote to USNA again, just a few days later. "Would it be possible for you to alert our overseas Joint representative not to select orthodox units for resettlement in our community?" he inquired. "It is practically impossible to find housing close enough to our *shuls* and employment opportunities which would not interfere with their religious preference." He went on to describe the W. family, who, "after two months of strenuous work, led to our sending them to Minneapolis. We consider this situation," he continued, "a waste in time, energy, and money, which could be easily avoided if our situation is known to the overseas selectors."[53] USNA, however, was not easily swayed by Dr. Neumann's request. In fact, Denver was not the only city that questioned the reception of religious functionaries. This had been a topic for discussion as early as 1948, when USNA's migration department reviewed the destinations of religious functionaries outside New York City. At that time, USNA took the position that

> refusal to accept such cases by any community is not acceptable to USNA. The location of the immigrant in one of these categories has been determined prior to his arrival by the sponsorship which made possible the migration. Failure to adhere to the agreement existing between the immigrant and the Government places the immigrant in jeopardy. In addition, there is ordinarily so little difference between the original plan and any that may thereafter be made, that there is no justification for a community other than that in which the sponsoring institution is located, to take responsibility.[54]

Nevertheless, when the Denver JFCS had any voice about a survivor's destination, it was loud and clear. It preferred not to accept religious functionaries or practicing observant Jews.

When the RFD at USNA and NYANA wanted to send a religious functionary to a given community, it negotiated with a local orthodox institution, not with the secular cooperating agency. As the orthodox institution paid the salary for the newcomer, the RFD saw no reason to include the local agency, such as the JFCS. Dr. Neumann did not agree. He argued that the religious functionaries used his agency's resources and he felt that they should be included in (not added to) the monthly quota of DPs arriving in Denver. USNA and the Denver agency quarreled about this. Rabbi Trainin insisted that this was the standard policy for the RFD's vocational planning all over the country, but Dr. Neumann remained adamant. The correspondence between the two agencies regarding the R. family, a husband and wife who were both hired by Denver's Rose Memorial Hospital, is a case in point. Esther Einbinder, settlement consultant at USNA, wrote, "Because there will be no waiting period for employment this situation is quite different from a general settlement case in which the Jewish community assumes full responsibility for a new arrival until he finds employment and becomes self-maintaining. Therefore, it will not be possible for us to consider the Rs settled on your community quota."[55] To which Dr. Neumann replied, "In case we shall be called upon to consider another religious functionary, we will receive them in this community only if we get credit for it on our community quota."[56]

Dr. Neumann appears to have lost the battle on this particular issue. Esther Einbinder sent him a letter a few months later informing him that "through the Religious Functionary Services Mr. Polak secured employment in Denver for the Vaad Hakashrut [rabbinic committee that oversees community standards of kashrut] as a schochet of fowl and cattle at a salary of $75.00 to $100.00 a week. We hope that this information will be helpful to you in the event that questions arise as to the status of the family."[57] Nevertheless, whenever Dr. Neumann had the opportunity to reject orthodox refugees destined for Denver he did so. When Esther Einbinder requested that Denver accept two refugee families for resettlement, including a young couple who could not obtain kosher meat in San Francisco, his reply, via telegram, was curt. "Accept Mr. M for resettlement . . . cannot accept B family because strict orthodox living impossible here."[58] And while JFCS may have not had control over the religious functionaries sent to Denver, its New Americans Committee passed a resolution in December 1950 that denied help to any needy religious functionary who had been sent to Denver without JFCS authorization.

Occasionally, Denver agreed to accept a religious immigrant "on quota," and the JFCS files allow us a glimpse of this secular agency's attitude toward its observant clients. Such phrases as "Mr. G. had also made excessive demands in relation to his religious practices. Pocatello [the town from which he was transferred to Denver] did not have a synagogue or Rabbi, and no facilities to buy kosher food."[59] Describing Mr. G.'s desire for a community with a synagogue and kosher food as being excessively demanding clearly reveals not just a lack of sympathy for but also a lack of knowledge about the fundamentals of orthodox life.

That Denver had a Jewish population of eighteen thousand people, eight synagogues, Jewish day schools, a Jewish hospital and Jewish TB facilities, the National Home for Jewish Children, and kosher slaughterhouses did not influence Dr. Neumann's decisions, over and over, to refuse to accept most orthodox refugees. As late as 1953, a casework supervisor at JFCS responded to USNA's request to allow two newcomers to settle in Denver by writing, "We also trust that these people are not orthodox. We can't place Sabbath observers."[60] It was an outrageous claim. As he well knew, a number of religious families had been able to make a home in Denver. These facts on the ground belied Dr. Neumann's position, but it was his ideology that had shaped the supervisor's reply. The history of Dr. Neumann in Denver shows how one individual, in a leadership position with few checks and the probable support of the larger community, could influence the course of resettlement in a locale.

Clearly Dr. Neumann did not see the remnants of orthodox European Jewry as potentially enriching to the Denver Jewish population. He only saw potential problems. One example is strikingly poignant. A twenty-six-year-old rabbi wrote to the JFCS inquiring about "the possibilities of getting settled in your city."[61] He explained that he had been graduated from both the Rabbinical Seminary and college in Poland, that he had a special interest in "bibliographie [sic], books, and librarianship," and that he had a good command of English, German, Polish, Hebrew, and Yiddish. He went on to mention his years in "the Ghetto and several concentration camps" and his postwar studies in philosophy and economics at the Goethe University in Frankfurt. Having just finished a three-year project for the organization Jewish Cultural Reconstruction, he was ready "to get out of the hustle-bustle city New York" and asked for "guidance, information and friendliness."[62] Dr. Theodore Salzberg, vocational counselor at JFCS, responded, "We feel we cannot recommend such a move for the following reasons: Many people of circumstances similar to yourself have moved here and desire to move here for the same reasons. This has resulted in a larger group of religious functionaries than the Jewish population can possibly absorb at any time."[63] Rabbi R. may have been unusual in his extensive experience and education, but the agency's response to him was not; Dr. Salzberg zeroed in on his rabbinical training and discouraged his move to Denver primarily on that basis.

One would hope that those involved with resettling orthodox refugees would have been able to transcend some of their own assumptions and prejudices. One wishes that they had been able to step back and broaden the lens. They were working with Holocaust survivors who wanted to preserve the religious life destroyed in Europe by the Germans and their allies in the way they knew best: by living full orthodox lives here in America. Notable as one of the few from the secular agencies to express this was Judah Shapiro, education consultant to the Joint Distribution Committee. The "American Jewish community ought to realize that a real upheaval has taken place in Jewish life," wrote Mr. Shapiro to Henry Levy of the emigration department of the committee in 1951. "I think that we have not yet seen a sufficiently radical approach to the problem in America, where for at least a generation a substantial number of Jews from Europe will continue to be and act as they were, and who will regard America with warmth because it gives them an opportunity to behave as Jews, defining 'Jews' by their standards."[64]

This radical approach eluded the agencies. USNA and NYANA were secular organizations wedded to their own ideologies. The creation of the RFD was one way to approach the problem of religious functionaries and still adhere to agency goals. Hundreds found appropriate positions under its auspices, even as local cooperating communities put up barriers. Others struggled to meet the same criteria demanded of all newcomers while maintaining their religious beliefs. They discovered that social workers at best had little understanding of orthodox traditions and values and at worst were openly hostile. Few understood or sympathized with the surviving remnant of orthodox Jewry's belief that they were obligated to continue Jewish life, not just for themselves but also for all that had been obliterated.

The agencies also viewed another group of newcomers through a communal lens. Like the orthodox refugees, this group was under the jurisdiction of a special department. It is to them, the orphan Holocaust survivors, that we now turn.

CHAPTER 5

"Unaccompanied Minors"

THE STORY OF THE DISPLACED ORPHANS

1 October 1946. The S.S. *Ernie Pyle* pulled into New York. Among the ship's passengers were a handful of war orphans whose plight was described in the *Herald-Tribune*: "20 War Orphans among 945 on The Ernie Pyle . . . Waifs' Ages Range from 8 Months to 18 Years; All Will Go to Foster Homes."[1] The journalist observed that the "youngest of the lot was eight-months-old Sigmund Tryangel, whose Polish father was killed by the Nazis during the last week of the war in Europe. His mother died at the baby's birth after enervating months in a Nazi concentration camp. Rosy and happy, the baby grinned at the flash of news cameras."[2] The article depicted a group of children whose "morale was high"; even "the babies did their part by not getting seasick."[3] The *Herald-Tribune* was one of many papers that recorded the arrival of these young refugees and predicted a future of promise and renewal. Like other accounts of refugees in the media, it cast the newcomers in an optimistic glow and emphasized the contribution they would make to America.

It quickly became clear to those involved that these particular newcomers were anything but rosy and happy babies. Few young children and even fewer babies had survived the Holocaust. Most were adolescents who had experienced years of deprivation and horror. Nevertheless, they were the most sympathetic of victims. Made parentless by Hitler, many had endured concentration camps and were their families' sole survivor. To some, they were motherless children; to relatives they were the surviving orphans of murdered sisters and brothers; to others they symbolized a youthful link between the devastated Jewish world and a Jewish future in America. While the public perception varied, one fact remained constant: they were alone and without means of support. To whom could they turn?

European-Jewish Children's Aid (EJCA) was the American agency that supervised the resettlement of at least one thousand "unaccompanied minors"—a benign designation that belied the Holocaust experiences, which had orphaned these few surviving Jewish children. EJCA took charge of these youth from the time they stepped off the boat in New York until the orphans were adopted, married, or came of age. EJCA located and supervised the children's placements, and for this it relied on local cooperating agencies such as the Jewish Family and Children's Services in Denver. How effective was the agency in meeting this challenge of settling and protecting their charges? How did the system shape the children's experiences? How did the orphans' traumatic past influence their assimilation into American life? The answer is not simple. A confluence of factors—agency policies, foster care placement, location of settlement, the children's wartime experience—shaped the resettlement of these most vulnerable charges. Some of the same questions and dilemmas that faced older refugees applied. But there were other considerations, unique to orphans, which necessitated different responses.

EJCA evolved out of German-Jewish Children's Aid (GJCA), which had been created in 1934 to care for German Jewish refugee children. GJCA was a landmark: the first agency in the United States to be involved with the protection of the rights of alien children. It developed placement guidelines for locating appropriate homes for refugee children as well as follow-up supervision of the placements. When the United States Committee for the Care of European Children (U.S. Committee), a voluntary agency, was founded in 1940 with the goal of rescuing children whose lives were endangered because of the war, GJCA became one of its cooperating agencies. The U.S. Committee then assumed the role of deciding which children were eligible to enter the United States.

In 1941, GJCA became EJCA, with sole responsibility for placing the small number of Jewish children that the U.S. Committee brought to this country. Like other refugee organizations, EJCA's activities withered during the war years. After the war, however, EJCA once again became the primary cooperating agency for the care of Jewish children in conjunction with the U.S. Committee.

The U.S. Committee decided whether a minor could enter the United States and supervised the process until EJCA met that child in New York. The former screened the children in Europe, provided temporary care while their applications were processed, made arrangements for travel, selected an escort when necessary, and assumed port and dock services in America. Unless they went directly to relatives, the orphans were temporarily housed at an EJCA reception center in New York. They spent several weeks at the center, where they were evaluated medically and psychologically. EJCA then worked with its own local cooperating Jewish agencies to place children in communities around the country.[4] In addition to overseeing general resettlement of the orphans, EJCA was required to submit semiannual reports to the U.S. Children's Bureau (a federal agency that set standards for local child-care agencies) and the immigration and naturalization authorities. The U.S. Children's Bureau also consulted with state welfare offices and decided which local child-care agencies met their standards for service.[5] The local agency assisted with family placements, but an orphan remained under EJCA's jurisdiction, unless fully self-supporting or married, until the age of twenty-one.[6]

Unlike the adult DPs, the majority of orphans, such as the twenty aboard the S.S. *Ernie Pyle*, came to America from 1946 until July 1948 under the Truman Directive. In this otherwise neutrally worded document, "orphaned children" were specifically named for immediate consideration for admittance to the United States.[7] While approximately one thousand unaccompanied Jewish minors entered the country with Truman's help, an additional unknown number arrived after the enactment of the Displaced Persons Act, on 1 July 1948, which terminated the Truman Directive. This allowed for the admission of three thousand nonquota orphans. To be eligible, the displaced orphan had to be living in the American zone by 25 June 1948. Nonquota admission was restricted to those under the age of sixteen. Those between the ages of sixteen and twenty-one received affidavits from the U.S. Committee to enter on the regular quota.[8]

As for adult refugees, the minor's first step toward leaving Europe was to procure an affidavit. Relatives provided the needed document for some DPs. EJCA could provide an affidavit for those who had no American relatives or whose families were not interested in sponsoring them. Sponsorship of orphans differed from that of adult DPs in one significant way: children went to live with their affiants until they married or became legal adults.

In some ways, but not all, the demographic patterns of orphan DPs mirror those of the adult refugee population. It appears that most were from Eastern Europe. Several studies based on small samples also support the supposition that, as with the adult refugee population, the majority were male.[9] Early media coverage of the war orphans generated the impression that most were young children. This was untrue. The average age was seventeen to eighteen years old.[10] Many in this group were ten to eleven years old at the onset of the war and a significant part of their short lives was lived during the Holocaust. This was camouflaged by their apparent recovery; many observers in 1946 were impressed by their outward good health.[11]

EJCA anticipated that the cooperating agencies would need assistance in their work with these newcomers and sent Deborah Portnoy, a field representative of EJCA, to meet with child-care agencies around the country to assess the situation. She reported that communal agency workers recognized immediately that this was a group with which they had little experience and that they would need to be flexible in their planning.[12] Whether or not these youngsters required treatment that differed from other foster children, however, provoked a debate among social workers. The question of "equal treatment" also emerged among agencies dealing with older DPs.

After spending two years in the field, Portnoy presented her observations at the National Conference of Jewish Social Welfare in May 1948:

> In this age group the usual conflicts of adolescence seem to be exaggerated. Since their problems could not be worked out in a normal setting of a family unit, the degree of maturity which one anticipates in this age had not yet occurred. We find the struggle between dependence and independence going on at full force. As one would expect, they seek love and acceptance but are ambivalent about taking it. They carry into their relationships the pattern of competition and drive for survival which has characterized so important a part of their formative years. Frequently they manipulate their environment in a manner and with cleverness beyond their years. Their tendency is to enter into a struggle of wills in order to force their environment to conform with their needs. They seem to adapt themselves to situations when they are actually only evading or temporizing. The situation is further complicated by other psychological and objective factors. They have the fear of the unknown which is common to the immigrant and which is often covered by exaggerated self-assurance and an unrealistic assertion that they can carry through their own plans.[13]

Portnoy's comments are remarkable for a number of reasons. On the one hand, she attempted to understand this group, to uncover their motivations and behavior through a psychological lens and to relate this to the agencies' approach to action. She clearly paid attention to the adolescents' emotional state and noted both the similarities and the differences between the development of members of this group and that of typical adolescents. Compared to the general approach to refugees, many of whom were barely older, this was extraordinary.

What Portnoy omitted is also striking. She discussed some "psychological factors," but said little about the reasons for the loss or grief that these adolescents had experienced. Her starting point was the norm. Her concern was with where these teenagers fit in the range of both normal adolescence and the typical immigrant experience. The assessment was insightful, but it was not without a certain judgmental reaction, as mention of how the young newcomers "manipulate their environment" and "enter into a struggle of wills" show. The perceptions of the newcomers' behavior on the part of Portnoy and her co-professionals were rooted in the scheme of normal adolescence. And this led to ambivalence toward these clients. The caseworkers recognized that orphan DPs differed from both adult DPs and other native foster children, but the magnitude of that difference eluded even the most well-intentioned professionals.

Editha Sterba, PhD, was a child analyst who had experience with young refugees in Michigan and, like Deborah Portnoy, shared her knowledge with her colleagues. Perhaps because she worked first with newcomers who arrived before 1945, her assessment of the adolescents who came after the war is more astute than Portnoy's. She believed that this group, indeed, required special care. When treating the adolescents, she urged her colleagues to remember the root cause of the young people's behavior:

> The difficult behavior which, to a certain degree, all displaced children present when they are placed in foster homes or with relatives after their arrival is a reaction to their terrible experiences, particularly to the loss of their parents, home, and country. This reaction, which heretofore had to be repressed completely due to the conditions under which the displaced children lived, must become manifest if these children are ever to be enabled to work through the depression brought on by the losses they suffered. Loss of parents and home, which usually occurred in a very traumatic way, must have been particularly upsetting emotionally because it was combined with the threat of complete annihilation for the child.[14]

Many young newcomers, however, did not have the benefit of both the professional expertise and the compassion expressed by Dr. Sterba. Alex, for example, was a seventeen-year-old boy from Czechoslovakia who arrived in Denver in November 1947 under EJCA's auspices. While most adult files have scanty details about what the individuals endured, his file, like others of the EJCA, reveals something about his wartime experiences. We learn that when Alex was fourteen years old, he and his parents and five brothers and sisters were deported to a concentration camp. Only he survived. After the war, while in a DP camp, he was diagnosed with TB and sent from Europe to the National Jewish Hospital in Denver. After a brief stay in the hospital, doctors determined that Alex did not have TB and could be discharged. The Social Service Department of the hospital recommended to the Jewish Family and Children's Services (JFCS) caseworker and the members of the Denver Coordinating Committee that Alex receive "foster care in an excellent home" because "he is definitely not ready to go out and face the world alone." The Denver Committee pledged that it was "completely willing to render any and all services that the boy will need."[15] Despite this commitment, the committee was unable to find a foster home that was willing or able to take in Alex. A room was located in one home and he took his meals in another. The latter was felt to be a good match because the woman had left Germany in 1939 and "would know how to help A. readjust."[16] In the parlance of the U.S. Committee, these were boarding homes; both foster families were paid by JFCS for the care they provided.

By the time Alex was twenty-one and released from JFCS/EJCA's responsibility, he was working full time in a men's store, spoke English fluently, and was supporting himself. Moreover, he was active in a Zionist group and had several friends. He had, as the semimonthly report to the U.S. Committee stated, "made a splendid adjustment."[17] This had not come easily. He had changed foster placements numerous times, once because the foster mother felt that the allowance was insufficient to cover Alex's board, another time because the foster parents felt that Alex was spending too much time at home, which interfered with their privacy. Despite an outwardly healthy appearance, he was under a doctor's care for an ulcerous condition.

Echoing Portnoy's comments, one of the most common themes in Alex's file was JFCS' belief that the adolescent was a dependent and manipulative boy who had tried to take advantage of the agency's resources by resisting finding work. "A., as you probably know, is quite a dependent and exploitative youngster," wrote Dr. Neumann in a letter to Lotte Marcuse, director of placements at EJCA, less than a year after Alex's arrival. "He clung to his childlike dependency," continued Dr. Neumann, until he was told that no spending money would be forthcoming unless he made an effort to find part-time work. "We think it is so very important for A. to be treated more like an adult than a child and offer him some responsibility which would enhance his growing up," said Dr. Neumann. He concluded this letter by adding, "We want to help him get away from exploiting case workers, friends, and foster parents."[18]

The facts of Alex's life stand in stark juxtaposition to Dr. Neumann's description. Alex was attending night school, learning English, and moving from one placement to another. When Dr. Neumann sent his semiannual report to the EJCA, he noted that Alex had "resisted for a long time acceptance of the fact that he must assume responsibility for his own welfare." This Dr. Neumann continued, was a result of the fact that "he is a very dependent, and in a way, passively aggressive sort of fellow who has pleaded, like so many others, for special consideration because of what he went through in Europe, and because of his hospitalization at the National Jewish Hospital in Denver."[19]

Dr. Neumann's feelings were clear. He was among those who adhered to the principle that these clients should be held to the same standard as nonrefugee clientele. And this attitude shaped agency refugee policy. Whether or not Alex and other survivors hoped for special consideration, they were not to be treated any differently from other clients. This is significant. It is not that JFCS withheld help from this orphan. Alex did receive support from JFCS while learning the watch-making trade. Yet until he was gainfully employed, he was criticized by the agency for what they perceived to be his excessive dependency and reluctance to make a new start.

The staff of JFCS in Denver did not have a great deal of patience for young people who had endured the Holocaust as children. Dr. Neumann did not see an orphan survivor in Alex. Rather, he saw a young adult who was expected to behave like other clients and achieve economic independence as rapidly as possible. When orphans like Alex did not, they were quickly labeled as dependent, childlike, passive. Given the agency's attitude, it seems that their battle was hardly over after the war.

The issue of home placement was crucial. Alex was not alone in experiencing several foster homes. In a study of thirty-eight refugee children who arrived in Detroit from 1946 to 1948, the authors wrote, "Many refugee children who have proved themselves able to get along adequately in other respects have trouble in a foster home."[20] A full 50 percent of the placements, noted the article, were deemed unsatisfactory. The explanations for this problem were threefold: such failure was caused by poor choice of home, problematic children, or a combination of the two. A crucial factor was the limited number of families who were willing to be foster parents. The supply of foster children exceeded the demand of foster parents. Moreover, the Detroit list of potential foster parents had existed before the refugees arrived. These parents had not necessarily signed up to take in refugee children and were ill prepared to do so.

The situation was no happier for those children who went to relatives. Some twenty of the thirty-eight foster families in Detroit were related to the orphans. The criteria for assessing these families were more lenient because they were relatives. All twenty families were accepted even though the case-workers felt that only twelve met their standards for foster care. Once the children were placed with relatives there was little supervision of the arrangement, as relatives sometimes resented what they perceived as the agency's meddlesome attitude. Indeed, of the twenty children so placed, fifteen were described as having made a poor adjustment. The authors concluded that both children and foster parents expected too much from each other; this would explain the high numbers of unworkable placements.

Expecting too much from one another is one possibility. Chana B., a sixteen-year-old from Poland, articulated another in a discussion with the EJCA social worker about her placement with an aunt and uncle. When asked what it had been like in her own home before the war, Chana burst into tears, "averting her head and trying to control herself," and then replied angrily, "Don't ever ask me about my family again."[21] When the social worker pressed on, inquiring if she had a particularly painful memory, Chana "continued to cry silently for a moment and then with a burst of feeling, which seemed to come from way down deep, she said, 'how do you think it will feel to me to live in that house and hear that 21 year old son call mama and papa and know that it can't be for me?' "[22] For Chana, the idea of living in a family constellation would be a constant reminder of the loss of her own parents.

The new relationship was complicated on many levels for both the orphans and the sponsors. The orphans' new families often had little understanding or desire to understand the young DPs' past. Undoubtedly, many thought that "moving on" would be advantageous to the youth. Sometimes the foster parents expected their charge to relate to them as parents right away. One woman, for example, recalled her aunt and uncle's insistence that she call them "mother and father" immediately after moving in with them.[23] This could evoke ambivalence in the newcomer. She may have wanted this closeness but may have felt it betrayed her murdered parents. Or, as with Chana, it may have signaled a continual recognition of her parents' death and their absence in her life. The American relatives were often unprepared for the turmoil that an adolescent survivor brought to their home and expressed disappointment that the refugee was not more grateful for their help. That was not an uncommon sentiment between natives and all new immigrants. In the case of the orphans, however, it was more pronounced by the minors' financial and legal dependency on their foster parents.

For Chana, her placements proved to be troublesome. From the beginning, three sets of relatives expressed interest in hosting her but could not agree on who would be responsible for their niece's living and financial arrangements. To the social worker's credit, she explained that relatives did not always offer the best solution and was ready to look elsewhere for Chana's foster care. The families were adamant about keeping her with them even though they were all ambivalent about her support. Chana went to one aunt and uncle's home with the agreement that it would be a trial period for everyone. Both sides were careful about making a long-term commitment. In this example, the social worker kept a close eye; she monitored the arrangement through almost weekly meetings with the girl. But lapses happened. After two months, Chana came to the center, very distraught, and asked to see her caseworker about a problem she was having. The secretary told her to come back the next day and Chana left, crying. Her uncle then called the agency and left a message that the girl "is mentally ill. He is afraid she will jump from the window."[24]

At the meeting the following day with her social worker, Chana calmly agreed to return to her foster home, but her aunt was immovable. She refused to take Chana back, because "she does not listen, she would not have a doctor when she was sick, she is very moody, does not talk to the aunt but talks to others."[25] Chana then stayed for a few weeks with another aunt and uncle, but all agreed that there was not enough room for her there. She seemed much more positive at the third placement, with an elderly couple who were more distantly related. Still, her file shows that she, with the agency's help, continued to consider the possibility of going to a foster home outside New York. Her case file also indicates that Chana began studies at two different high schools during this three-month period, a reminder that the young refugees not only had to cope with foster families but negotiate new schools, too. As with many of these children, Chana's postwar years were anything but stable. The aftermath of the war period was often a merciless series of disruptions.

Lea W. also had difficulties with her foster parents who were relatives.[26] She was twelve years old when the war ended; she had survived with her sister in hiding. She and her family had been deported from Germany to France, where her mother contacted the Oeuvre de Secours aux Enfants (OSE). OSE placed the two girls in orphanages for three years and then with a French family for two years. After the war, OSE moved the pair to a home for survivor children. Lea's maternal grandfather, with whom she had had contact before the war, had fled to New York from Germany in 1938. He saw his granddaughters' names in a newspaper and contacted OSE. "I was told," recalled Lea, "that a man who claimed to be our grandfather wanted us to come here and we started getting packages with candy from him." Although Lea remembered initially being excited by the idea of going to America, her arrival in New York in September 1946 "was very traumatic because I didn't recognize him [her grandfather] and he was a stranger with gray hair." Lea's bewilderment is reflected in her words. "It was traumatic," she stated again. "It was tough, it was rough . . . and this man—I was afraid of men—all the bad things that happened was because of men . . . so our grandfather who we hadn't seen in so many years, we didn't know him— I don't know—we didn't understand what was happening."[27] Their grand-father took Lea and her sister from the dock to an aunt and uncle's house and left them there. That was their first and only encounter with their grand-father in America. He died suddenly six months later without having man-aged to see his granddaughters again.

Lea believes that the relatives, particularly her aunt, did not really want the girls but took them in because she and her husband received payment for doing so. Soon after their arrival, Lea and her sister infected their sixteen-year-old cousin with lice, so her aunt shaved their heads. "We weren't allowed to go in the living room or to the fridge," Lea stated. "We weren't allowed to speak French—she thought we were talking about her." In her first few months in New York, she felt that she had gone "from one hell to another." The situation did not improve. Sometime in 1949, her aunt decided that she no longer wished to care for the girls. When the social worker asked where they wanted to go, Lea and her sister chose Houston, Texas, partially because of a romantic notion of adventure that Texas conjured up and partially because it was far from New York City. They were placed in the Wolf Home, a Jewish orphanage, where Lea discovered three other survivors, all boys, among its charges.[28]

Once Lea was in Texas, JFCS took over responsibility for her care until she finished high school. Shortly after she arrived in the Dallas orphanage, the social worker asked Lea if she wanted to earn her own keep. This meant separating from her sister, but they agreed to try. Before long, Lea was working for a well-to-do Jewish family. She cared for their three children and attended high school at night. She continued to receive a small allowance from the local JFCS and recalls her caseworker, Miss Jamison, with great fondness. "She was wonderful. I remember the warmth she pro-jected." Lea graduated from high school and, through Miss Jamison, met another survivor. He was unstable, but she eventually married him because "I thought I'd never find anyone else who'd love me."[29]

Lea and her husband had four children together before they divorced in 1979, and she is proud of her children's accomplishments. She derives much pleasure from the fact that they all live nearby and are involved in one another's lives. She is now happily remarried to a native Texan. Still, Lea remarked, "there are times when I wished I had stayed in France." She believes that the pain and disruption of her first years here, after the trauma of the war years, obstructed pursuing a meaningful education and career path. As with other refugee children, a sense of irrevocable rupture, despite certain successes, punctuates Lea's life.

Marion Nachman, like Lea, was sponsored by relatives.[30] But her story is unusual for two reasons: she was younger than most orphan DPs, and her aunt and uncle adopted her. As we know, very few young children survived. Marion, who was seven years old in 1945, had been saved by her parents and two non-Jewish families in Holland. Her parents, who were deported and murdered, had the courage and the means to place her with a family named Bruning in 1941. When one of the Brunings' eleven children announced to her class that a little Jewish girl was living with them, Marion was sent to the Martin family. She lived with the Martins for four years.

At the end of the war, her paternal uncle, whom she did not know, came to claim her. "It was horrible leaving the Martins," Marion recalled. That they seemed to give her up so easily devastated her. She arrived in New York in July 1946 and moved into her aunt and uncle's home. "It was not a good situation," she reflected. "I became a very sad child, I think, and I had not been … I had been happy." She did not speak at all for a while in her new home and remembered that she was "very lonely and homesick for Holland." Although she excelled in school, she thinks of herself as being depressed as she grew up in New York. Her aunt and uncle adopted her during the first year after her arrival, but she never felt close to them.[31]

Several years ago, Marion learned that the Martins had initiated procedures to adopt her after the war, which is some consolation to her now. In many ways Marion's resettlement in the United States would be deemed successful. She was one of the few Jewish children to survive the Holocaust, her father's brother and wife adopted her, she learned English quickly, and she finished high school and went onto higher education. She married and raised two children. Yet her life was shaped by loss that dealt her an emotional blow, and with which she continues, until today, to struggle.

Different factors motivated people to sponsor their young European relatives. Sometimes it was a sincere desire to help a young survivor. Sometimes it was a feeling of obligation. Often it was a combination of reasons. These factors were similar to those that motivated people to sponsor adult DPs. There was one fundamental difference; the orphans went to live with their relatives. The foster families then became eligible for financial aid from the agencies, which could further complicate their motives.

Michel Jeruchim's story illustrates how conflicting factors influenced his maternal uncle to sponsor him, his brother, and his sister. Michel was twelve when he arrived in the United States with two older siblings.[32] All survived by hiding with French farmers. They went to live with their uncle and his second wife and children in a small apartment in Brooklyn. Michel believed that his uncle felt directly responsible for them but that his uncle's wife did not. He sensed that they were not too welcome there and believed that they received less food than the others. "Not scraps," he recalled, "but we didn't get grapes when they did." Michel recognized that it was not easy for this already large family to take in three others, which mitigates his criticism. Still, he remembers his overriding feeling of being an intruder and trying "to be a fly on the wall." When Michel and his brother left to find an apartment on their own, the exchange was unpleasant "because they [the relatives] were upset about the associated loss of income." They did not see each other again for many years. Thus, Michel's family helped for a combination of reasons: his uncle's feeling of responsibility to his sister's children along with the financial supplement he received from them.

Some young DPs were positive about their relatives. Such was the case of Frances N., who, along with her three siblings, managed to survive several labor and concentration camps in Poland. She and one sibling, because of their ages, benefited from the Truman Directive, while their married sisters came later on the DP quota. Frances and her brother, sixteen and eighteen years old, respectively, disembarked from the S.S. *Marine Perch* in New York in 1947 and went to the EJCA reception center in New York. "They put us in this home in the Bronx—in a house where the Children's—the Jewish Children's Bureau had arranged." And she added, "They had clothes for us, they had food."[33]

Shortly after Frances and her brother's arrival, their grandmother's sister and nieces came to visit them in the reception center. "From then on, every few days, they brought us things, they took us to their houses, they gave us nice meals, they treated us nice." Still, when it came down to where the siblings would live, the relatives decided that they wanted the pair to go to an aunt in Cleveland because she was well-to-do. "She had her own home. . . . [T]he husband had [a] business," Frances explained.[34] Thus, after some ten days in the Bronx, Frances and her brother left on a train for Cleveland.

The siblings lived with these relatives for a few years. Her brother worked in their uncle's beauty supply business. Frances is grateful that her aunt decided that she was too young to go to work. She attended high school and took a beauty course at night, finishing in two and a half years, rather than three. Her brother gave her an allowance out of his earnings because "we didn't want to take so much" from their relatives. But Frances emphasized her closeness to her brother above all. "I love my brother. He was . . . we were the closest . . . we were only two years apart and we were orphans together. He took care of me until I got married." While she felt her relationship with her brother was paramount, Frances praised her aunt and uncle, too. "They were older people," she explained, "but they did as best as they could for us."[35]

Robert Berger also had positive memories of relatives. He, too, arrived in New York in 1947 and, like Frances, went to the EJCA reception center in the Bronx. Shortly thereafter, he met several relatives. "There was one couple in the Bronx who were really very nice to me—people of very, very modest means," he remembered. "I think he had a grocery store," Robert added, "and they had a small apartment somewhere in the Bronx and they took me for supper a couple of times. I stayed with them and probably slept a week on the couch in the living room. . . . [T]hey were very nice people."[36] Still, none of his relatives sponsored him, and he was resettled elsewhere. They were too poor to offer much help, but the family's kindness made a lasting impression on the boy.

Miriam W. had no American relatives. She arrived on a corporate affidavit in 1946 at the age of sixteen.[37] She had wanted to go to Palestine, but while she was in a DP camp her brother-in-law heard that the United States was accepting children without parents and signed her up. She ended up in Cleveland. The H. family there had registered with the local cooperating agency in the hopes of receiving a young girl who would be company for their five-year-old daughter. Miriam recalled in 1984 that the agency alerted Mr. H. "that they [had] a child but the child [was] a little older than what he wanted and he said okay and when he came to get me he found a big girl." Nevertheless, Miriam went to live with the H. family. It was not always easy, in part, she admitted, because "I would not communicate. . . . I went to the library downtown, came home with a pile of Polish books and went upstairs and shut the door and sat there with the books and I wouldn't come out." The family, however, "had a lot of understanding and worked with the agency on my behalf." After a series of placements in various schools, Miriam enrolled in John Jay High School. It was a lucky move. The school had a special class for foreign students and the teacher took Miriam under her wing. The girl excelled academically and befriended other refugee teens.

She did not fit in well with American students, but "was very, very happy in that class," as she remembered.[38]

Abraham was a nineteen-year-old who arrived on the S.S. *Ernie Pyle*, noted earlier.[39] Although the news article describing the ship's arrival reported that all the children would be sent to foster homes, Abraham had a different experience. Like Miriam, he arrived on a corporate affidavit of the U.S. Committee and EJCA was responsible for placing him. Having lived his early years in a Polish shtetl with a population of a few thousand, Abraham accepted the agency's recommendation that he go to a small town.

Although Abraham expected to go to a foster family, his file reveals that the agency sent him to a residential institution for troubled boys in Cleveland as a temporary measure. Abraham was extremely unhappy there and "voiced considerable resentment against the personnell [*sic*] at the New York Reception Center." He told the caseworker at the Bellefaire reception center that "he felt that they had played a 'trick' on him by sending him to Cleveland." The agency, instead of having his best interest at heart, he believed, had only been interested in getting him out of New York. Perhaps Abraham found the institutional setting distasteful because he was a concentration camp survivor. "He implied that he had no use for the cottage father and resented his dictatorial methods," his caseworker wrote. "He was anxious to leave here as soon as possible."[40] Fortunately, a rabbi from another state telephoned less than a week later. A man in his community believed that Abraham was a second cousin and wanted to sponsor the teenager to live with him. It then fell to EJCA to locate a designated children's agency near the relative that could supervise the arrangement. The file does not indicate whether this happened, although the removal of the boy from the institution did seem to be the plan. Abraham's experience underscores the role of EJCA. The agency made this decision without the young man's consent. While he may have then wanted to leave the Bellefaire for his cousin's home, he and his cousin were powerless to effect the move.

The EJCA's ostensible goal was to protect the orphans. What the agency perceived as acceptable, however, the orphan might view as intolerable. When there was no ready foster placement or when the orphan was deemed "difficult," juvenile institutions sufficed. Abraham's story, like others in the case files, tells us about this.[41] These placements were most upsetting to the young DPs. As Abraham's words show, he felt angry and abandoned rather than protected.

One exception shines bright as an example of an institutional or quasi-institutional program that served a number of young people well. The

Boston JFCS decided in 1946 to experiment with placement strategies for New American children who were beginning to arrive in the United States. The agency created a special refugee unit at an already existing Jewish summer camp, Camp Kingswood, in Bridgton, Maine. The new unit, slightly separated from the regular girls' camp, was intended to offer a supportive setting in which the youth "are able to utilize many of the skills acquired in European experiences to master the rugged environment, which the new campsite offers."[42] This special program began with seven children in 1946 and by 1949 had grown to include nineteen orphans. Beatrice Carter, JFCS agency case consultant and camp supervisor, stressed the therapeutic nature of this initiative. In a presentation delivered at the National Conference of Social Work, she described this program:

> The children operated in a tri-polar situation: the classroom, the living and social accommodations, and the cabin of the caseworker. The latter was also a canteen. We early recognized that the regularity of meals for the New American children was a distasteful and frustrating experience, and until the children were more socialized in their food habits, free access to and availability of food carried with it the symbol of home.[43]

Mrs. Carter's description of the camp structure and the example of food illustrates the administration's sympathetic stance. Leonard Serkess was a young social worker whose involvement with the New Americans began in 1947 at the summer camp. Speaking in 2002, he, too, noted the staff's response to the refugees' attitude toward food. "One of the biggest problems we had was the kids would steal food and bring it back to the tents. And we tried to explain to them, there was a mild language problem, mild, because we had enough people that could convey the different languages, that there would be plenty of food," he remembered. "They found it hard to believe. There was a perpetual hunger. . . . [T]hey just never felt secure that there would be enough food for them."[44] The staff recognized the special significance of food for the young DPs and allowed for it. The manner in which the camp staff responded to this and other issues reflects its attempt to understand the psychological aspects of these children's behavior.

The camp gave the young people a great deal of latitude in their actions. "So, if they got angry and urinated on a tree . . . we were out in the woods," said Mr. Serkess; "you could allow more freedom." That tolerance and understanding pervaded the camp. The youngsters spent some of their time learning English, Mr. Serkess explained, and there were also art therapists and opportunities for creative expression.[45] At the end of each summer, the New American unit published a collection of their stories, essays, and poetry.

EJCA sent Robert Berger to Camp Kingswood in summer 1947. He was not happy about leaving New York. It had become familiar to him during his brief stay. Moreover, an accidental encounter shortly before he was slated to leave for Maine cemented his feelings. On that day, he was traveling on the subway and became separated from his New American group. He rode the train all day because he spoke no English and had neither money nor a sense of how to return to the Bronx reception center. finally, he approached a policeman in the station who asked Robert if he spoke Yiddish. "The last thing I expected is a uniformed policeman to speak Yiddish. I was in seventh heaven." That chance meeting made a deep impression on him. "I wanted to stay in New York for the very simple reason I found a cop who spoke Yiddish . . . and I thought that's that. I knew New York and I knew that I was going to be comfortable and the rest of America seemed to me like Siberia. But they wouldn't let me."[46] As we have seen, none of Robert's New York relatives would agree to sponsor him, and EJCA, disregarding the boy's wishes, decided to send him to Boston. In protest, he ran away from the reception center and spent several nights sleeping in public parks. The familiarity of Yiddish and its connection to his past life was enough, in that one brief exchange, to influence his wish for resettlement. But without a ready sponsor in New York, EJCA remained steadfast in its decision to send the boy to New England. Because it was summertime, Robert went directly to Camp Kingswood.

Despite his initial reluctance, Robert found a place for himself in Maine partially because it was a summer camp and partially because he was among others like himself. "You're on the lake, you can go swimming," he reminisced. "It was very milk and honey . . . and we had each other. I'm pretty sure there was an element of isolation, of loneliness . . ." Still, Robert said, "I just don't recall wallowing in it. I mean, there were so many things to do and so many positive things."[47] Robert's remarks emphasize the camp's ideology. Although the summer experience was therapeutic in nature, the staff discouraged their campers from dwelling too long on their traumatic past.

The camp's philosophy, as described by a visiting journalist from the *Boston Herald*, was "to help these young folk face and forget their pogrom experiences."[48] Today this principle would be considered naive. In the context of the time and the message to forget the past that most adult DPs received, however, it was exceptional. Even more extraordinary: in order to face their past, the unit created and performed a play based on their lives

Robert Berger, left, with English teacher, and Mrs. Beatrice Carter, right, director, Camp Kingswood, at camp, summer, circa 1949. Courtesy of Robert Berger, M.D.

during the Holocaust. In a collection of campers' short stories printed at summer's end, one boy wrote a piece titled "Why We Put the Play On" which gives us a glimpse of that unusual production:

> Other people rehearse for weeks and then put on a mediocre show. Not so with us. To this day we don't even have a name for our show. We needn't—because it just simply is the showing of part of our life experience. One day Szmul came out with the idea of a play about concentration camp events, and, in talking, he had already acted out parts of the future play. At first we were stunned and resented to be overcome again by the flood of evil memories. Then we resolved to face once more the reality that had been. We only needed to pass out roles, never learned any parts and never twice said quite the same words during the life-like rehearsals. Within a week we were ready to perform in front of the entire camp. During that week we had little time for classes. We lived only partly in the present. Some of us sang the songs of the concentration camps; some, who were to act as Nazis, sang the songs which before we so often had heard and hated. Then the Friday night came. We were deeply steeped into the past and we played from our hearts. People were impressed. We were asked to perform in other camps. That, we could not do. We did something to ourselves by acting as we did. Something we cannot now "re-enact." In some way we are freer now to live for the future.[49]

Many of the youths did seem to live for the future. Not all. Robert described Danny, a young boy at Camp Kingswood who had witnessed the murder of both of his parents and had survived afterward in the forests of Poland. He did fairly well at the summer camp, where he could spend much of his time outdoors. Back in Boston, however, he had difficulty functioning. After a suicide attempt, he was sent to a school for troubled boys in Pennsylvania.[50]

Were it not for an unexpected turn of events, the refugee children who subsequently arrived in Boston might all have been placed by JFCS in foster care. At the end of its first summer of operation in 1946, Beatrice Carter took three of the children who were having adjustment problems into her home in Boston. The number of refugees grew and Mrs. Carter was evicted from her apartment. As a result, in January 1948 JFCS created Bradshaw House, a group home for the young refugees in Dorchester, then a primarily Jewish neighborhood of Boston. Bradshaw House became the first of two group homes that JFCS established for New Americans in the Boston area. This afforded the teens a way to continue living with other DP orphans while still under adult supervision. "They clung and were very supportive of one another," emphasized Mr. Serkess.[51] Indeed, Robert Berger spoke about how he, even as a college student, continued to spend weekends with friends who were still in the group home.

While the JFCS approach was unusually understanding, there were limits beyond which it would not go. Mrs. Carter accused two teenaged boys who had survived the camps together and remained inseparable of being homosexuals. A refugee who recalled the incident remembered that Mrs. Carter referred the boys to a psychiatrist.[52] Ironically, the two women who directed the New American program at JFCS, Dora Margolis and Beatrice Carter, herself, were noted by three separate observers to have been involved in a lesbian relationship during this time.[53]

Mrs. Carter's leadership exemplifies the difference that individuals could make in a communal institution. Her exceptional devotion to these young people stands out. Some, however, found the behavior of Mrs. Carter as not being entirely healthy. "You know, she tried to be very mothering," said Robert, adding, "She was in many ways very possessive."[54] He remembered that she always had a small group of younger children in whom she took a special interest. Did she cross the boundaries of propriety? Both Robert and Mr. Serkess believed that she could be difficult and demanding in her actions. They also agreed, however, that she cared deeply for the children and that she had never abused their trust in any way.

A number of examples support the impression that the staff of JFCS in Boston responded to this refugee group differently from how their counterparts elsewhere did. In addition to the availability of social workers and psychiatrists and the willingness to use them, the innovative program at Camp Kingswood allowed the youngsters to be together in a particularly tolerant environment. The residential home also offered a transitional place where the orphans could step into the world of America yet still retreat to one another's company. It was a circle of friendship and mutual understanding that the "children" share to this day.

Aside from these structures, the social workers' attitudes appeared to have transcended the traditional professional-client relationship. Beatrice Carter is one example. Leonard Serkess is another. When he married, he invited all the children. "We had twenty-two of the kids at our wedding," he remembered. Moreover, the newlyweds brought trinkets from their honeymoon for each of the teens. "We wanted them to feel that my getting married was not separating from them but we were bringing someone in . . . an acquisition for them," Leonard Serkess explained.[55]

The Boston agency, unlike JFCS in Denver, believed that their New American orphans needed differential treatment and created special programs accordingly. Other policies already in place for their local clients benefited the New Americans as well. One was a strict rule about clothes. The staff believed that only new clothes should be given to foster children, and this was extended to the newcomers. Nothing secondhand would do. A seemingly small gesture, this was profoundly important to the teenagers, Mr. Serkess recalled.[56] In other ways, too, the agency showed a unique respect for their charges. Art therapy was an integral part of the agency's treatment for all children, both native and refugee. Ms. Margolis, the director, insisted that only the agency's clients' artwork should be used to decorate their offices. Thus, the teenagers' work was among those framed and displayed on the JFCS walls. How different this approach was from that of Denver.

JFCS supported the youth in many ways, but sometimes it was the youth who created their own opportunities. Robert Berger felt very strongly about his education. "I learned it basically during the war that if you have a big piece of gold they can take it away from you but if you have something up here [tapping his head], it stays with you," he reflected.[57] That belief prompted him to approach Boston Latin, an elite public school, for admission. JFCS would have supported him but the school did not initially accept him. Undeterred, he approached several colleges, including Harvard and MIT, and asked what he needed to do to gain acceptance. He was told that as long as he earned a certain number of course credits a high school diploma was not mandatory. As best as he could reconstruct of this time in his life, Robert remembered discovering that Boston Latin had a refresher course for returning GIs. Despite his DP status, he convinced the administration to permit him to take it.

Robert completed the course and applied to four colleges. Three accepted him, including Harvard. Robert turned to JFCS to help him pay his tuition bill. He recalled his dismay when Mrs. Carter told him, "You can't go to college, you have to go to work." The young man persisted in pursuing his goals, working first at a law firm, and later as a laborer in construction and as a dishwasher at Camp Kingswood, to pay for a part of his college tuition. In the end, JFCS helped as well. It turned out to be a wise investment. Robert finished college and medical school and became chief of cardiac surgery at Boston University Medical Center. He pointed out that his case was not exceptional, noting that many of the orphans achieved professional and financial success. Still, he acknowledged that the Holocaust shadowed all these children's lives, making them "very vulnerable to certain things that we had a very difficult time coping with." Of their group of approximately twenty-five orphans who were together in camp and the home, two committed suicide and another two were institutionalized.[58]

The story of the orphan DPs is complex. The United States had the mechanisms in place to protect these unaccompanied minors, but after their arrival they were subjected to the vicissitudes of agency and relatives' perceptions and decisions. As the child-care agencies and foster parents quickly discovered, these were not young children. They were adolescents who had experienced years of violence, trauma, and displacement in their still-young lives. One agency recognized this and established an innovative program.[59] For most DP orphans, however, finding a place in America often meant a series of mismatched foster homes and mutual family disappointments. The majority set about creating new lives. A small but not insignificant number were irrevocably shattered. Over time, many achieved spectacular success both professionally and financially and others exalted in the presence of their children and grandchildren. Still, the past is always there. As one of the now adult orphans reflected, "Very few of us don't have some kind of a sad story behind the good story."[60]

CHAPTER 6

The Bumpy Road

PUBLIC PERCEPTION AND
THE REALITY OF SURVIVAL

*I*n a front-page article in the *New York Times* of 19 January 1950, the writer's conclusions were summed up in the headline: "DPs Quick to Catch Tempo of America, Survey Shows: New Immigrants Become Self-Sustaining in Short Time and Offer Few Problems—Language Barriers Most Serious."[1] The reporter emphasized the rapidity with which refugees adjusted to life in the United States and cited a survey that demonstrated that their acculturation "is proceeding so fast that they are different from older residents only in their stumbling English."[2] Indeed, this assessment of a quick and successful adaptation of the newcomers, in great measure a result of the host communities' help, was the impression commonly reported and accepted at the time. Today's scholars, among them William Helmreich, in *Against All Odds* (1996), arrive at the same conclusion and emphasize the triumph of the survivors in rebuilding their lives after the war.[3]

As I showed in Chapter 3, employment, more than anything else, defined success in the DPs' adjustment. This was what the agencies communicated and what was depicted in the media. Time after time, in publications ranging from USNA's *New Neighbors* to the *New York Times*, stories boasted of the speed with which the immigrants had entered America's workforce. That the main objective of NYANA, for one, was to remove the DPs from the agency relief load within a year was not mentioned. Nor were the many examples of those individuals for whom one year was simply not sufficient time to find a place to live, become self-supporting, begin to learn a new language, and adapt to a new culture.

These were survivors of the Holocaust, and they were still reeling from their experiences. Even as they endeavored to meet agency agendas, the

Holocaust intervened. A close examination of the agency files reflects this. Not that refugees did not make great strides in their new lives. Many did. But others did not. For both groups, the early years in America were fraught with difficulties, which have been not only ignored or minimized, but also transformed into a heroic and victorious story.

Important as employment was, it would be myopic to infer adjustment according to that criterion alone. And comforting as it might be to look only at those who appear to have been successful, it is historically inaccurate. The survivors' path was long and bumpy. Some never regained wholeness. Others pieced together a life as best they could. All were scarred. To suggest a unanimous victory belittles the grave challenges with which they struggled, the depths to which they were misunderstood, and the pain of those who were irrevocably damaged.

Lawrence Langer, the scholar of Holocaust testimonies, art, and literature, has identified the phenomenon of the "disintegrated self" among Holocaust survivors.[4] Survivors coexist, Langer has asserted, with the presence of those who did not survive. Their deaths are an essential part of the survivors' beings and hover over them throughout their lives. In a similar vein, Langer also has described how survivors experience two separate notions of time: chronological and durational.[5] In the former, survivors mark their lives within a conventional calendar noted by the usual milestones that typify our days: work, holidays, birthdays. At the same time, they live according to the latter—the narrative of their Holocaust experiences.

Langer formulated his ideas from his analysis of hundreds of videotaped interviews with Holocaust survivors. They are equally applicable to the case files that are assessed in this study. So much of what the survivors confronted when they arrived in the United States was experienced through a veil of irrevocable loss: of mothers, fathers, husbands, wives, children, siblings, friends, youth, status, place, home. The refugees moved through two parallel universes. One consisted of their new life and the demands of finding a place in America. The other was a universe of death from which there was no escape. How the survivors experienced this tension between past and present in the context of their postwar experience is at the heart of this chapter.

The survivors' records dramatically illustrate the impact of the refugees' recently endured trauma on their life in America and how it affected their perceptions, their family, and their health. These records also shatter the myth that survivors chose to be silent about their wartime experiences in the early years because they were too painful, too raw to acknowledge. Telling, scholars hold, came later, beginning with the Eichmann trial. It gained momentum after the survivors had led fruitful lives. In the later years, during the quietude of retirement, after the business of work and raising children had diminished in focus, survivors would be better able to confront their past. Their readiness, so goes popular theory, was part of the reason behind the proliferation of oral history projects and Holocaust memorials that began in the 1980s.

The case files and survivors' oral histories reveal an entirely different sentiment. They are filled, loud and clear, with the refugees' desire and need to address the past. This need at times seems uncontrollable and at other times ambivalently expressed: bringing these feelings to light also awakens the accompanying anguished memories. What the case files show, too, is how little anyone listened. The conspiracy of silence started not with the survivors, but with the agencies and the greater society, which just did not want to hear.

The DPs arrived in a country that needed to be convinced of their value. In light of this, the media endeavored to promote positive impressions of the refugees to combat both antisemitic and nativist sentiments. The intent was to reinforce the notion that the refugees were the kind of people who belonged in the United States. To that end, the United Jewish Appeal and USNA sponsored a series of radio programs titled *I Am an American Day*, which marked the anniversary of the arrival of the first DPs in the United States in May 1946. Three New York stations, WQXR, WNYC, and WMCA, aired programs on 18 May 1947 dedicated to "the new Americans who have recently reached these shores from war-torn countries, and are now making important contributions to life in America."[6]

The choice of personalities determined by the United Jewish Appeal and USNA for this program reflects the images that the organizations wanted to portray. It also reflects the contemporary Jewish establishment, which was of German, not East European, descent. One *I Am an American Day* radio show featured guest Newbold Morris, a leading New York citizen "whose ancestors came to America 300 years ago as refugees from religious persecution and helped formulate democratic foundations in this country—Lewis Morris signed the Declaration of Independence, Governor Morris drafted the Bill of Rights."[7] This reminded the listening public that even some of America's founding fathers were once refugees too. Another guest was Dr. Maurice Davie, chair of Yale University's sociology department, whose book *Refugees in America*, about the settlement and contribution of German Jews, had recently appeared. The two refugee participants had escaped Nazi Germany by 1939. One was both a baritone with the Metropolitan Opera and a cantor. The other had been an insurance broker in Germany and became a successful farmer in New Jersey. Both men had been in the United States for nearly ten years and were hardly representative of the DPs who began to arrive after the war. Moreover, their Jewish identity was minimized. USNA's programming served several goals: universalizing the refugee, negating any *ostjuden* (unflattering term for Eastern European Jews) image, and assuring its audience that the DPs not only were not troublesome but were adjusting well and making significant contributions to American life.

One year later, in May 1948, other cities joined New York in observing I Am an American Day. A ceremony in Central Park marked the occasion and Governor Thomas Dewey issued a proclamation from Albany urging wide observance of the day. One newspaper highlighted the stories of a few of these "hopeless refugees who have received a new lease on hope, the homeless wanderers who have put down fresh roots in the fruitful soil of American tradition, to whom the 'I am an American' Day ceremonies, inspired and staged on a coast-to-coast scale by the Hearst newspapers, are a symbol and a beacon."[8]

The cast had changed since 1947, but the press was still careful to universalize the victims. Morris Cohen, an Italian refugee who was interviewed for this article, described himself as a man who hated the Fascists. "Because of this hate," the authors wrote, "he was sent to various concentration camps, Italian and German, including Auschwitz and Belsen."[9] Again, the virtues of American democracy were championed and each DP's desire to become a U.S. citizen was duly noted. While brief mention was made of terrible, degrading experiences, and even of the shattered nerves of the newcomers, the writer emphasized the DPs' eagerness to become full-fledged citizens and their joy at being on American soil.

Certainly many New Americans expressed these positive sentiments. They also described a great deal else about their state of being and the reality of their lives in the postliberation world. Often it was not happy. In direct contradiction to the media reports, DPs in both case files and postwar oral histories almost universally anguished over how very, very difficult it was to start life in America. The shiny veneer of the PR images belied the newcomers' torment.

The process of settling in a new land is multilayered—it is complicated and fraught with difficulty for any immigrant. The DPs faced the expected challenges and more. The process of moving forward in America was invaded by the tensions suggested earlier: the presence of the Holocaust and the unfamiliar demands of daily living. Added to this were the agency requirements. What were the manifestations of these conflicting pressures and how did the agencies' staff respond?

The social workers articulated their expectations for the refugees but they were mute about their clients' wartime history, and there is little—if any—evidence of their recognition or acknowledgment of the significance of that history. This reflects the attitude they communicated to their clients: do not spend too much time thinking about the past. Despite the lack of encouragement they received, the refugees often referred to their past when discussing employment and other issues of resettlement with the agency staff.

One recurring theme that newcomers expressed was a lack of purpose or meaning to their lives after what they had lived through. Mr. B., who was having trouble beginning his search for employment, illustrates this bleakness perfectly. He confided to his social worker that he felt guilty that he had survived, while his first wife and three children had not. "People live on," he told her, "but after such experiences somehow lose their meaning for living or their desire for living. They more or less exist." And he felt "that he [was] in such a state at this time."[10] The social worker responded in a way that no doubt was meant to be sympathetic but that minimized the depth of her client's grief. She encouraged Mr. B. to find satisfaction in his role as breadwinner for his new wife and their three children. Mr. B. responded that her suggestion might help, but he was pessimistic. At the same time, he did want to learn a trade so that he could take care of his family. Mr. B. saw the necessity of working, but he was also struggling to live with his pain over the murder of his first family at the hands of the Germans and their allies.

Facing a new life in America sometimes elicited emotions that were the antithesis of those the media depicted. Like those of Mr. B., Mr. G.'s wife and children had been killed. Mr. G. talked about how "'dark' he [was] finding life here in America."[11] He was nearly paralyzed by the prospect of beginning anew in a strange place. "All of this was extremely frightening to Mr. G.," wrote his caseworker. She noted that "he would need a great deal of help in moving out of this total fear into some sort of ability to begin picking up one piece at a time." He was having trouble locating work in the first several months in New York and "spoke of the pains he has had and his nervousness now."[12]

One woman, after her arrival in 1949, described the past ten years of her life to the social worker so that the latter might better understand why beginning in America was a nightmare for her client. "While she was hiding from Hitler, her main preoccupation was that she may survive. Then when she went to a DP Camp, her thoughts were preoccupied for herself and her family about coming to this wonderful land, America," her social worker recorded. The narrative abruptly changed course, and this survivor then articulated something quite different. Now that she was here, she confided, "she [wished] that she were not alive."[13] The murder of two of her children tormented her. Although she was sixty-five years old, she begged the agency to help her find work so that she would be occupied.

The idea that being occupied would help block out the past was reiterated by others and dovetailed fortuitously with the agencies' aims. Both client and professional sought the same goal—but for very different reasons. Mr. L., a thirty-nine-year-old Polish man who arrived in Denver in 1951, wanted to find work because he "was very much alone." Expressing his loneliness unleashed his longing for his murdered family, and the social worker listened to his story at length. "Living was very hard," reported the social worker. "Many times in thinking over his experiences he cries quietly. His first night in America he had gone to bed and couldn't sleep, thinking over what had happened and had finally cried himself to sleep. He said that he cannot forget his experiences and he will carry the memory as long as he lives." Mr. L. told the worker, "You can understand why life is not worth very much after all I have seen."[14]

The social worker was not uncaring. She responded that "while he could no doubt never forget his experiences he could adjust and be able to live with those experiences and be a better man because of them." The woman was trying to be helpful, but was she listening? One wonders how the murder of his entire family and two years in a concentration camp made him a better person. At Mr. L.'s next meeting, one week later, his social worker "spoke to him of his being strong and that he survived." She also recognized that although "he would not forget what had happened to him and others in the past, it was something he had to try to put aside and work on his readjustment here in America."[15] The agency's sympathy only went so far. Focusing on the future was the order of the day.

Sometimes the professionals were much less kind about their clients' need to talk about their past. One couple was referred to a psychiatrist who stated that "neither of them revealed any psychotic manifestations but were neurotic individuals, self absorbed [sic] and preoccupied with their past."[16] Another refugee, a young woman plagued by memories of her murdered mother, father, three brothers, and sister, said that she tried "not to think about it" and that she had "the future to start over again in." Her social worker agreed and advised her that "it was hard to forget, but we must all descipline [sic] ourselves to that direction." That the client and her husband were so young "was a big thing in their favor." She was sure that the couple would make a good adjustment.[17] The psychiatric diagnosis and the happy future were two sides of the same coin: finding a way to package the new-comers' past in a way that the agencies could more easily handle.

There were many refugees who did not see work as an immediate panacea and requested a recovery period in America so that they could gar-ner the strength to begin looking for work. Chana L.'s social worker wrote in her NYANA file that the young woman did want to work eventually, but did not believe that she was employable at present, since she felt "weak and tired." Chana's uncle, who accompanied her to the interview, "interjected that she had spent a year and a half in a dark, dank cellar with little food and water."[18] The social worker referred Chana to a clinic for a medical evaluation in order to determine her client's condition, employability, and eligibility for financial aid. The agency was willing to support her if she was deemed medically unfit. For the following nine months NYANA did just that. All the while she was tested, without conclusion, to determine the source of numerous symptoms, including headaches, dizziness, and nausea. Eventually, her uncle found her a job that was not physically taxing and she entered the workforce with her physical symptoms unabated.

It is interesting to note that NYANA would, within certain limitations, support those whom a physician confirmed to be ill. Support is not to be con-fused with sympathy, however. It was an economic equation. Chana did not need relief beyond her one-year allotment. There was little long-term sympa-thy or financial support for those whose ailments were not so easy to diagnose.

Comments about returning to Europe in the face of what seemed insur-mountable obstacles were not uncommon. Mr. K., a nineteen-year-old, said, weeping, to the USNA worker that "he had hoped that things would be bet-ter in this country. Life had not been so bad for him in Germany where the Joint Distribution Committee had arranged for him to attend University. Disappointment in America," he told the social worker, "hardly described how he felt."[19] He was lonesome, confused, and "miserable." Another new-comer said that "had he known what difficulties he would meet here and what adventures, he would have stayed over there."[20]

Part of this despair was attributable to the refugees' unhappiness and part to the differing messages that the overseas and American agencies con-veyed. Many refugees said that the overseas agencies had promised that the U.S. agencies would take care of them in America. Upon arrival, however, the DPs quickly learned the nature and extent of the agencies' help. Morris L., a Czech Jew, had been sent to England on a children's program after the war. For three years, he was cared for under the auspices of the Central British Fund, a Jewish organization located in London, which serviced refugees.[21] He received full support while he learned a trade. He came to New York in 1950 after he learned of the existence of an uncle, his only living relative. He had also been told by the European agency that USNA would support him until he was self-sufficient. When he learned that the agency could not "go along with this plan," he expressed extreme disappointment. His uncle was too poor to help him and his sponsor had provided an affidavit with the understanding that he "would not be bothered about any-thing."[22] Morris felt as though he had nowhere to turn. Through his own efforts he found work after several months, feeling very much abandoned by the agency.

Many articulated the desire to join the American mainstream quickly. One young, single man "made up his mind to make a good adjustment as fast as possible," wrote a caseworker at the Jewish Family and Children's Services (JFCS) in Denver.[23] Another married man said that his aim was "to get a job and become completely independent."[24] Mrs. L., mentioned earlier, pleaded for help in finding employment. There are echoes of these comments throughout the files in both New York and Denver. What is compelling, however, is the way that the refugees' recent past seemed to seep through unbidden and manifest itself in ways that disrupted their lives and both their own and the agencies' plans for their future.

One tragic consequence of the traumatic aftermath of the Holocaust was the impact of the survivors' experiences on their family relationships. This was varied and complex, but in many cases the aftereffects were dev-astating. These histories contradict the comforting notion, still in circula-tion, of a triumphant return to life after the war.

For example, although recent studies emphasize the extremely high birthrate in the DP camps to support the thesis of the DPs' postwar affirma-tion of life,[25] not all women wanted to have children right away or were pleased when they became pregnant. The Denver file of Mr. B. is one among many that illustrates the complexity of this issue.[26] Mr. B. was sent from New York to Denver after he was diagnosed with TB. While he was at a sanitarium, the Jewish Consumptive Relief Society, he met a young woman, another DP, and they became lovers. When the woman became pregnant, the two married, but they decided that they did not want to keep the baby. The husband was taking a training course and his bride wanted to support him. She did not feel that she could do this while caring for a baby.

Despite her glowing descriptions of Jewish family life in Europe before the war, Mrs. B. insisted on putting the baby up for adoption. The couple did change their minds after Mrs. B. gave birth, since "she never dreamed that she would actually be able to come through a pregnancy and bear a live healthy child as she had done."[27] Mrs. B.'s change of heart was short lived. When Mr. B. refused to give up his training in order to support his new family, Mrs. B. panicked and again asked the agency to place the baby boy with a family, stating that "she wished both she and the baby were dead."[28] JFCS obliged and the baby was placed with a foster family. Six months later, however, the parents decided to have their son come back to live with them. They did not live happily ever after.

The B. family exemplifies one of the ways that the Holocaust continued to warp its way through the lives of the survivors. Yes, the family was reunited, but each member functioned poorly. Mrs. B. suffered from a serious heart condition as a result of her concentration camp experience. Mr. B. collapsed at work because of his compromised health condition. He had trouble holding on to a job. Their son was diagnosed with kidney disease. Mother and child were in an automobile accident. The couple's marriage was affected. After three years, Mrs. B. returned to relatives in Hartford and Mr. B. remained in Denver. Seven months after her departure, Mr. B. established that he wanted to leave Denver. His destination, however, was undecided. He disliked the weather in Connecticut and considered going to California. Finally, he decided to join his wife and son. After nearly six years, the case in Denver was closed.[29] What became of this family is unknown. What is known, however, is that eight years after the refugees arrived, the Holocaust was still very much a part of their lives.

There were times when families were torn apart with the help of the agencies, not because the agencies sought the dissolution of the families but because the former perceived that there was no other choice or way of helping the family. Mr. and Mrs. D. turned to JFCS when Chaim, their twelve-year-old son, ran away from Denver.[30] He managed to get as far as New York, where he was found staying at a public welfare shelter. Chaim's father told the social worker about "the difficulty which he [had] had in Europe and in adjusting in this country and was able to say that he was impatient with the boy because of his own nervousness and unhappiness." Surviving the war in hiding was brutal and the murder of their daughter was devastating, but after one and a half years in the United States, the family's struggles were hardly over.

For a short time after his return, Chaim was a model of good behavior, assiduously attending both school and his appointments with his social worker. Once again, however, the story did not end there. When the youth began to withdraw from his parents and stayed away from home, sometimes overnight, the couple returned to the agency for guidance. This time there was a psychological evaluation. Chaim "is neither psychotic or neurotic," the psychiatrist wrote, "but . . . this is a simple behavior and [*sic*] disorder."[31] The parents were at their wits' end. Simple, orthodox people, who spoke little English, they seemed adrift in their new home and puzzled over the agency's explanation of their son's hostile behavior. The agency suggested a solution: give JFCS custody of the boy and he would be sent to Bellefaire, a residential treatment center in Cleveland (where Abraham, mentioned in Chapter 5, had also been sent).[32] The parents agreed, but the decision was taken with heartache. "Having survived, which in itself to them constitutes a miracle," the social worker reported, "it seems particularly tragic to them now that they have to be separated when an opportunity finally presents itself for them to live together normally as a family."[33] Chaim spent nearly three years at Bellefaire. The reports about his progress there and his visits home were mixed. He finally returned to live with his parents in 1953, planning to finish high school. Whether or not he did is an open question; the parents refused to continue working with JFCS. The case was closed.

That the D. family's wartime experiences had a profound impact on their lives in America seems obvious, yet the agency approached their treatment as they would that of any dysfunctional family. The family's wartime experiences seemed to have had little bearing on how the agency handled the family. One woman, a children's worker, did appear to recognize the after-effects of the trauma that the newcomers had endured and responded with sensitivity. Unfortunately, her contact with Chaim was brief. The agency, however, looked at this family as though their difficulties had begun the day that Chaim first ran away. There is another possibility, too. The social workers' references to the mother's dull mental status, the father's rigidity, and their orthodoxy, raises a question about the agency's attitude toward this family. Did the agency seek what was best for the family, or did the social worker see little hope that these Eastern European Jews were capable of coping with their son in the way that the agency deemed effective? The possible tension between the agency, whose executive director was an Austrian Jew, and the worldview of the immigrants brings another level of complexity to JFCS's response to this family crisis.

Occasionally, parents requested that their children be placed in foster care or an institution because they did not feel able to raise them. This was more common with widowed parents who were caring for their children on their own. Mr. B. placed his daughter, Jan, and her older sister in the Jewish National Home for Asthmatic Children in Denver. He was ill, needed to find work, and could not "establish a home for the children."[34] But Jan's file reveals another wrinkle: Mr. B. was not entirely convinced that the child was, in fact, his daughter. He and his wife had placed their daughter, a toddler at the time, in a convent. His wife was killed and he survived. Two years had elapsed by the time he claimed the girl. The child he took away from the convent school did not completely match his memory's image, but he felt fairly confident that he had made the right choice. Still, doubt lingered. That uncertainty combined with Jan's "serious personality difficulties" had provoked "definite signs of rejection on the part of Mr. B."[35] Then, too, Mr. B. felt himself to be "emotionally and physically broken" and not up to the challenge of caring for an extremely rebellious adolescent. Jan lived at the home for nearly five years, at the end of which time it was determined that there was no longer a place for the girl; she was getting older and more difficult to handle. Her father talked about buying a house and having Jan and her college-age sister come to live with him. He was involved in a relationship with a woman, however, and the plan for the girls did not materialize. At the age of sixteen Jan was discharged from the institution and went to live with a foster family. For most of her early life and in the eleven years after the war's end, she never lived as part of her nuclear family. Jan was not an orphan, but the Holocaust had nonetheless devastated her family life. This was as clear in 1956 as it had been in 1951 when the family came to the United States to start a new life.

The issue of illness looms astonishingly large in these files, and when the file includes both husband and wife, it is not unusual for each to describe somatic complaints. While the agencies tended to view "real" symptoms more seriously than those they considered "merely" psychosomatic, even the former were minimized. Agencies, after all, evaluated illness in the context of the immigrant's employability. And they saw employment as a form of rehabilitation.

Dr. Gary Zucker was a volunteer physician for NYANA whose first encounter with the agency was as a consultant on some recent arrivals who had inactive TB.[36] His wife, a social worker at NYANA, was working with these refugees, who had spent time in sanitariums in Europe and had recovered to the point where they were acceptable to U.S. Immigration Service. Since Dr. Zucker had completed a two-year fellowship in chest disease, including work with active TB cases, his wife suggested that it would be helpful to the agency if he consulted with NYANA social workers. Thus, he gave two seminars in 1950 on "the medical nature of TB; the degree of infectivity and the capacity of rehabilitated TB sufferers to resume gainful employment." The message of his seminars was exactly what NYANA wanted to hear; Dr. Zucker educated the social workers "so that they would know how to shorten [the refugees'] period of dependency."[37]

Dr. Zucker wanted the social workers at NYANA to understand the cutting-edge treatment of and attitude toward TB patients in the United States. In America, TB was no longer considered a lifetime disability; one could put in a normal workday according to one's abilities and professional training. The agency embraced this approach; Dr. Zucker commented that the real problem was "a reluctance on the part of the refugees to give up what they were accustomed to and that was drawing a modest pension and having a continuing claim against Germany; and the feeling that they would not be able or were afraid of being gainfully employed for fear that they would get sicker." Dr. Zucker emphasized to the staff that TB was not a disease that was permanently disabling and that the refugees' former dependency on sanitarium care was incompatible with the American philosophy of rehabilitation. Said Dr. Zucker, "You know, it was more humanitarian to get people independent and self-employed or working for other people than just to coddle them."[38]

The doctor's statement was emblematic of the fundamental attitude of NYANA and perhaps even also of the times. It was better for the refugee not to be coddled. It was for their own good. Indeed it was for a higher humanitarian purpose: personal independence as quickly as possible. This attitude is a striking example of how lopsided the ideology was. Little attempt was made to address anything besides the DPs' ability to work. Dr. Zucker proudly estimated that the NYANA budget for prolonged care dropped from 1.3 million dollars to less than three hundred thousand dollars after his recommendations were put into action, as though this reflected the success of the DPs' rehabilitation.[39]

With both the budget reduction and the consonance of the doctor's and NYANA's beliefs, it is no surprise that Dr. Zucker was asked to remain as the agency's medical consultant. Once the pressing problem of ex-TB patients was handled, there were other concerns. "You were dealing with a population that had many other diseases," reported Dr. Zucker, enumerating them, "heart disease, diabetes, strange to say, obesity, and psychological disorders with many psychosomatic complaints."[40] This comment is startling. While it certainly reinforces the patterns in the case files, the mention of illness in the administrative documents is barely hinted at. Yet it was clearly known. Certainly, this side of the refugees' lives flies in the face of the public image that was projected, and it was most certainly kept away from the public

arena. It also suggests a outlook that saw an illness such as TB as worth noting but viewed complaints about others, which could not be easily diagnosed, as indications that the refugees were not really sick.

Nevertheless, one discovery gleaned from analysis of hundreds of case
files and oral histories is the great amount of data that show that the newcomers were clearly suffering from a wide array of psychosomatic ailments.
Today, we recognize posttraumatic stress disorder as an illness. It is no surprise that survivors fell victim to this syndrome. What is surprising is that
the social workers and physicians, including psychiatrists, made little connection between the numerous somatic complaints and their clients' recent
history. Clearly, workers seemed quite averse to delving too deeply into the
source of their clients' pain. Not surprisingly, when newcomers were referred
for psychological help, it was often because their problems interfered with
employment. This was the case with a fifty-year-old woman, Mrs. F., who
arrived in Denver alone; her husband and daughter had been killed in
Europe. She was determined to reclaim some semblance of her former life
as a successful cosmetologist by studying for a Colorado license in this
field. Her dreams of opening a small shop of her own remained distant as
she struggled with preparing for the exam in English, as well as with
JFCS's attitude that her time would be better spent by taking a job. During
this period Mrs. F. lived alone in a rundown hotel in the city, anxious for
companionship but unsure about how to expand her social circle. She began
to manifest a number of ailments for which there appeared to be no organic
basis. Finally, the agency recommended psychiatric treatment. The psychiatrist's assessment after their initial meeting was that Mrs. F. suffered from
depression resulting from menopause. He treated her accordingly. Mrs. F.
accepted the doctor's diagnosis.[41]

Even in extreme cases of psychological disorder, the professionals recommended work as the best medicine. Mr. K.'s history illustrates this dramatically. In conversation with his social worker, he said, "'Then I must tell
you' and poured our [*sic*] rapidly his story presenting himself as mentally
ill." Thus, his file has a brief but fairly detailed description of his wartime
and immediate postliberation experiences. His family was from a shtetl near
Kraków. They lived in the ghetto from 1940 to 1942 and then were deported.
He managed to escape and survived by hiding in a hole in the ground. He
had several breakdowns in the DP camp. "He had headaches, lost his hearing, lost all knowledge of reading and writing," the social worker recorded.[42]
When the American Joint Distribution Committee located a relative in the
United States, there was a question of whether the consulate would grant

him a visa. Despite the official's reservations, he arrived in New York in 1949; even though his relatives found him work in a bakery he could not hold down a job. Although he wanted to work, he continually complained of headaches. He had trouble operating within the agency guidelines for seeking employment. His social worker, at a loss about how to approach the problem, asked the consulting psychiatrist to meet with Mr. K. and make a recommendation. The psychiatrist wrote:

> On the basis of this single interview and the appearance he presented I am wondering whether he isn't showing some sort of depressive residuals from his original psychosis. It seems to me that the approach in this case would be to try to have him taken on by some mental hygiene clinic such as Beth Israel or Lebanon. There he could be observed by the psychiatrists and given psychotherapy and a more definite diagnostic impression of his present behavior pattern can be arrived at. If it should be felt by them that we are indeed dealing with a depressive condition, then they might consider giving him a short series of electric shock treatments. On the other hand, it is possible that with time and encouragement his depression might be alleviated and he might find himself. In any event, I think that you or your Vocational Department should make every effort to continue to find employment for him.[43]

Mr. K.'s file ends there. How his emotional state was reconciled with the agency demands remains unanswered. It seems highly likely that this conflict would continue. What is crystal clear is that putting the refugee to work was the aim, even if his condition dictated electric shock treatments.

Infrequently, the refugee himself realized the connection between his physical symptoms and emotional state and attempted to convey that to the professionals. Mr. H., a widower who arrived in New York City in August 1949, exemplifies how futile this could be. Mr. H.'s wife was murdered in 1942 and he still struggled with this loss in 1950.[44] One social worker, with stunning insensitivity, suggested that he find a new girl to overcome his grief. When he continued to have a number of undiagnosed physical symptoms that interfered with finding work, Mr. H. was referred to a psychiatrist, who wrote:

> Mr. H., 43 years old, was examined by me on June 1, 1950. The patient told me that he had never been seriously ill before, and that he had developed no complaints during 4 years in concentration camps

but that his complaints started after his liberation. He has been here for 9 months, and complains now that he perspires excessively, that sometimes he has a weakness in his hands and gets severe headaches. He attributes his complaints to the severe emotional upsets he has suffered during the last 10 years. He says that he would gladly do any kind of work, but that he is unable to find any position in this country. He told me in particular that it is not his complaints which keep him from working, but the impossibility to get a job.

He seemed slightly depressed, but did not show any signs of a deep depression. On physical examination there was no evidence of an organic disease of the nervous system but he showed increased perspiration and some trembling of the hands, disappearing when distracted. This patient suffers from a psychoneurosis with depressive and hysterical symptoms. I told him that the best way to get over his complaints would be to start a new life here by getting a regular occupation, and that his chances for recovery would not be good if he would have to spend the whole day without useful work. To this he reacted rather violently, saying that this meant an accusation that he was not willing to work. Nothing of this kind has been expressed by the examiner.

It is my opinion that this patient should be put to work as soon as feasible and should continue in any case the training course which he is taking now. It might be well to refer him to some psychiatric clinic where he can talk over his problems as well as find further encouragement.[45]

In the cases of both Mr. H. and Mrs. F., work was seen as a remedy for the client's ills, which underscores the agencies' primary goal for their clients. In both files, too, the newcomers themselves articulate that they want nothing more than to find productive work. Despite that, their depression interferes with the objectives that they and the agencies share.

Mr. H.'s history raises another point. He emphasized that he had never been ill before, even in the concentration camp. He fell sick only after liberation. Many others shared Mr. H.'s experience. Sometimes the newcomer observed this in puzzling frustration: why should I be sick now when I am living in freedom and need to work? The Holocaust continued to shadow the refugees even when they were most intent on making a new life in America. Despite survivors' willingness and determination to get settled, their past quickly came back to haunt them and undermine their great efforts.

We last saw Mr. F. in Chapter 3. He and his wife came to Denver in 1950 and he began to study immediately for his barber's license. A month after their arrival, he passed the required exam and received the license. A few days later, he called the agency to report enthusiastically that he would be starting a job imminently.[46]

Shortly thereafter, his wife came into the office for her appointment with the caseworker. She said that both she and her husband were very happy about his new position but she was concerned about his health; he could not sleep at night and had chest pains and terrible headaches. She also commented that her husband was never ill. When asked if he had visited the agency's physician, Mrs. F. said that he had but that the doctor had found nothing wrong with him.

For several months, Mr. F.'s symptoms persisted. He said that "he was dragging himself to work and hardly [knew] how he [could] go on."[47] This was said despite his new glasses, treatment for a possible infection, and numerous doctor visits. A tonsillectomy was performed, with no visible improvement in his overall well-being. His marriage began to show the strains of his constant health issues.

Nearly five months later, Mr. F. called his caseworker to say that he was not at all well. He had seen five specialists and all reports were negative. He wanted to discuss the possibility of moving to California because he thought that the climate there might benefit his health. At present, he said, "from his right eye down the back of his head and into his back he had constant pains." After that conversation, his social worker conferred with his physician, who recommended a psychiatric evaluation. The patient agreed, although he could not think of any particular problems, "since he was very happy with his wife and work, and was already very nicely settled here."[48]

Mr. F. made no connection between his physical symptoms and his Holocaust experiences. Initially, neither did Dr. Shere, the agency psychiatrist, as recorded by the caseworker, who first explored other possibilities. He concluded, however, according to the caseworker, "This is not a marital problem case from the interviews which he has had with Mr. F, but rather Mr. F is suffering from a persecution complex." The psychiatrist explained that his patient had a deep sense of guilt because "his whole family had perished by the hands of the Nazis, yet he, himself, was in a concentration camp working for them as a barber, and lived rather well, considering the times and how other people were getting along." The psychiatrist noted, "Mr. F. feels he cannot afford to be well, and his many symptoms relate to his guilt complex."[49]

Dr. Shere's analysis of Mr. F.'s problems reflected conventional psychiatry of the early 1950s. He did attempt to link the patient's chronic illness to his concentration camp experiences. But the psychiatrist's ability to help was limited. After Dr. Shere presented his diagnosis to the caseworker and to Dr. Neumann, the former recorded, "We thanked Dr. S for his cooperation and services in the case." There is no mention of treatment. Perhaps the agency was at a loss about how to help. Mr. F.'s case was closed when the agency refused to pay for his request for chiropractic visits. Still ill, the patient searched for a way to ease his suffering.

Unfortunately, both Mr. F.'s story and the way that JFCS responded are typical. It illustrates the newcomer's genuine desire and initial success in rapidly getting on his feet, which the agency supported and applauded. The triumph quickly soured, however, when Mr. F., who had "never been sick not even in the concentration camp" began to suffer from a host of symptoms.[50] The agency responded in what appears to be a sympathetic fashion. It accepted that Mr. F. was sick and facilitated doctors' appointments. But, as noted earlier, this was also an economic equation. In barely more than a month after his arrival in Denver, the newcomer was working and supporting himself. The agency offered advice, direction, and an agency discount for medical referrals, but Mr. F. footed the bill. However, Mr. F.'s caseworker did finally suggest psychological intervention when her client seemed to exhaust all other possibilities. Again, it was an ambivalent show of sympathy. The psychiatrist labeled his patient with a host of complexes and sent him on his way. The agency would not finance any other treatment. The case was closed, but it is hard to imagine that Mr. F.'s troubles were over.

An analysis such as this that challenges the idea of the survivors' triumphant return to life must look, too, at the darkest end of the spectrum: those who were irrevocably shattered. The most extreme were the instances of suicide. These were rare, but they did happen.[51] There were those who made an attempt to end their lives but did not succeed.[52] The files reveal that some survivors became transients, traveling from one Jewish community to another, depending on charity for food and a bed.[53] Others struggled to live within normal society but their spirits were broken beyond repair. Pueblo State Hospital in Colorado was host to several; even electroshock treatment, popular at the time, could not cure their ailments. Children, too, found themselves in institutions, helped along by the agencies, when their parents were too devastated to cope with both their own and their youngsters' sufferings. Where do these stories fit in the accepted narrative about the survivors' experiences in America? To confront them is shattering, but a critical analysis of this period must include their history too.

Holocaust survivors' postwar narrative has been constructed as a triumph: lives once destroyed rebuilt in freedom. This myth has its roots in the immediate postwar years when the refugees first arrived. Politics, antisemitism, and the national mood shaped their stories and cast them in a victorious glow. Underneath this public patina of hope and success that the media promulgated, the DPs struggled to begin life in America with the constant companionship of their recent Holocaust experiences. Moreover, it is generally accepted that survivors would not or could not speak then about their painful memories and instead endeavored to put the past behind them as they moved forward. Contemporary documents voice exactly the opposite. The survivors had much to say, but their listeners were deaf to what the survivors had to tell them.

CHAPTER 7

The Helping Process

MENTAL HEALTH PROFESSIONALS'
POSTWAR RESPONSE TO SURVIVORS

"*A*re these the files of Holocaust survivors?" I often asked myself as I read hundreds of social workers' reports in the agency files. The agency caseworkers, who met regularly with their clients and kept detailed accounts, exhibited a nearly universal blindness to the fact that these newcomers were among the few who had survived the destruction of European Jewry. As the professionals went about their business of helping the immigrants on the path to a reconstructed life in America, they seemed very nearly oblivious to the aftereffects of the Holocaust for their clients. That they minimized survivors' references to the past and rarely raised questions is baffling. The agency workers had front-row seats to the internal drama in the survivors' lives and yet they appear to have missed the obvious. How can we comprehend the way in which the social workers danced around this enormous black hole without ever falling in?

This question plagued me. What kept the social workers' probing at bay? Did they simply believe that by providing their clients with a stipend and advising them on employment, they were charting the best possible course for them? Did those who worked most closely with survivors lack the tools and expertise to deal with this experience for which there was not yet even a name, for which there was no precedent in their repertoire? Is it unfair to even raise this point from a twenty-first-century vantage point? I think not. To pursue this question, however, an examination of the context in which the social workers operated was essential. Therefore, I explored the prewar status quo of mental health and social work practice and its changing postwar emphasis. The contemporary psychiatric and social work literature about survivors was also scrutinized. I immersed myself in the social workers' reports and interviewed professionals who had worked with the refugees.

Oral histories of survivors added another perspective. Sifting through the literature, the files, and oral histories confirmed my original observations and permitted me to formulate some preliminary conclusions. I contend that given the professional context of the times, social workers indeed had the tools with which to help survivors beyond superficial aid. These were rarely made use of. Instead, the recently endured trauma in the newcomers' lives was deemphasized both in agency policy and through the attitudes of social workers when they came face to face with the newcomers. Why?

By 1946, when the first survivors began arriving in the United States, social work was still a relatively new profession, but it had come a long way from the nineteenth-century charity organizations' early attempts to construct a scientific and preventative approach to almsgiving.[1] Modern social work, born during the Progressive Era, embraced a systematic effort to help the poor through provision by trained personnel of both relief and intervention. This movement heralded the beginning of social work as a profession. In 1904 the New York School for Applied Philanthropy (the predecessor of the Columbia University School of Social Work) became the first university-affiliated school for the professional training of the "friendly visitor."[2] The formalization of casework, by social work pioneer Mary Richmond, provided the "treatment" of the poor with a scientific methodology and enhanced the profession's status.[3]

Richmond laid the foundations of the psychosocial approach to casework, although her work, rooted in the individual's social milieu and environment, espoused a sociological approach.[4] As her ideas gained in popularity, so did the nascent mental hygiene movement, which the profession enthusiastically embraced in the 1920s. This interest in psychiatry fostered a new orientation toward the individual's psychic as well as physical world.

Until World War I, the perception of psychiatry as the domain of asylums had relegated the discipline to the bottom of the medical hierarchy. Its link to soldiers both during and after the war gave the field increased credibility and captured social workers' attention.[5] In response, in 1918 Smith College established the first course for psychiatric social workers, which included training students to work with shell-shocked veterans and their families.[6]

The dissemination of Sigmund Freud's ideas in the 1920s, on the heels of the Great War and the concomitant entry of psychiatry into the mainstream, had a fundamental impact on the growth of psychiatric social work. Freudian theory gave social work a cohesive structure and a framework for understanding individual differences. Increasing numbers of social workers began to view analysis and insight into an individual's emotional life as the measure of skilled casework. Again, this directed social work away from relief giving and the association of social work with charity, which social workers hoped would bolster their professional status.[7]

The arrival in the 1930s of émigré Jewish analysts reinforced the initial impact of Freudian theory. They infused New York circles in particular with energy and sparked interest in their specialization.[8] In addition, some psychiatrists who lacked American credentials became practicing social workers instead.

As the growth of psychiatric social work drew psychiatry and social work ever closer, it created a major split in the social work profession. As a result, the 1930s witnessed the emergence of two main schools of thought: diagnostic and functional social work theory.[9] The differences between the two are important; these developments in the 1920s and 1930s sowed the seeds for the later training and orientation of the social workers who worked with the DPs in the 1940s and 1950s.

The diagnostic method, first taught at the New York, University of Chicago, and Smith College Schools of Social Work, adapted Freudian psychoanalysis to the practice of social casework. This practice was predicated on the assumption of pathology, and the social worker was responsible for diagnosing and treating the client. Functional theory, based on the writings of Freud's disciple Otto Rank and first taught at the University of Pennsylvania School of Social Work, relied on a model of growth and saw the impetus for change coming from the social worker rather than from the client. It stressed the interrelationship of the "helping process" and use of agency function. To a much greater degree than the diagnostic school, the functional approach emphasized the agency's role, rather than the individual's, in setting the agenda for the process.[10] This development would have far-reaching effects on the way that refugee agencies would dispense aid to survivors.

These differences in approach are clearly illustrated in both the psychiatric and the social work literature and practice of this period. While the immediate postwar literature is not exactly replete with articles about survivors' mental health, they certainly claimed a presence. Psychologists and psychiatrists today repeatedly note that discussion of survivors in the immediate postwar period was nearly absent until the 1960s but a careful exploration reveals that this is not the case.[11] Psychiatrists and psychologists studied survivors, graduate students wrote theses about them, and social workers attended conferences devoted to the topic.[12] There was indeed interest in the late 1940s and early 1950s. Ample evidence confirms this.

Published in 1947, "The Psychology of the Deportees," by French psychiatrist Eugene Minkowski, was one of the earliest postwar articles to appear in a professional journal, the *American OSE Review*.[13] It is noteworthy for its timing, its contents, and its influence on subsequent studies by American psychiatrists. Based on interviews with an unspecified number of Jews who had been deported from France during the war, the article was one of the first to mention "the emotional reaction of these people to their experiences."[14] Minkowski, a French Jew who had worked as a battalion physician during the Great War, survived World War II in Paris. Perhaps his own understanding of the war in Europe brought a sensitivity and sympathy to his analysis.[15]

Minkowski described the aftereffects of prolonged starvation on those who had endured World War II. He also studied "emotional anesthesia," the depression that set in after survivors began to "go on living."[16] Minkowski recognized the magnitude of the deportees' loss and expressed apprehension over their future mental health.[17] "Who knows," he asked, "what will happen when those who know that they are left all alone in the world suddenly comprehend the terrible void in which they are left?"[18] He was unable to answer his own query: to predict the survivors' future was impossible because there had been no precedent. Minkowski beseeched his peers to help these unfortunates by creating "an auspicious framework for the new beginning which we all long for."[19] He did not detail what this should be. Nevertheless, he recognized and noted to his peers, early on, that the aftereffects of these incomparable experiences on survivors would necessitate special care.[20]

In the United States, psychologists and psychiatrists were also taking note of this group of people who had lived through unprecedented circumstances. David Boder, a psychologist, is one whose response was groundbreaking. When the war ended, Dr. Boder, who was born in Lithuania and immigrated to America in 1922, was teaching at the Illinois Institute of Technology. After viewing newsreels of the concentration camps, he was convinced that it was important to capture the stories of DPs. In 1946, he set off for Europe armed with a new technology—a wire recorder—and two hundred spools of carbon steel wire. His collection of one hundred interviews is the first example of recorded survivor oral histories. It is pathbreaking both because of the technology as well as his methodology, which prefigured similar projects to come. Like others, Dr. Boder wanted to study the effects of wartime experiences on individuals. Unlike others, he allowed the interviewees to speak for themselves rather than impose his own orientation onto them. He wanted to make the experiences of the DPs available not through others' lenses but through their own. In 1949, his book *I Did Not Interview the Dead* appeared.[21] With only a brief introduction, this slim volume features eight of the interviews. Renowned psychologist and Harvard professor Gordon Allport remarked, "It is material that mankind should have wide access to—and ought to be required reading of mankind until the problems so vividly laid before the reader are solved."[22]

Paul Friedman, a Polish-born psychiatrist, also went to Europe in 1946. His early observations on the effects of the war on survivors appeared in 1948 in the American Jewish magazine *Commentary*.[23] Dr. Friedman brought the plight of the DPs to professional venues as well. He presented a paper titled "Some Aspects of Concentration Camp Psychology" to the American Psychiatric Association in 1948; it was published in the *American Journal of Psychiatry* in 1949 and reflected the psychoanalytic training he received in Vienna and Switzerland before immigrating to the United States in 1938.[24]

In his *Commentary* article, "The Road Back for the DPs: Healing the Scars of Nazism," Dr. Friedman shared some of Minkowski's concerns. He, too, recognized that survivors' psychological needs did not end with liberation. "It seems altogether incredible today that when the first plans for the rehabilitation of Europe's surviving Jews were outlined the psychiatric aspect of the problem was overlooked entirely," he remarked. "Everyone engaged in directing the relief work thought solely in terms of material assistance to the DPs. It took months of first-hand practical experience before anyone would acknowledge a similar, equally pressing need for psychological assistance."[25] This line of thinking should have boded well for survivors' postwar care.

In Friedman's view, DPs simply did not receive the kind of help they needed. Return to a normal life required much more than finding work and a place to live, he noted. The DPs needed treatment before they could resume living. And, he admitted, this treatment had been denied because of "the indifference and even often downright opposition on the part of many people to psychiatric aid for the survivors."[26]

It seems astonishing, today, that people would oppose offering psychological help to survivors. Friedman's explanation of this resistance illuminates some of the attitudes toward survivors' mental health immediately after the war on the part of the very people who should have been the most vocal advocates. Guilt, he averred, rather than lack of interest, kept the professionals' involvement to a minimum. He explained that psychiatrists, himself included, felt discomfort because they were safe in America while the Jews of Europe were massacred.

Then, too, Friedman pointed out, the first relief workers in the DP camps, untrained in psychological matters, had reported that the survivors were "miraculously unaffected by their recent terrible experiences."[27] This news encouraged mental health professionals to ignore or minimize stories of emotional ruin. Instead, in what appears to be the cornerstone of the triumphalist view of survival, mental health workers immediately after the war emphasized the physical and psychological superiority of those who had survived over those who had not.

Physicians were pleased to learn that they had wrongly imagined Europe "as a huge, unattended hospital for neurotics, psychotics, and the hopelessly insane."[28] The DPs had endured because they were the strong, resilient ones: it was a Darwinian explanation of survival. They had succeeded in staying alive, and once they were liberated, their suffering had ended. What terrible dishonor, the author remarked astutely, to impute to those who did not survive. In addition to trivializing or, worse, rationalizing the deaths of millions, he believed, attributing special strength to those victims who lived would not help their future treatment.

Dr. Friedman went to Europe twice to survey the DPs' emotional state and make recommendations for a mental health program for Jews in the DP camps and in Palestine. He surveyed the DP camps in 1946 and returned to Europe one year later to observe survivors' reactions to the detention camp in Cyprus. Friedman examined 172 people in Cyprus: 84 children under the age of 18, and 88 adults.

The DPs' condition and experiences, particularly those of the children, moved Friedman. He commented on their state of emotional apathy, or, referencing Minkowski, "affective anesthesia," when "they recounted horrible experiences."[29] Even more curious to him was the marked tendency toward fatigue among adolescents who showed no physical pathology yet slept for seventy-two hours without waking.[30] Friedman clearly recognized his visits to the DP and detention camps as a scientific as well as humanitarian opportunity. "The purgatory of Cyprus," wrote Dr. Friedman, "was a real psychological laboratory, in which one could study a wide range of ego defenses, ranging from rational attempts to ward off and deny new threats to real states of panic and psychotic manifestations."[31]

Dr. Friedman was a sensitive physician. His observations include recognition of the unparalleled nature of the Holocaust. Although his powerful insights hint at a new interpretation, he remained a product of his Freudian training. His study in Cyprus reflected this. "The abstention from sex was one of the most striking effects of life in the concentration camps," he concluded. The proof was in the Rorschach tests, which "showed in all cases a deep sexual repression with underlying anxiety."[32] What explained this repression, asked the doctor. In their struggle to survive, he suggested, the prisoners' libido focused on the instinct to live. Nowhere in his discussion does Dr. Friedman address aspects of camp conditions that would affect sexuality. Absent was mention of the starvation diet of the inmates or forced separation of men and women. The orthodox Freudian model prevailed.

Psychiatrists' studies focused on camp survivors because concentration camps were both unprecedented and the most widely publicized effects of "Hitlerism." The effects of concentration camp experiences on the individual's personality fascinated psychiatrists. The specialists clearly regarded their "subjects" as fertile ground for the study of human behavior in extreme situations. And this was viewed through a Freudian lens. These were the professional norms of the time.[33]

It is not surprising that psychiatrists and psychologists studied survivors from this perspective; it was an initial effort to grasp the incomprehensible by applying their own professional framework. On the one hand, the mental health professionals did recognize that concentration camp experiences had lasting impact on individuals. On the other hand, they were reluctant to allow the traumatic events to dominate their diagnoses. In one case, for example, Dr. Friedman administered sodium amytal to an eighteen-year-old Polish woman in order to determine the source of her violent headaches. So done, he determined that her neurotic symptoms were the result of childhood problems of attachment and were "activated by the recent hardships of [DP] camp life after liberation."[34] In many cases, psychiatrists decided that their interviewee's problems originated not from wartime experiences but from earlier developmental difficulties. Had Dr. Friedman looked at both the wartime experiences and prewar personality, his assessment would have truly been ahead of his time. But this eluded him.

The strict application of this model prevented an understanding of the profound impact of the Holocaust on survivors. The psychiatrists tried to understand survivors' experiences within the normal range of human experience, their postwar reactions as a function of prewar personality. Over and over, their findings seem to miss the boat. They did not or could not yet recognize the unprecedented nature of this catastrophe.

Applying classic Freudian terminology such as *infantilization* to survivors universalized the Holocaust. Through discussion of the Final Solution as an extreme case of Thanatos winning over Eros, the individual and the Jewish context was obliterated.[35] An already established distance between the psychiatrists and their Eastern European co-religionists may have furthered this. In the attempt to understand how an individual could survive the dehumanization of the camp, the strict psychoanalytic lens seems forced, misplaced, and unsympathetic. In 1982, Martin Bergmann and Milton Jucovy, psychoanalysts and the editors of *Generations of the Holocaust*, suggested that the approach belied something deeper. Psychiatrists and psychoanalysts themselves were not ready to confront the enormity of the destruction of European Jewry. Their professional orientation allowed for and facilitated a gulf between themselves and survivors, and by extension the Holocaust.[36]

Agency records support this conclusion. As consultants, psychiatrists carried out face-to-face meetings with refugees that often led to diagnoses lacking in fundamental sensitivity or even understanding. One psychiatrist who interviewed a couple requesting a transfer from Memphis to Denver wrote that "neither of them revealed any psychotic manifestations but were neurotic individuals, self absorbed [*sic*] and preoccupied with their past."[37] Another observed, "This patient suffers from a psycho-neurosis with depressive and hysterical symptoms."[38] Both these agency-appointed psychiatrists recommended vocational counseling to help the clients. They treated these patients as they would any of their other American patients. Or worse.

Dr. Emanuel Tanay, formerly a child who had been hidden during the Holocaust, reached the United States in 1949. He was not a patient. Rather, he applied to do a psychiatric residency at the Michael Reese Hospital in Chicago. Prior to his acceptance, three Jewish staff psychiatrists interviewed him. One asked how he had managed to survive the war. When he answered that he lived on false documents, his interviewer inquired if he had also falsified his medical school documents. Outraged, Emanuel stood up to leave and told the panel why. The doctor immediately urged him to stay. His comments, he said, "were part of the admissions' test."[39] Dr. Tanay did stay and went on to become a psychiatrist. He acknowledges that he and his interviewer later became good friends. At the time, however, he was so livid that a psychiatrist—Jewish, no less—could be so insensitive and ill informed that he was prepared to walk out on the interview and not return.

One Auschwitz survivor who currently lives in Washington, DC, spoke on condition of anonymity. Her experience with an American psychiatrist illustrates a different response. She remembers with deep appreciation the psychiatrist who helped her nearly sixty years after her arrival in the United States. Mrs. W. feels that the woman was her lifeline and guided her through an especially rocky time in her early years in America.[40] Mrs. G., of Columbia, South Carolina, also reflected on a positive relationship with a psychiatrist in the early 1950s.[41] There are surely other cases like these buried in psychiatrists' files. We do not know how many. What the examples show, however, is that there were physicians who approached these patients in a sensitive and caring manner and it made a lasting difference in the newcomers' lives.

An attempt to apply research to practice appears in the literature in 1951. "A Case History of a Concentration Camp Survivor" was published in the *American OSE Review*.[42] The article described a man who was the subject of a study by three psychologists on concentration camp survivors in New York City. The project "was undertaken for the purpose of investigating the immediate and long-range effects of concentration camp experience on personality and attitude."[43] In 1951, the interest was still focused on the camp survivors as the worthiest subjects for clinical research.

Conducted through the Graduate Faculty of the New School for Social Research, the New York project was financed by the U.S. Public Health Service. In this study, the researchers administered a battery of psychological tests, such as the Rorschach and the Thematic Apperception Test, with the goal of "gaining insight into the underlying personality dynamics."[44] The authors concluded that the individual described in this case history did undergo personality changes that were consonant with his traumatic wartime experiences. The psychologists carefully mentioned that participants' behavior, in some cases, was a function of their prewar personality. Nevertheless, the examination of behavior in the context of wartime experiences was an important step for the times. Clearly, even in 1951, there were professionals who recognized the impact of the Holocaust, per se, on survivors.

The authors noted that their study was directed primarily toward research. Nevertheless, they hoped that their results would be helpful to those involved directly with survivors' problems of adjustment. Whether their information was ever shared with the staff of NYANA, located a short distance from the New School, or any refugee agency is unknown. There is nothing in agency records to suggest that there was contact between them.

One of the last psychiatric accounts to appear in this period was a medical-psychological study, *Human Behavior in the Concentration Camp*, by Elie Cohen, a psychiatrist and survivor of Auschwitz.[45] Public attention to his subject had waned, the author noted in 1953, since the heightened curiosity toward the victims of Nazism immediately after the war. Cohen's assessment was accurate. Little, if anything, appeared in this arena for the remainder of the decade. Whether this was the result of flagging interest or other reasons is difficult to assess. The interest, while certainly there, was never ubiquitous. And then it began to fade away. A curtain of near-total silence descended after 1953 and lifted dramatically in the 1960s with an awakening of renewed psychiatric inquiry that gained further momentum in the 1970s and the 1980s.[46] Nevertheless, survivors, especially of concentration camps, piqued psychiatrists' and psychologists' interest in the first decade after the war and undoubtedly social workers were thinking about them, too.

The subject of refugees, in fact, was not new to the social work profession even before the DPs' arrival. The topic arose during the 1930s and 1940s, when a trickle of Jewish émigrés reached America.[47] It hit full force in 1948 with the enactment of the Displaced Persons Act and the subsequent new arrivals. Articles immediately cropped up in social work journals. One of the first that appeared that year in the *Journal of Casework* was titled "Can Freedom Be Taught?" The author was the very same Dr. Paul Friedman who wrote about the DPs in Europe for *Commentary* magazine and the *Journal of American Psychiatry*.[48]

A few months earlier, in April 1948, Dr. Friedman had presented "Can Freedom Be Taught?" at the National Conference of Social Work. He was one of many speakers at the conference to discuss refugees. DP issues predominated at both the National Conference of Social Work in April and the National Conference of Jewish Social Welfare in May 1948. No doubt this interest was encouraged by upcoming DP legislation, which Congress would pass in June 1948. Social workers readied themselves for the imminent arrival of DPs.

Just as the psychiatric literature highlights that professions' view of survivors, the papers presented at national social work conferences and others (numbering at least forty) published in contemporary social work journals also provide further context to this story. They reflect how social workers imagined the DPs and how they responded to their arrival. The articles clearly show that social workers around the country struggled with their response to the refugees and were aware that these newcomers were different from native clients.

If the psychiatrists' earlier papers were rooted in the European experience, the social workers' conference presentations and articles clearly demonstrated a shift to the treatment of survivors as newcomers on American soil.[49] Psychiatrists concerned themselves primarily with studying the concentration camp experience at arm's length. The social workers were in the postwar trenches battling with "the helping process."

Dr. Friedman's presentation to social workers attending the conference in 1948 was surprisingly abstract and peppered with generalizations. From a discussion of Kafka and an excerpt from Freud's *Civilization and Its Discontents*, he went on to concede that "it is not my intention to outline here a full program for the guidance of the immigrant; only empirical, day-to-day experience can really furnish that." His goal was to describe "certain basic facts and attitudes with which you will have to cope."[50] Friedman endeavored to point out subtleties such as the variations in Holocaust experiences, yet told his listeners that all newcomers had to relearn freedom and emerge from an attitude of suspicion and distrust.

One point that Dr. Friedman emphasized is noteworthy. "We cannot help [refugees]," he announced, "by saying, 'Forget the past,' but by giving [them] specific recommendations for the present."[51] He restated this even more strongly and cautioned social workers to avoid mistakes made by the first fieldworkers. Unqualified personnel had "used certain repressive techniques" by saying " 'Forget all that—don't discuss it—put it out of your mind.' This is no way to deal with the long memories of horror," he exhorted the audience.[52] When social workers and DPs finally met face to face, despite Friedman's admonition, most social workers did indeed urge their clients to do just that.

Did these newcomers require treatment that differed from that of any other immigrant or even any other native client? This was the question that dominated the day in 1948. The social workers had a great deal to say about this topic and their responses are revealing. One would anticipate and hope that adherents of the diagnostic school of casework would advocate for an approach that dealt with this groups' differences.

Sanford Sherman of the Association for Jewish Children in Philadelphia was one who argued for "important differences in case work with refugees— or newcomers—than with native clientele."[53] He believed that imposing old standards on and assessments of these newcomers by universalizing the helping process impeded progress in the profession in general and help for the newcomer in particular. It was essential, he stressed, "to push ahead and identify the distinguishing features of helping special groups of people whose needs stem from special kinds of experiences."[54]

Sherman's description of the new refugees is striking. They have "been shaped by [their] earliest and pre-war experiences; by years of living in a hostile, authoritarian society where [they were] in constant hiding, in concentration camp, or, in active, partisan conflict with this authority; by being stripped of status, occupation, home, and friends; by being given the

awful burden of surviving where family and friends were killed; and finally
by living two or three years in post-war Europe in flight, in displaced persons
camps, in black markets, in work or in formal education, etc."[55] It was an
insightful assessment in 1948; he recognized the range of experiences that distinguished these newcomers from other clients *and* from other immigrants.
Indeed, he noted that "in all the Jewish history of immigration here, there
has never been so complete a burning of bridges behind the immigrant."[56]

Sherman was deeply concerned about the newcomers. He realized
that they were different from previous immigrants. These very differences
also presented challenges that social workers faced when relating to these
refugees. The incomprehensibility of what the DPs endured evoked a spectrum of response among social workers, Sherman explained. The professionals imagined that the wartime experiences inevitably resulted in "some kind
of mass psychosis" and were taken aback by "what surprisingly *whole* people
the newcomers were."[57] This dissonance led to social workers' "psychological disappointment" in the refugees for the latter's failure in meeting the
social workers' expectations. This in turn provoked the feeling, echoing the
sentiments of Dr. Friedman, that the clients needed less help because of
the strengths that allowed them to survive.[58] In addition, Sherman averred,
guilt played an important role. Upon observing the newcomers' guilt over
surviving, some caseworkers, too, experienced guilt because they were safe
in America. This, claimed Sherman, led to an overidentification with survivors and a desire to compensate them for their past suffering. Eventually,
the author remarked, this also provoked resentment toward the survivors,
"who confront us with their own uneasiness."[59]

While some social workers appeared to need to make restitution to
survivors, others consistently expressed the feeling that some refugees
"believed that the agency and the community owed them a living because of
the severe indignities and deprivations they had suffered."[60] These comments shed light on the complexity of the relationship between the survivors and the social workers and the range of conflicting emotions in both
the agencies' professionals and the newcomers. They reveal that social workers understood that there was, indeed, something unique about this group
and their interactions with it.

In another article, "Techniques in Casework with Displaced Persons,"
Rita Spaulding, district supervisor in the Jewish Family and Community
Service in Chicago, also advocated for special care for the DPs.[61] Spaulding
urged her colleagues to understand individual differences. "The individual, in
most cases, has been severely traumatized," she emphasized.[62] The agency

must be accepting and flexible. "Emphasis on planning geared primarily to relieve our own pressures and decrease our case loads is not helpful to the client," she stressed, adding, "In some instances it is punitive and harmful to his total adjustment."[63] Few heeded her words.

Others spoke more about the hardships that the influx of refugees brought to bear on the agency than about how they could help the DPs. "The problem of integrating the newcomer of the post-war period into the life of an American community as a responsible, mature individual and member of that community," wrote an agency worker, "has placed a great burden on the agencies which have accepted this responsibility."[64] Working with refugees "created anxiety, tension and often hostility in the case worker,"[65] noted Allan Cowett, of the Jewish Family Service Bureau in Cincinnati. The social workers at his agency were frustrated. They had to abandon their progressive psychiatric social work techniques and revert to relationships based only on dispensing financial aid. Apparently, it did not occur to this staff that the newcomers needed anything more.

Cowett believed in the inherent similarity of the native client and the refugee. He was convinced that treatment toward the newcomers should be no different from that of "many clients who have suffered much adversity, whether from loss of employment in the long depression, family breakdown, war casualties, or similar traumatic experiences."[66] The two essential differences were of a practical nature. The numbers of refugees and the urgency of dispensing relief (food, housing, and clothing until the newcomer was self-supporting) demanded an immediate response. Cowett noted that 40 percent of agency time was spent trying to solve refugee problems to the exclusion of other agency responsibilities, which incurred the staff's ill will toward the newcomers rather than engendering sympathy for them.

Social workers debated these issues at national conferences and in professional journals. The everyday treatment of the social worker toward survivors mirrored a spectrum of other sensibilities. On the ground level, the caseworkers' personal attitude as well as the agency limitations often eclipsed theoretical discussions. When it came to direct encounters with survivors, advocates of a diagnostic-oriented approach were scarce. In fact, there seemed to be an assumption that aid to newcomers was to be oriented almost exclusively toward relief giving.

In the postwar period, private agencies, especially the Jewish agencies in New York, were at the forefront of social work practice.[67] These agencies tended to attract professionally trained and experienced social workers. They could close their doors when the caseload grew too unwieldy; they had the luxury of limiting the size of their client population and considered thirty-five cases per worker to be the maximum ratio. Moreover, these agencies saw themselves as laboratories for the latest social work techniques. They emphasized staff development, which would benefit the agency as well as the field of professional social work.[68]

NYANA was a private agency funded by the United Jewish Appeal.[69] It initially shared these progressive, even cutting-edge, goals. The large influx of DPs in 1949, however, quickly turned their intentions around. The Family Service Department did at first follow the model of other Jewish family agencies. When the caseload exceeded fifty per worker and the budget soared, the agency reached a decision. It chose to substitute the "more practical and realistic concept of the public agency's methods of dealing with a mass relief problem."[70]

The private-agency model was one of the first casualties of the New York crisis. Within a few months, economic strains on the agency propelled its agenda. "Regardless of whatever other reasons may have prevailed for differing pre-existing policies," read NYANA's *Statement of Services and Functions*, "certainly the compelling financial considerations which make it necessary for NYANA to limit its services only to those of an adjustment nature and not to continue services for a defined period of time, present a sound reason for this concept of NYANA's function."[71] In February 1949, NYANA cut the duration of its services to the DPs from five years to one.

NYANA did not lament its reduction in support to the refugees. On the contrary. The agency insisted that this approach benefited the survivors. "It is sound from a casework standpoint to adopt such a policy," its mission statement detailed, "because it really facilitates the adjustment process when we focus on integrating an immigrant wholly into the community."[72]

This was not just the NYANA way, it was also the American way. Other agencies outside New York also believed in the notion that it was up to the individual, first and foremost, to take charge of his or her own future. "American agencies customarily start with the premise that the primary responsibility for helping the immigrant (or any individual) rests with himself; the agency is prepared to help him, but only to the extent that he cannot help himself, and only in a manner which will increase his capacity for self-dependence," asserted Marcel Kovarsky, executive director of the Jewish Family and Children's Services in Pittsburgh.[73] Kovarsky emphasized the immigrant as primary agent in his or her own future. Mention of "the immigrant (or any individual)" also underscores his agency's uniform approach to treatment regardless of the client.

The agency limitations were not dictated solely by financial constraints, but were in keeping with the best interests of the refugee and also backed up by contemporary American social work philosophy and practice. Gone was the diagnostic, therapeutic approach embraced by other private Jewish agencies. NYANA soon resembled "the minimum maintenance and emergency service program of the New York City Department of Welfare."[74] This included an increase of the caseload per social worker from thirty-five to fifty. As the total caseload grew by 53 percent from July to December 1949, the staff increased by less than 22 percent.[75]

Like so many of the contemporary writers' coverage of the DPs in the media, L. C. White's chronicle of USNA's history put a positive spin on what transpired. "The greatest achievement of USNA, its predecessor organizations and cooperating agencies," he wrote, "was the extent to which they speeded up the gradual process by which immigrants became active participants in the economic, social, civic, cultural, and spiritual affairs of America—a process by which they came to feel 'at home' and were Americanized to the point where we felt that they were no longer foreigners."[76] The problems of integration were helped, White stated, "in accordance with the highest professional standards of social casework techniques."[77] The social workers were the enablers that used both agency objectives and that of current social work guidelines to hasten the immigrants' adjustment.

Despite White's characterization, this adoption of "minimum standards of service" had a negative impact on its recipients.[78] Social workers were, indeed, burdened, but it was the refugees who lost out. Case files give evidence of recurring discussions between refugee and social worker that centered on accepting and working within agency limitations.

"With the policy of limitation of services," wrote one caseworker, "the Ps began to become even more anxious about what would be their future."[79] The clock was ticking on their one-year assistance plan, even though this family had been trying for weeks without success to make an appointment with NYANA's overburdened Vocational Service Department. NYANA social workers commented frequently on the inability of the refugees to relate "to agency structure and limitations."[80]

The theme of agency limits is one that echoed in both the social work journals and the agency files. Social workers often bundled their perception of their clients' reactions to limits together with descriptions of dependency, which was anathema to the agencies' goals. "He impressed me as a passive, reticent, dependent kind of person who apparently is not too well oriented to agency purposes and services," commented one social worker after her first meeting with Mr. P., a forty-four-year-old unattached man.[81] "Mr. and Mrs. H. are individuals who have difficulty in accepting agency limitations and are dependent individuals who will need a great deal of help in working thru [sic] the way in which we can help them make a beginning," wrote another social worker.[82]

If some survivors met agency constraints with confusion, others viewed them with disbelief and anger. "Any number of newcomers," stated Kovarsky, "asked, 'Was this what you brought me to the US for? Why, it was better in the concentration camp. Send me back.'"[83] Despite this, Kovarsky defended his agency, which remained committed to limited help because "it is grounded in American culture and that for them to do otherwise would serve to retard the newcomer's adjustment."[84] This tension between what survivors expected and what they received is a constant in the files.

As the immigrant population grew, the number of professionals arguing for differentiated treatment for the refugees fell. Widespread opinion concurred that the best approach to helping the refugees was to offer limited help, which would quicken the pace of their adjustment. This approach was not limited to the larger urban communities of New York and Philadelphia. In Denver, for example, which committed itself to an annual quota of 166 DPs, the staff at Jewish Family and Children's Services felt that the newcomers would be best served by limited treatment (as befitted the native clientele) and acted accordingly.

Agency policy, even of a limited nature, is one facet of this story. Attitude, that elusive yet perceptible quality of an interaction, is another. Attitudes are communicated in the case files and are, at times, shocking. When Mr. H. had difficulty completing the NYANA application, for example, his caseworker reported that Mr. H. had "made a big issue of the fact that he was a newcomer and tried to give me the impression that he knew absolutely nothing about anything."[85] This was six days after Mr. and Mrs. H.'s arrival in the United States. The caseworker's descriptions of the couple over the following four months show little warmth or expression of compassion.

A young survivor's story illustrates another surprising reaction by a social worker. There is little in the file about his life before or during the war. What is known is this: he came to New York, alone, on a corporate affidavit as a nineteen-year-old concentration camp survivor in 1948. USNA permitted him to stay in New York "on the basis that he had need of family relationships which were not available to him else where [sic]—namely a 60 year old cousin living in N.Y.C."[86] Despite this, the young man received little help of any kind from his American relative. He had no surviving members of his immediate family, no skills, no knowledge of English. In the initial meetings with his caseworker he seemed completely lost. He often cried when he spoke with her and remarked on several physical ailments that troubled him.[87] The young man's caseworker was not empathetic. "He then went on again," she noted, "to give some fantastic tale about how he had been able to take care of himself the last couple of years in Europe and had wandered around Europe himself and had to do a great deal for himself."[88] Said in the context of the young man's inability to find work, perhaps his supposed self-reliance in Europe evoked her suspicion. Nevertheless, her doubt may also shed light on some social workers' avoidance of engaging their clients in discussions about the past. If a refugee's history was a "fantastic tale," it was better not to dwell on it than to take it too seriously.

Many years later, a former social work intern at the Montefiore Hospital recalled her own and her colleagues' reactions to her refugee clients. "We had no sense of the Holocaust as we know now, with a capital H. We really didn't understand what people were telling us," she remembered. "The stories were too horrible. We simply did not believe them."[89]

Gabi Schiff, a German Jewish émigré, received her degree in social work from Swarthmore College and asked the American Jewish Joint Distribution Committee to send her to Europe after the war so that she could work with refugees.[90] She devoted five years to working in DP camps, married a Polish Jewish survivor, and returned to New York and a job at NYANA. Because of her experiences working with DPs in Europe and her marriage, Gabi felt that she was more attuned to the refugees than most other social workers at NYANA. A half century later, she recalled how much the new immigrants struggled and how lost they were in America.

Mrs. Schiff believed that it was not for lack of concern that the agencies' workers misunderstood the DPs. The staff simply had no experience with the likes of the new arrivals. She believed that the refugee organization "meant so well and knew so little. We didn't think about the feelings of people," she remembered.[91]

Overlooking the newcomers' feelings is illustrated in a comment by a caseworker in Denver. Mrs. F. came into the office to request a coat. The social worker stated that while Mrs. F. was talking "she had her arm on the desk and as she spoke, expressing how she needed the coat, she kept pushing the sleeve of her dress which revealed a tattooed arm, which she had received at the concentration camp. She made no reference to the concentration camp or to the numbers," the social worker continued. As she talked "she kept pushing the sleeve of her dress up so that I could notice them." The caseworker authorized thirty-five dollars for a new coat. She did not ask Mrs. F. about the numbers on her arm.[92]

Many social workers' reports contain language that illustrates their diagnostic orientation. The focus, however, was on the clients' present and future rather than the past. Psychological factors often described the client's inability to become self-maintaining and frequently implied character weakness as well. One NYANA social worker wrote:

> Miss A. appears to be a very immature hostile individual who apparently establishes relationship on a demanding dependent level. She seems so involved with her emotional conflict that mobilization toward self-realization and self-sufficiency seems stifeled [*sic*]. There is no spontaneity about her behavior. She cannot venture out on her own. Any change in status quo appears threatening. She is prone to blame all her difficulties on the external world in an almost paranoid manner—the world is irrational, America impossible, the agency cruel, the worker heartless, the doctor unsympathetic, the nurse ignorant, etc.[93]

Miss A.'s history indicates that she was not an easy client. She was often sick and prone to emotional outbursts. Her "adjustment to this agency has been a very difficult one," wrote the caseworker. The reason for this? Because, the professional noted, "she seems so involved with her emotional problems that she was unable to move constructively towards self-sufficiency."[94]

The phrase "moving constructively towards self-sufficiency" (or not, in this case) is one that appears repeatedly throughout the files. The words are a euphemism, an expression of tension between the agency representative and the newcomer. It belies the survivors' anguish, the daily struggle to resume life, to live with excruciating memories and still meet the agency's time limit. In the twenty-five pages that document Miss A.'s initial two years in the United States, much of the focus is on her adjustment problems—her adjusting to the agency and accepting the manner in which it could best help her—more than anything else. The caseworkers virtually ignored the aftereffects of her trauma as part of her difficulties. The woman met with several social workers over the course of her two-year relationship with the agency. While the tones vary from kindly to hostile, their message to Miss A. remains consistent: she must move on.

Another document in this file is illuminating and serves as a reminder of what stymied Miss A.'s progress. Also a report by a social worker, it comes from the social service department of the Hospital for Joint Diseases, where

Miss A. was referred because of health issues that interfered with her employability. Upon the social worker's examination of her, he suspected psychogenic factors. A staff social worker followed up with a medical-social employability report. In this interview the social worker noted that the "patient related her personal and family hardships in Europe under the Nazi regime and war time conditions and felt now she was 'suffering from a hangover of these experiences.' She appreciates the help she has received from your agency but 'lacked the energy to move ahead,' due to feelings of overwhelming pressures that she must hurry on with social adjustment, which was beyond her present emotional pace."[95] It is a glaring reminder of what shadows—yet is absent—from the vast majority of the files.

Some social workers observed that their clients did not understand the basic purpose of the agency and the clients' relationship to it. Sometimes, the social worker perceived this as a means of resisting adjustment. There were those for whom the notion of a social worker was a completely novel concept and this resulted in much miscommunication. Again, the minimization of agency services also had an impact on this. One of the ways that NYANA cut costs was by offering a group orientation for the DPs. This resulted in a reduction of the length and number of individual interviews.

One caseworker reported that it had been necessary to explain to her client just what the former's function was, and by extension the agency's, and how they would work together. She noted that the client "came into the office meekly and gave the impression of being 'the little boy.' Immediately told me that he had no idea of the purpose of the appointment which he did not keep last week."[96] She tried to explain agency procedure but "he did not seem to understand we would be having a regular appointment structure, and that I would be seeing him regularly."[97]

This confusion on the part of the young man seems genuine enough. He was adrift in a bureaucratic and cultural sea, alone and unhappy. To the social worker "he showed a great deal of difficulty in relating to agency structure and limitations and resistance to job referrals, stemming from his high and unrealistic job aspirations."[98] The caseworkers' perception that the DPs expressed resistance to looking for work is a constant in their written reports.

Many social workers insisted that their clients were using sickness to avoid work and, by extension, to obstruct their adjustment. "It did seem apparent that client was using these illnesses to further prevent her from making a move on her own," wrote one social worker in her closing summary.[99] It was common for refugees to use illness, another agreed, "when you couldn't make the goals that were set for you."[100] Still another stated that illness was a "respectable excuse" for not working.[101] One social worker had an ambivalent reaction to her clients' numerous symptoms. Even though she eventually referred this client to a psychiatrist, she hesitated initially because "we felt this might make him believe he was sick and unable to get along."[102] Despite the preponderance of illness the social workers made no connection to the DPs' past experiences.[103] They saw the root cause as the immigrants' inability, or lack of real interest in, becoming independent.

In a few rare instances, survivors had the opportunity to delve into their past with their social workers. E. K. was one who did so. E. K.'s case-worker noted that this client found "life much harder since he [was] in America, because as long as he was in camp, he shared the same fate and the same misery with thousands of other people." The worker concluded, "Here in America he is all alone and memories keep piling up on him." She reported what E. K. had confided: "He makes efforts to blot some of the memories which are haunting him, but sometimes he is overcome by misery and finds his loneliness unbearable."[104] The social worker was sympathetic. She praised E. K. for speaking openly with her and told him that she identified with him and what he had gone through and "brought in our desire and our responsibility in helping him." She added that she saw a "dual personality in him; the one who drives forward and functions very well and positively in the world of reality and the other who is all passivity and who is constantly interfering with his forward drive." When E. K. again brought up his loneliness and that " 'he was different from other people,' " she responded that "it was not easy for a young man with so much feeling of deprivation to have a more positive outlook on life. Was it not possible," she asked, "that he was expecting too much from others and how much had he tried to give himself more fully and use himself more constructively?" She urged him to join a neighborhood center and to be realistic about what he could expect from new friendships.

E. K.'s social worker did not ignore the young man's feelings. But the bulk of his thirty-seven-page file skirted his Holocaust memories. Details were scanty and reduced to a few sentences. Meetings revolved instead around his job search, his perceived independence/dependence struggle, and his numerous illnesses. E. K. met with this social worker only five times. But she was kind to him. And he appreciated this. Still, her kindness was proscribed by policy and could only go so far. When he landed a referral for a manufacturing position, he was no longer eligible for assistance from NYANA.[105] He was on his own.

Simona Frajndlich remembers well the interactions she had with her social worker at USNA. The memories still rankle. The young woman grew up in a wealthy and well-educated family and aspired to a career as a physician. She feels that the young social worker with whom she met in New York had preconceived ideas about her as a newcomer. Simona believes that instead of seeing the cultured and refined individual that she was, the agency worker saw an immigrant—as the worker's parents may well have been—from an Eastern European shtetl, from *Fiddler on the Roof.*[106] Simona believes that this prejudice and condescension drove the American-born social worker's attitude toward the young Polish survivor.

Simona's perspective is one worth examining further in the broader context of American Jewish identity and demographics in the postwar period. If the young professionals directly serving the newcomers in the agency settings were themselves the first generation born to their immigrant parents, then their response to these newcomers—who were largely Eastern European, unskilled, uneducated, and Yiddish speaking—may very well have evoked condescension, impatience, and even hostility, rather than sympathy, toward this reminder of what their parents had left behind and they had grown beyond.

When all the contributing factors are scrutinized, can the question posed at the outset of this chapter be answered? Why was the topic of the Holocaust absent from the majority of case files of those assisting survivors? Can or should the helping profession be faulted for its approach to survivors? After all, the elements were there for offering good diagnostic psychiatric social work to the refugees. Discussions about newcomers certainly existed. Trained professionals and agencies were at the ready. The agencies indeed stepped up to the plate, but the help they gave the survivors missed by a mile. Dollars and cents dictated treatment, but so did attitudes. It could have and should have been different. There were no doubt caring and sympathetic individuals among the social workers. Most, however, failed to understand the impact of the recent clients' past on the process of acculturation. Perhaps the source of this failure was the workers' inability to confront the depths of the Holocaust's destruction or the idea that survivors were imbued with great strength. It may have been the result of guilt at having had the good fortune to escape the claws of Nazism in the safety of America while European Jewry burned. They may have preferred to concentrate on the mechanics of practical concerns, carefully prescribed by agency policy, which allowed for a feeling of purpose and accomplishment. This inability of most helpers to see the newcomers as anything but immigrants whose speedy Americanization would make both parties feel more comfortable was a way of masking what was plainly in front of them. It was so much simpler than confronting the messy, emotional, complicated needs of survivors.

It was this rush to get the refugees out of their offices, not the Holocaust—even as it stared them in the face—that framed the treatment of these newcomers. One social worker in Denver summed up this philosophy succinctly. He told the refugee that "the agency [could not] be a father or mother or a sister or the brothers or any of the relatives or any of the friends that he the displaced person had lost or left behind." Instead, "the purpose of the agency was to help the newcomer become self-sufficient and to help himself."[107] Survivors, however, needed more and found other ways to address this deeper need.

CHAPTER 8

The Myth of Silence

A DIFFERENT STORY

━━◄╋►━━

"When I came to the United States, even my aunt who loved
me, who helped me, my cousins that were dear to me, they
always said, you suffered enough, don't talk about it. So who
did we talk to about it? Survivors to each other!"
(Nessie Godin, 14 December 1995)[1]

Soon after their arrival, survivors
began the process of acculturating to life in America. They looked for jobs,
searched for and settled into apartments, and started to learn English.
Although urged to abandon their past and look to the future, they found that
moving forward was possible but ignoring the past less so. Forgetting was
difficult. They could not forget, nor did they want to. Few outside their own
circles, however, wished to remember with them. At that time, it was largely
among themselves that they found the persistent desire to recall, a common
language of mutual grief, and sympathetic ears.

There is close to universal agreement among survivors that no one—
not their relatives, the social workers, or the outside world—wanted to hear
about the Holocaust. Survivors' reactions to this are vivid. "We were very bitter," said one camp survivor. Because "in the beginning—in the beginning
the people in America didn't want . . ." his voice failed. "We started to tell
stories, nobody wanted to listen. And if somebody listened, they thought
that we are . . . we told them stories that it is not true. From the first minute
I spoke." He continued, "When I came to America, when I told the people,
they thought I'm crazy . . . they didn't want to listen," he repeated again.[2]

One new arrival, who wrote for the Yiddish daily the *Forverts*, was
invited to speak at a fund-raising event for a women's organization in
Baltimore in 1949. She looked out at her audience and told them that their
faces reminded her of her mother, whom the Nazis had murdered. The

organization's president quickly interrupted her and reminded the guest that the bad memories were in the past. As the host urged the band to resume playing, the survivor fled, resolving never to speak publicly about her experiences again.[3]

Another woman was ready to talk but when her American cousin asked her if she had orange juice for breakfast in Auschwitz, she knew she could not and would not share her story with her American family. "People had no—no understanding," said Hanne, explaining her cousin's crushing insensitivity and ignorance. Perhaps more telling, she added that they "didn't really want to know."[4]

A.'s experience confirms that, as well. None of her relatives believed the extent of the atrocities she had witnessed. She agreed, too, that Americans were not ready to hear. She posed a possible reason: guilt. "They felt guilty for number of years Jews and non-Jews," she suggested. But she also remembered that (American) "Jews were also complaining that they suffered . . . they didn't have enough meat and sugar." The attempt to equate their wartime experiences with survivors or to suggest that they empathized with their European relatives' suffering because of their own did not sit well with the newcomers. To the newcomers, this signaled a deep, even unbridgeable chasm between the two groups and reinforced the belief that their American hosts did not care to hear about what survivors had endured. This prevented one woman from talking to her relatives. "[I] saw the lack of understanding in the first years, so I decided not to waste my time," she remembered. "It was too emotional to open my wounds," she explained.[5]

The conspiracy of silence started not with the survivors, but with their relatives, the agencies, and the greater society. Some tried to broach the subject with their American kin. For others, the topic never came up. "How could the relatives not ask about their murdered aunts and uncles?" wondered one woman, whose father was the only child out of his large family who survived Auschwitz. But they did not. And the silence hung like a curtain separating the newcomers from their hosts. "No one asked," said Amalie Sandelowski with finality.[6]

Certainly there were survivors who chose not to speak. Some simply could not. Bernie Sayonne of Denver believes that many of his friends were quiet because they could not shake the internalized fear of persecution that shadowed their lives in America; better to keep a low profile, some survivors reasoned, than to become a possible target of antisemitism.[7]

What these sources make excruciatingly clear is how little the outside world encouraged survivors to talk or seemed interested in learning about their Holocaust experiences. Even simple sympathy about the past was rare and for that reason important to note. When it happened it was deeply appreciated and remembered. One survivor recalled her despair after arriving in America. She mourned her murdered family so intensely that she could not stop weeping. At night she screamed from her nightmares and woke her young cousins. "Why are you crying?" they wanted to know. The young woman told her relatives. Their response was simple and direct. "Cry, if this will help you," they encouraged her. Moreover, her aunt told her, "I know it's not easy for you, but we love you and we want you to be happy." Their understanding meant a great deal. "I appreciate those words what [sic] she said to me," recalled the woman in an interview nearly forty years later. "Till now I remember them," she emphasized.[8] Such instances are glaringly absent from survivor testimonies. But it exemplifies that survivors could and would speak, especially when encouraged with sensitivity and kindness.

For the vast majority this did not happen. "We, the survivors, even me, I'm talking personally, I wanted to, I wanted to talk about it," emphasized Nessie Godin, who settled in Washington, DC, in 1949. "Why?" she asks. Because "in the most horrible times during the Holocaust, we used to sit and talk to each other, the women, hungry, cold, all the women used to say, please don't forget us. If you survive," she was instructed, "tell the world of what happened." Nessie, as do others, take this obligation seriously. "Those women asked me to talk about it," she affirmed.[9] And talk she did. But at first it was with other refugees, not her American family, that she spoke. Nessie recalled "five, six couples, survivors coming to our house on the Sabbath, having a little lunch, what did we talk about? . . . comparing each other's suffering, telling how it was, talking about how by miracle we survived this selection and that selection and in a way, I think this was really beneficial to us . . . we didn't keep it inside."[10]

Mr. Weingarten of the New Cracow Friendship Society unequivocally stated, "There was no conversation that did not end up on the subject." "Even in social situations," remarked one woman, "the topic always came up."[11] When Denver's New Americans Club socialized, the discussion "always came back to the same thing," recalled Auschwitz survivor Bernie Sayonne.[12] Paul Krell continues to meet to this day (2003) with a small cadre of other male survivors at a local coffee shop in the Bronx. "No matter what we start talking about, politics, the stock market . . . we always end up talking about the war," he asserted.[13]

These comments recur so often and with such insistence that one wonders how the myth that survivors were silent after the war evolved. Perhaps this perception prevailed in the greater Jewish world in part because of a lack of genuine interest in the agony of the Holocaust. Other factors, however, compounded this apathy. Some may have truly felt that it would be an unacceptable breach of privacy to ask. For others, it may have been a way to avoid confronting the murder of their own European relatives. Some Americans Jews, in the postwar mood, may have believed that it was better for the survivor to look ahead rather than back. Others may have felt that the refugees preferred to keep to themselves. A follow-up study of one hundred DPs in Cleveland in 1956 supports this. The author of this report noted that the typical DP was not isolated or lonely. "On the contrary," the report stated. "He was found to be a very socially-minded person who did not reach out into the community for these contacts, but rather continued to lead a social life within the DP group."[14]

Survivors did indeed lead social lives with other survivors. They sought one another out and formed many types of groups. The structures varied but the intent was clear: they wanted the comfort of others like themselves. These networks were critical to their well-being. They provided sustenance on many levels, from mutual aid to casual socializing to profound emotional succor. For many, these groups became the family and the community that had been brutally and irrevocably destroyed. They also became the mechanisms through which they preserved their memories.

Those whose physical and existential past had been savagely shattered longed to be with others who shared a common history. After the obliteration there was a need to reclaim their history and ensure that it existed outside their imagination. Whether created by their refugee status, their Holocaust experiences, or a hometown connection, these new bonds formed the basis of new communities. Within these communities, the newcomers spoke about their painful past and mourned their losses. Talking was not the sole form of expression; they built monuments, created memorial books, and conducted commemorative services. Nor were groups the only avenues through which survivors found their voice in the immediate postwar years. They wrote books and plays and even choreographed modern-dance pieces. The public may not have been receptive, but it was not because survivors were silent. Numerous and varied examples attest to this.

Many survivors who settled in New York turned to hometown social clubs, or *landsmanschaftn*, as a vital source of support. During the wave of immigration that began in the 1880s, Jews from Eastern Europe had established thousands of self-help societies.[15] The membership was made up of *landslayt*, those who came from the same hometown, area, or even country in Europe.[16]

The societies served a variety of functions. They were mutual-aid groups and met a number of important practical needs. They provided medical assistance from an affiliated doctor, financial help to unemployed members, life insurance, sick funds, interest-free loans, funeral arrangements, and a plot in their group's cemetery.

Just as crucial, these organizations offered much in the way of social support. Through informal contacts as well as at dinners, picnics, and other events that the groups organized, they eased the way into American life. They provided safe places where landslayt could hold on to the old country while securing a footing in the new.

From their inception in the late 1800s, the popularity and focus of these associations rose and fell with the needs of their members. By 1920, many immigrants no longer depended on landsmanschaftn as they once had. New activities and goals arose that reflected both the societies' population in America and that of their hometowns in Europe. As the immigrants in the United States aged, for example, they established landsmanschaftn old-age homes for their members. As the situation for Jews worsened in Europe, first during the Great War and then with the rise of Nazism, the American landslayt threw themselves into relief work.[17]

During World War I, the majority of landslayt in America still had strong and direct attachments to the European towns of their birth. Many had parents, siblings, and other close relations living overseas. They responded immediately to the destruction visited upon the Eastern European Jewish communities after the Great War. Societies organized special committees such as the Bialystoker Relief Committee, one subsidiary of the numerous Bialystoker landsmanschaftn, and raised millions of dollars for those back home.[18] This revitalized established groups and sometimes resulted in the creation of new associations. During this time, the greater American Jewish community demonstrated enormous sympathy for the plight of Jewish victims in Europe. The American Jewish Joint Distribution Committee, for example, was born during the Great War to send relief to Jews overseas.[19]

World War II not only infused the landsmanschaftn with a new sense of purpose, it also reasserted its members' bonds with their faraway hometowns. This, however, did not reaffirm an identity with their former communities. "Paradoxically," historian Daniel Soyer has pointed out, "as the hometowns became more central to official *landsmanschaft* activity than they had ever been, the increase in formal contact made society members more conscious of the differences separating them from those they had left behind."[20] The immigrants in America were aware of their growing financial comfort compared to the poverty of their landslayt in Europe. The new-comers were also conscious of a shift in their identity. "During the war," Soyer has noted, "the immigrants came to see themselves clearly as American Jews, a community distinct from those in the countries in Eastern Europe."[21] This distinction would frame the future connection between the Americanized immigrants and the postwar refugee landslayt.

Communication between the societies in America and overseas communities ground to a halt during World War II. Lack of contact with Europe along with American landslayt's diminished emotional connection to their hometowns encouraged a reduction of activity and even collapse of some landsmanschaftn. The Ladies' and Men's Society of Konin was one of many that all but died.[22] Toward the end of the war, a growing knowledge of the murder of European Jewry prompted a flurry of landsmanschaftn activity and the formation of new associations, such as the Kamenetz-Poloder Relief Organization, established in 1944.[23]

After World War II, the societies once again focused on relief work. Most American landsmanschaftn concentrated their initial efforts on assisting landslayt still alive in Europe just as they had after the first World War. The *Grodner*, a newsletter of United Grodner Relief, urged their readers to translate sympathy for Grodno survivors into genuine help. The Passover appeal in March 1948 summoned its members to action:

> $10 WILL FEED ONE HUNGRY GRODNER PERSON FOR 8 DAYS!
>
> The starving Grodner survivor in Germany, Austria, Italy, Poland, France and other places can't eat sympathy! It is our duty . . . YOUR Responsibility . . . to see that the Grodner father, mother and children in Europe's DP Camps will have sufficient FOOD this Passover and after Passover. Too many Passovers have they suffered as Nazi slaves . . . for us to dare neglect them now.
>
> We send food packages and clothing to them, but it isn't enough and besides our treasury is empty.
>
> This Passover the needs are greater. Every $10 donation supplies Kosher food for 8 days of Passover for ONE HUNGRY PERSON. How many needy souls will you provide for? Give today . . . PLEASE![24]

Societies' members responded to the call for help, but it was, at times, with diminished enthusiasm. More Americanized, their connection to and memories of their hometowns grew fainter. "During World War I when the real Grodner *landslayt* of the Independent Grodner Sick Support Society were alive we didn't have to beg them to help Grodno," announced an editor of the society's newsletter, the *Grodner*. "Now, there are new birds and new songs," he poetically entreated his readers in an effort to encourage his audience to help the few surviving, needy landslayt in Europe.[25] While initially slow to respond, the group eventually organized numerous fund-raisers to raise money for the handful of Grodners still alive.

Immediately after World War II, landsmanschaftn helped their DP landslayt in Europe. This soon grew to include those who emigrated to the fledgling Jewish state. In March 1949, the secretary of United Grodno Relief informed its membership that the Federation of Grodner Relief groups (there were at least nine affiliates in New York) had agreed to raise one hundred thousand dollars to build a Grodner kibbutz in Israel.[26] The federation was responding to desperate landslayt in Israel and urged New Yorkers to do the same through memorializing their relatives. "This *Kibbutz* will be in honor of your dead mothers and fathers, sisters and brothers, and all the other members of your family who were murdered by the Germans," the appeal promised.[27] The United Bialystokers, too, supported a Bialystok village in Israel.[28]

While landsmanschaftn, like so many other American Jewish organizations at the time, raised money for their brethren in Israel, other surviving landslayt in need reached the United States and sought out their people. Hiller Bell, current (2003) president of the United Belchatower Assistance Committee, reflected on his first experience with the existing landsmanschaft soon after he arrived. Mr. Bell learned about the American group while still in Europe and met his landslayt shortly after he reached New York in February 1950. "We Belchatowers knew from the other side what's going on in America so we found them and we joined the organization," he recalled.[29] While the clubs attracted DPs in search of connection to their hometowns, the societies' importance had diminished for many Americanized landslayt. The growing number of refugees in New York like Mr. Bell jump-started existing societies, many of which were on the decline or defunct.[30]

While the groups mobilized to send money to Israel, their reception of landslayt in America, who were both part of the surviving remnant of European Jewry and also the last link to their own communities, was mixed. In some cases, the American members of the landsmanschaft did not accept the refugees unconditionally. "In the beginning they didn't have the trust in us," Mr. Bell remembered.[31] Membership in the society required dues so that "you had to earn a living before you became a member," he added. The lack of unconditional acceptance by his fellow Belchatowers that betrayed an absence of sympathy for the newcomers still rankles him more than fifty years later. He noted with some irony that he was not "so happy about it, to say the least . . . I was from Belchatower." In the intervening years, however, Mr. Bell has reflected on the divergent expectations between the old-timers and the DP landslayt. He has come to understand how different the newcomers were from the American Belchatowers and has accepted their early treatment of the DPs. "I think it's natural when you grow up in different circumstances," he explained more than fifty years later.[32]

The experience of survivors who infused the Ladies' and Men's Society of Konin with new energy offers another perspective. The old-timers were no longer involved but then were pleased that newcomers expressed an interest and warmly encouraged the immigrants to carry the Konin torch forward.[33] The new Koniners did so without the help of the old-timers.

Still other survivors formed new groups within established groups. Such was the case with a core of surviving Bialystokers who met at a preexisting Bialystok landsmanschaft. Within the context of the Club of Bialystoker Friends, these survivors promised "to preserve the cultural and spiritual heritage of Bialystok."[34] Thus, some created new survivor organizations within the already existing landsmanschaftn.

The Kamenetz-Poloder Relief Organization, founded in 1944 to help the members' surviving European landslayt, welcomed several newcomers at a meeting in 1947.[35] In the group's bulletin the editor summed up the evening for his readers. "Let's hope that our new *landslayt* will settle down quickly in America and will free themselves from the memories of their horrible existence during the war years."[36] The Americanized hosts expected their new guests to leave the past behind. Rather than freeing new members of their memories, however, many landsmanschaftn became the conduits of memory when the newcomers used them to establish memorial services.

In some cases, survivors felt estranged from the older and more Americanized landslayt. These feelings were often mutual. Just as earlier immigrants felt an attenuation of their identification with hometown relations after World War I, this identification was nearly erased by the end of World War II. Since the average age of survivors in New York was twenty-nine years old, a generation gap also existed.[37] In addition, some European hometowns had drastically changed by the late 1940s from the places old-timers remembered from the 1920s.[38] Some survivors, therefore, created their own societies that were intentionally separate from the old-timers' groups.

The New Cracow Friendship Society was one such group that carefully distinguished itself from an earlier established Cracow Friendship Society.[39] Another was the Sosnowice-Bedzin Society composed entirely of newcomers.[40] The members of groups such as these had no interest in being part of an older landsmanschaftn but preferred to restrict membership to survivors. They felt that being landslayt *and* survivors was necessary for membership because their Holocaust experiences transcended identity based solely on their hometown. Indeed, many survivor landsmanschaftn, like the Sosnowice-Bedzin Society, included members from a general area rather than a specific town.[41] This reinforces the notion that Holocaust experiences, more than hometowns, were the most vital common denominator.

Whether newly formed or recently revamped, landsmanschaftn promised survivors a connection to their lost homes and murdered families. Within these circles, they discovered people who might have known their parents and who, in turn, wanted to learn what had happened to their own relatives. Imagine the joy when a survivor discovered "someone who knew something about the family," remembered Belchatower Hiller Bell. For many newcomers these connections were bonds that symbolized a bridge to both their past and their future. Emphasized Roman Weingarten, president of the New Cracow Friendship Society, "We came together as survivors and as friends; half of us . . . we knew each other from Cracow or we knew the family. You must understand [that] people who came here after the war . . . they had no family. We were each other's families."[42] Indeed, the groups provided structures in which survivors celebrated such occasions as birthdays and holidays with fellow landslayt.[43]

Family connections were paramount, but they were not the only benefit for refugees. One shy twenty-seven-year-old man told his NYANA social worker that he had reluctantly approached a landsmanschaft and found himself accepted warmly. It was, he said, a group of "mostly older men of his parents' generation, some of them remembering his parents or grandparents."[44] He was the youngest man in the group. "It seemed," reported his caseworker, "that the paternal interest that was extended to him was just what Mr. O needed to alleviate some of his fears against [*sic*] strangers."[45] For Mr. O. the group meant forging bonds with people who remembered his family. With that, other considerations also came into play. Mr. O. told his social worker that he had "requested help with employment and not with money and that he had some hope that the men in the *landsmanschaft* would try to be helpful to him in this direction."[46] As this case indicates, refugees sometimes turned to the societies as previous immigrants had for practical help in addition to social contact.

The need to be with other survivors was consuming. In the absence of landsmanschaftn, or where there was no critical mass of landslayt to form a hometown group, the immigrants created alternatives. In such cases, being a survivor, not country of origin, defined one's membership. The New Americans Club, a common form of survivor group, dotted the postwar landscape outside New York.

In 1952, twelve Polish newcomers in Los Angeles banded together to form the 1939 Club, named to commemorate Hitler's invasion of Poland.[47] In Boston, refugees established a New Americans Club in 1951. Denver was home to two clubs: Club 1939 for German Jews who had survived the war in Shanghai and the New Americans Club for those from Eastern Europe.[48] In 1950, newcomers in Indianapolis also created a New Americans Club.[49] Some DPs in Dallas dubbed their association "New Texans."[50] In Kansas City, Missouri newcomers quickly joined together.[51] Refugees in Cleveland, Ohio, formed the Menorah group.[52] In community after community, New Americans Clubs sprang up and took root.

Other kinds of groups also coalesced. In smaller communities, survivors met informally without an official organizational framework. Approximately fifty refugee families in Providence, Rhode Island, for example, congregated in one another's homes on a weekly basis. Heinz Sandelowski (z"1), a German survivor who arrived in 1947, recounted his memories of those early social gatherings nearly fifty years later. "We got together at our houses, every Saturday night at somebody else's house. One brought one record, I think I had a phonograph. This we played together and the next time, another brought a record. We played cards and in the summertime, we went to the ocean or the park. Yes, we got together," he recalled.[53]

Informal meetings occurred even in large cities such as New York where like-minded survivors somehow found one another. Sidi Natansohn, an Auschwitz survivor, described how young adult refugees met regularly at a certain spot on the boardwalk of New York's Brighton Beach. It was there that she met a young man, Sam, whom she later married.[54] Paul Krell, a Polish refugee, began meeting with a small circle of other men in a local coffee shop. Soon it became a regular event.[55] So great was his need to be with other newcomers after his arrival in 1949 that Naftali Lis traveled by train from Hartford, Connecticut, to New York City every Sunday. He recalled going to the temporary refugee hotels in New York in order to be with DPs even if they just "walked the streets together."[56] This need to be with others who share a common past is not unique to survivors, of course. Immigrants commonly socialize, live, and work together. These survivors, however, shared other powerful needs to which their networks soon gave expression.

The desire to be together and re-create communities clearly motivated the formation of their first groups, but many quickly came to address the pressing and complex need to remember. "I promised my father that if I survived I would never forget," emphasized Bernard Sayonne of Denver.[57] Mr. Sayonne's words capture a sentiment that many survivors expressed: the obligation to murdered family members that their son or daughter would remember by telling the world what had happened to their people. Indeed, this promise often became an answer to the question, Why did I alone survive? I survived to remember and to tell.

Translating this need to "tell the world" into meaningful action soon found expression through Jewish rituals of mourning. Because Judaism is a communal religion and its rituals of mourning are performed, in part, within the context of a community, survivor groups thus became the community in which the rituals were performed. Drawing from Jewish tradition, they created many structures through which they took the first steps in remembering and memorializing their traumatic past. Most were collective efforts to put shape and form to their inconsolable grief. The confrontation with the past took many guises. Most were communal; the survivors found some comfort in mutual mourning, in commemorative services, in tangible monuments, and in talking among themselves. Others were individual creative means to give voice to the past.

The rituals provided survivors with a way to articulate both the loss and the need to remember. Many found meaning in the familiarity and comfort of ritual and its link to their vanished world. Religious or not, most felt that the Jewish obligation to say *kaddish* (a mourner's prayer) for a parent, sibling, spouse, or child was simply what one adhered to. Furthermore, the traditional prayers supplied the very words to use; survivors did not have to struggle to find a way to express the vast gulf of their grief.

Yizkor, the memorial service for the departed, was a natural choice. Written centuries ago, the yizkor prayer for Jewish martyrs is chillingly appropriate for Holocaust victims. Its words capture the breadth and depth of genocide: "O God, full of mercy, Who dwells on high, grant proper rest on the wings of the Divine Presence—in the lofty levels of the holy and pure ones, who shine like the glow of the firmament—for the souls of the holy and pure who were killed, murdered, slaughtered, burned, drowned, and strangled."[58] The words of yizkor are significant, as is the manner in which it is chanted. One traditionally recites it in the context of a *minyan*, or quorum, of other mourners. Along with yizkor, survivors also recited the kaddish, which affirms life. Both allow the living to remember a personal loss,

Picnic, new American family and friends (back, from left, Rosa and Henik Abramowicz, Amalie Sandelowski; front, from left, Dora Weinberg, Margarete Sandelowski, Chana Weinberg), July 1954. Courtesy of the Sandelowski family.

but require a community to do so. At the same time, the service provided a framework for survivors to remember entire communities, while simultaneously reciting memorial prayers for murdered families who had no one left alive to say yizkor or kaddish for them.

Survivors from numerous landsmanschaft and New American groups recall that communal yizkor services began as soon as, or very soon after, the groups were established. The services varied somewhat but all seemed to draw their commemorations from Jewish traditions. They followed a simple format: elements of yizkor, the kaddish, and reciting names of family members. Eventually candle-lighting became an integral part of commemoration. In many yizkor services, participants lit six candles (symbolizing six million murdered Jews), which replaced the traditional lighting of one candle on a *yahrzeit* (anniversary date of an individual's death). Doing this also gave a date to those who did not know a family member's *yahrzeit*. The verbal recitation of names was of primary importance to the consecration of a loved one's memory and recurs in other commemorative efforts by survivors.

Traditional Judaism mandates the individual's recitation of yizkor on specific Jewish holidays. Survivors adapted the tradition by saying yizkor on a date that was linked to the murder of European Jewry. The landsmanschaftn typically chose a date for their service that was significant for their community. "Every year the organization [New Cracow Friendship Society] commemorates the liquidation of the ghetto in March 1943," Roman Weingarten explained.[59] "At first we chose August 11 when they sent out all the people from our little ghetto," commented Belchatower Hiller Bell.[60] The Grodners in New York picked the date in March that marked the deportation of their hometown's twenty-nine thousand Jews.[61]

Groups not connected to a specific place chose other significant dates that symbolized the Holocaust for its members. The Denver New Americans Club chose the anniversary of the Warsaw Ghetto Uprising as the annual date for their service.[62] The 1939 Club in Los Angeles did likewise.[63] Still others, such as the Providence group, extrapolated the date from another Jewish tradition. Based on the custom of visiting graves between Rosh Hashana (New Year) and Yom Kippur (the Day of Atonement), they chose a day that fell between the two High Holidays.

Survivors also began to erect monuments to honor their murdered loved ones. While these could never be genuine graves, setting up memorial stones gave many a sense that they had a permanent place for their relatives. Refugees commonly chose a Jewish cemetery in which to situate their monument.

For landsmanschaftn, which counted burial services among its membership benefits, their own cemeteries were the natural place for these structures. "We have a monument for the people who died by the Nazis and every year we go there for yizkor to remember our people" emphasized Mr. Bell of Belchatower.[64]

Providence survivors purchased a plot in the city's Jewish cemetery for their stone. Groups without cemetery space found other locations. The Hillel Academy, an Orthodox Jewish day school in Denver, donated space on their grounds to the New American Club. Beginning in the middle to late 1950s, monuments began to crop up in many cities or towns with a survivor community. The New Cracow Friendship Society erected three stones. "Our first monument that went up has our parents' names," explained Cracower Roman Weingarten. Again, the inclusion of names on a permanent monument is deeply significant. It not only guards against oblivion, but also acts as a symbolic grave for those who have none.

Monuments were by no means the sole tangible expression of memory. A profound and compelling example of survivors' early acts of remembrance are *yizkor bikher* (memorial books), which sprang directly from the landsmanschaftn.[65] Culled from members' collections of photographs, stories, and anecdotes, these books paid homage to the destroyed Jewish world in general, and specific communities in particular. "For Lithuanian Jews, like Jews from all of the murdered communities in Europe," wrote Uriah Katzenelenbogen in the introduction to a two-thousand-page Lithuanian memorial book, "are in mourning."[66] While the content of the great majority of the memorial books focused on chronological descriptions of the life and people of the community, they inevitably ended with survivors' accounts of the final days of their hometown during the *khurbn* (Holocaust).[67]

James Young, a scholar of Holocaust memorials, calls yizkor bikher the first Holocaust memorials. Drawing from the "bookish, iconoclastic side of Jewish tradition," he suggests, survivors created these "interior spaces," rather than physical memorials, as their first monuments to the Holocaust.[68] Historians Jack Kugelmass and Jonathan Boyarin, in their analysis of many of the hundreds of existing memorial books, identify them as "the single most important act of commemorating the dead."[69] Indeed, these books represent a worldwide effort by survivors to give expression to their grief, perhaps, as Young argues, in response to a "missing gravestone syndrome."[70] The memorial book becomes a tangible to which mourners can turn. While the final outcome—a memorial book—is supremely important, the process also addresses another significant dimension of remembrance. Within a short time after arriving in new homes, landslayt collectively responded by meeting, gathering information, and contacting others around the world.

Yizkor books, like the yizkor service, grew from previous Jewish practice. While the postwar yizkor service came from liturgy, the chronicling of a community's existence was a historic tradition. Indeed, the impetus to leave written testimonies to destroyed communities was a longstanding Jewish response that started centuries before the Holocaust.[71] In the midst of persecution, Jews historically drew upon an imperative to record.

Historian Abraham Wein notes that efforts such as the Ringleblum "Oneg Shabbes" archives and other underground attempts to produce a record for the future were the beginning of Holocaust memorialization that came into full force after liberation.[72] But these efforts occurred outside Europe, too. A Lodz landsmanschaft in New York recognized the depths of destruction and created the first official yizkor book to preserve the memory of that city.[73] Published in New York in 1943, it was the work of American landslayt and not of Holocaust survivors.

Immediately after the war, survivors in Europe began the task of collecting data on their hometowns. DPs created historical committees in Munich and Lodz to address this task. Survivor testimonies and documentary material was amassed for the historical record and also because of an immediate and persistent desire to remember. Indeed, a flurry of yizkor books appeared after 1947.[74] The number swelled in the 1960s and continues to this day. A recent yizkor book of the Lithuanian shtetl of Riteve, first published in Hebrew in 1977, was reissued in English by its South African landsmanschaft in 2000.[75]

There are close to eight hundred memorial books in existence that sprang from landsmanschaftn.[76] Some are mere pamphlets, while others are two-thousand-page, multivolume tomes. Just as the size varies so does the quality. Significantly, for the most part they were not written by historians; anyone with an anecdote, story, picture, or document was welcome to participate. In fact, remembering collectively lay at the heart of their success. In any one volume and from book to book the quality ranges from sentimental to scholarly. What they all share is a pledge to remember—before it is too late—for now and for the future. An announcement in bold type appears several times in the pages of the *Bialystoker Memorial Book* urging its readers, "Tell the New Generations of the Holocaust and Resistance."[77] The title page of the Riteve yizkor book includes a quote from Psalms (78:6) that captures the hope of all memorial books: "That the generation to come might know them, even the children that should be born, who should arise and tell them to their children."

As part of this mission to remember, yizkor books include the names of townspeople murdered during the Holocaust. This may assume different formats, but the names of the communities' "martyred" are inevitably inscribed. In some cases, photographs accompany the names. This mirrors the reading of victims' names at yizkor commemorations and also parallels the etching of names on monuments. The need to somehow render the names concrete is profoundly significant for survivors who do not have the graves, dates, or any physical reminder of those who were murdered.

Many of the first books were, by necessity, pooled memories of survivors and American landslayt. In the United Grodner Relief's flier announcing its 1954 yizkor program, a small notice at the bottom of the page called readers' attention to a new project. "We have decided to create a *yizkor* book about Grodno. Do you possibly have Grodno photographs, books, newspapers, magazines, proclamations or letters and other documents and materials?" it asked.[78] In their attempt to record the prewar life of the community, often in minute detail, survivors had to depend on older landslayt for documents as well as reminiscences. In turn, the survivors clearly had the task of describing the destruction of Jewish life in their hometown. The *Konin Memorial Book* affirms, as do many others, the need for this cooperative and interdependent effort between survivors and the older generation of landslayt. Historian Elias Schulman writes that nostalgia and compassion motivated the old-timers to contribute to yizkor books, while the need to recount Holocaust experiences pushed survivors.[79] For different reasons, both groups worked toward creating the memorial books. However, as the years passed, the task fell increasingly to survivors.

While yizkor commemorative services seem ubiquitous, not all landsmanschaftn created yizkor books. The New Cracow Friendship Society holds a memorial service and has erected a monument. It has also published a few small commemorative books including one on Mordechai Gebertig. But the members focused mainly on charity work for Israel. They purchased an ambulance and support a home for soldiers. They also continue to help survivors in Kraków who remained after the war. The group continues to this day (2003) to send funds to the shrinking population of eighty needy Jews there.[80] Numerous landsmanschaftn, in keeping with the goals of the original societies, support poor landslayt in the United States, Israel, and Europe. The Sosnowice-Bedzin group never reached an agreement on a yizkor book. The members help out local landslayt and continue to host memorial services, which now include their children and grandchildren.[81] Keeping the names of the dead in public memory is a deeply felt and ongoing objective among survivor groups that does not wane as time passes. Now it is important that "the younger generation should not forget to pay respects to our *kedoshim*" (holy ones), pronounced Belchatower Hiller Bell.[82]

Some memorial books looked to the future as well as the past. Their primary focus addressed the need for a community's symbolic final resting place. But some groups wished to conclude their books on a note of continuity. The last pages of *The Bialystoker Memorial Book*, for example, are devoted to landslayt activities in locations around the globe. In its final section, titled "Bialystokers All Over the World," there are descriptions of branch activities in the United States, Australia, Argentina, France, and, of course, Eretz Yisrael.[83]

Examples of survivors' literary and artistic works, from the early postwar years, further contradict the notion of silence. The first diary of the Warsaw Ghetto appeared in the United States in 1945 while the war still raged.[84] Before its publication in book form, it was serialized in the Yiddish press.[85] Indeed, many literary responses to the Holocaust first appeared in Yiddish. A *Jewish Book Annual* article surveyed "one hundred Yiddish books on destruction and bravery" from 1949 to 1951, which included some yizkor books as well as memoirs.[86] According to Holocaust scholar Jan Schwartz, more than one hundred works on the Holocaust (representing about 250,000 books) were in circulation by 1954.[87]

Had writing been limited solely to the Yiddish press and, therefore, unknown to most of the American public, the idea that survivors were silent might have more weight. However, this was not the case. Books appeared in English, too. "A number of refugees and others began the process of recording and exploring the harrowing experiences of Nazi persecution in Europe, especially the destruction of Polish Jewry, the situations of the displaced persons, and the migrations to Palestine and elsewhere," wrote Sholom J. Kahn in 1948. His bibliography lists ten books on the subject as compared to seven on the American Jewish community.[88] Memoirs continued to appear as well as other creative responses. Folk and theatrical dancers choreographed pieces based on their experiences and showed them in Jewish venues. Chaja Goldstein, a European dancer, performed her works portraying ghetto life in Eastern Europe, at Jewish centers around the United States in March 1949.

Survivors were by no means silent immediately after the Holocaust. While their American hosts encouraged the newcomers to move on and abandon their traumatic memories, the surviving remnant found this impossible. As they acculturated to American life, refugees joined forces and created a wide range of social networks. These groups became the vehicles in which survivors confronted their painful past and the need to remember. And remember they did. In a world largely apart from American Jews, newcomers talked about their wartime experiences, held yizkor services, erected monuments, and assembled memorial books. Others wrote memoirs and found their voice through creative works. Ample evidence contradicts the myth of silence. Survivors spoke, but few, outside their own circles, took notice.

Conclusion

By mid-1954, annual European Jewish immigration to America had slowed to a trickle. Fewer than seven thousand newcomers arrived that year.[1] USNA, whose offices had bustled in 1949 with a staff of 787, was reduced to 51 people.[2] The agency had outlived its original purpose. It merged with the Hebrew Sheltering and Immigrant Aid Society (HIAS) in August and formed the United HIAS Service. NYANA's doors remained open to its New York clientele, but it also felt the effects of the slowed immigration. Once an agency with 568 employees in 1950, NYANA cut its staff to 46 by the conclusion of 1954.[3] The era of Holocaust survivors' postwar immigration to the United States drew to a close.

Of the surviving remnant of European Jewry, 140,000 immigrated to America. In this study I have explored what happened to those men, women, and children in their first years in America and Americans' first face-to-face confrontation with the Holocaust through those who survived. It illuminates a time before survivors were "survivors" in their own eyes and in those of the greater society and the term "the Holocaust" was yet to become ubiquitous. Their numbers are relatively small, but the impact of this group transcends the statistic. And its impact grows even as the numbers shrink.

If the only impressions we had of their reception were gleaned from contemporary media reports and Jewish organizations' accounts, or from the place of honor that survivors hold in our society today, we would be led to believe that America had welcomed survivors warmly and the refugees had acclimated without delay. It is a comforting thought from many perspectives. But, unfortunately, it is false.

The experience of Holocaust survivors in America has generally been narrated as a victory. The mere ability to go on living has been viewed as ample proof of their triumph over Hitler. Such blanket statements veil important issues. As *Case Closed* shows, the postwar reality was exceedingly complicated. For many survivors, this era was imbued with vast and irrevocable loss. Through the focus on an external and uniformly happy ending, the complex and arduous period immediately after the Holocaust has been trivialized, minimized, obscured. It has been reinvented into a story that is comforting but untrue.

This myth hides another painful truth. It masks the way that survivors were treated when they arrived in America. How can we understand a survivor confined to life after Auschwitz in a state asylum? An orphan banished from a foster family's home? The downward spiraling of a family when its case was closed because the year of agency support was up? A new arrival waiting at the dock for a sponsor who never shows? These are not stories of triumph or welcome.

Undoubtedly, these postwar immigrants presented an enormous challenge to their hosts, battered as they were in body and spirit. The Jewish communities' response to the Holocaust survivors in America, however, was shaped by other concerns and other receptions in immigration history. But these new Americans were unlike any immigrants before them.

This was the surviving remnant of the Holocaust's obliteration; that tiny fraction still alive after *the* cataclysmic event of the twentieth century. That is precisely why, presented with the opportunity, the communities and individuals should have responded differently. Giving short-term material relief and pushing the DPs to work privileged the agencies' agenda first and the survivors' needs second. On both the community and the personal level, this pattern was repeated; it was the survivors' needs that were secondary.

Conventional wisdom holds that the survivors themselves wanted to move on, forget their past, live normal lives after the chaos they had recently experienced. And that their memories were too raw, too painful, to confront. They repressed them, the accepted account insists, and forged ahead, becoming successful "survivors." But *Case Closed* shows otherwise. Yes, many survivors did go forward, but it was hardly a seamless progression. There were those whose energy was depleted. There were those whose grief prevailed. Even when survivors seemed to be acculturating according to plan, a host of ailments cropped up unbidden. Births, eagerly anticipated, evoked loss that could not be staved off. Other pitfalls materialized. The road was bumpy and fraught with dangers. Over and over, survivors emphasize the difficulty rather than the ease that characterized this period.

Despite what refugees felt, despite the enormous bureaucratic efforts, the world around them was largely unsympathetic to the pain they harbored. Other concerns occupied people's attention. America was caught up in the postwar mood and anxious to leave World War II behind. After all, the refugees were not the only ones who had been in Europe. American troops returned to civilian life, eager to rejoin society. And it was expected that the newcomers, grateful to be in the United States, would do the same.

The postwar Jewish community was growing increasingly part of the American mainstream yet mindful of the virulent antisemitism of the earlier part of the decade. The refugees, as had immigrants before them, threatened the host community. Not just because they flocked to the main urban centers and competed for jobs, but also because they embodied the old-world sensibilities that the American-born Jewish community eschewed. Some claimed that they could not confront survivors because of guilt. They distanced themselves from this tangible reminder that they had been safe in America, had been spared Hitler's wrath, while European Jewry burned. Others simply did not believe the depths of the Holocaust's atrocities. Some simply did not want the burden of relatives they did not know or care to know.

Given the host of factors, could the reception of Holocaust survivors in America have been otherwise? Yes. Because in a few instances it was different, very different. Even exceptional. The examples of Columbia, South Carolina; Jewish Family and Children's Services, Boston; and the San Francisco sheltered workshop show that other, more generous practices were possible. Survivors mention individuals who reached out. Acts of kindness evoked deep gratitude. Sadly, these were the anomalies rather than the norm.

This subjugation of survivors' needs communicated to them that what they had experienced was inconsequential. Yes, survivors needed financial help, but they needed, wanted, and merited more. Despite the fact that these people had endured the Holocaust, the American community chose to see the newcomers as new Americans, *not* as survivors of genocide. In the immediate aftermath of the tragedy it was expedient to forget this essential fact; indeed, to erase it, when possible. The tragedy was effaced by the emphasis on the newcomers' successful acculturation, which eased the conscience of Americans but ignored survivors' deeper needs. The country wanted to see the refugees as such fade quickly into the community. No one cared to know them as Holocaust survivors.

This perception changed radically, beginning in the 1960s. Scholars credit the Eichmann trial as the turning point. It brought simmering agendas to the fore and forced a confrontation between survivors and the world. Curious, hostile, or indifferent before, our society became receptive to a new accounting of the catastrophe. Soon refugees became "survivors." The murder of European Jewry became the Holocaust—not a subject to shun, but the opposite: a torch that lit the center of our ethical universe. It pervaded our vocabulary and became a moral compass, the standard by which other atrocities are judged. For the vast majority of the Jewish community, the genocide of its people was embraced eagerly as a cornerstone of its identity. The Holocaust also materialized and flourished on the cultural landscape. Films and television programs on the subject proliferated. Music composed in ghettos and camps was heard once again in concert halls. Novels and memoirs multiplied. Museums were built to tell the story of "man's inhumanity to man."

Recording survivors' accounts became important, deeply so. First called *oral histories* and eventually *video testimonies*, this shift in nomenclature signaled their value, as the witnesses' legacy to the world, and defined our society as the grateful heir apparent. Survivors, once a cause for embarrassment, were recast as heroes, the title a badge of honor. Is it any wonder that survivors, finally welcomed, eagerly seized this transformation? It cast their past in a new and validating light and provided an opportunity to fulfill their obligation to "tell the world." Their survival, we are often reminded, is "testament to the human spirit," and many survivors found comfort in this redemptive message and became its emissaries. This cemented the narrative of hope and human potential for endurance and triumph rather than one of annihilation.

This narrative, now convention, was set in survivors' first years here. The spotlight was on their smooth transition from refugee to New American, while the manifestations of their survivorship were relegated to the shadows. It is troubling, indeed shocking, to examine the files from the mid-twentieth century and feel the weight of survivors' distress pressing on them while the media trumpeted their success. The reports are a glimpse into that universe where the Holocaust was very much a presence for the survivors but still a distant planet to the rest of the world. Unconstrained by any heroic notion of this population, their helpers wrote without preconceptions. Most striking is how completely the newcomers were perceived as newcomers or even refugees, but not survivors of the unprecedented tragedy they had so recently endured. These records stand in sharp relief to the focus on Holocaust experiences and the identity of the survivors as survivors, captured in later oral histories and video testimonies.

Postwar testimonies echo the distress that runs through the earlier accounts. But, as Americans did earlier, we choose to see and identify with other aspects and ignore what seems to be blatantly before us: the survivor's postwar career or children and grandchildren, for example, as emblematic of the human ability to endure rather than the lingering despair. We, in the words of Holocaust scholar Lawrence Langer, "change the impact of a disastrous event simply by renaming it."[4]

Many survivors, of course, are spectacularly successful financially, educationally, and personally. Some would not agree to be interviewed about their reception in the United States. They believe their recollections would throw a negative light on their American relatives and their story. That they were treated shabbily—or worse—is an uncomfortable splinter in their memory, best left untouched.

If the myriad testimonies in which survivors speak candidly about the black thread of the Holocaust—about the effort that goes into getting out of bed in the morning or the inability to be happy—do not convince, we have only to read the reports of Jewish organizations to learn that not all Holocaust survivors leave us a legacy of hope.[5] Many have never been able to put their lives in order. Thousands living in this country are below the poverty line and are in dire need of assistance.[6] They are hidden from the public eye. How do we fit them into the triumphant narrative? We cannot. We do not want to hear stories that offer a conflicting or contrary message, that whisper of the possibility not of triumph but of defeat. Once again, this is relegated to the shadows.

NOTES

Introduction

1. *New Neighbors* (New York: United Service for New Americans), May 1950, 3.
2. Leonard Dinnerstein, *America and the Survivors of the Holocaust* (New York: Columbia University Press, 1982), 288.
3. Ibid., 113.
4. There were exceptions made for orphans during the war, which allowed them to come to the United States on corporate sponsorship.

CHAPTER 1 *What to Do with the DPs?*

1. The terms *DP, refugee, newcomer,* and *immigrant* are words that reflect the period of this study. I use them interchangeably with *survivor,* a term that is widely used today but did not become part of our vocabulary until the 1960s.
2. For a contemporary demographic analysis of Jewish DPs and DP camps, see Kurt Grossman, *The Jewish DP Problem: Its Origin, Scope, and Liquidation* (New York: Institute of Jewish Affairs, 1951). For description of life and culture in the DP camps, see Menachem Rosensaft, ed., *Life Reborn: Jewish Displaced Persons, 1945–1951* (proceedings of the "Life Reborn" conference, United States Holocaust Memorial Museum, Washington, DC, 2001) and Susan Bachrach, ed., *Liberation 1945* (Washington, DC: United States Holocaust Memorial Museum, 1995). For background on the DP question that includes, but is not limited to, Jewish DPs, see Mark Wyman, *DPs: Europe's Displaced Persons, 1945–1951* (Ithaca: Cornell University Press, 1998), part 1; Haim Genizi, *America's Fair Share: The Admission and Resettlement of Displaced Persons, 1945–1952* (Detroit: Wayne State University Press, 1933).
3. Letter from Moses Auerbach to the *Forverts,* 14 November 1945, Box 49, File 108, Record Group I-065, American Jewish Historical Society.
4. On the White Paper, see Aaron Berman, *Nazism, the Jews, and American Zionism* (Detroit: Wayne State University Press, 1990), 66–70; Arieh Kochavi, *Post-Holocaust Politics: Britain, the U.S., and Jewish Refugees, 1945–1948* (Chapel

Hill: University of North Carolina Press, 2001), 60–64; Michael Marrus, *The Unwanted: European Refugees in the Twentieth Century* (Oxford: Oxford University Press, 1985), 152–153, 274–276.

5. On the Harrison Report, see Leonard Dinnerstein, *America and the Survivors of the Holocaust* (New York: Columbia University Press, 1982), 38–71; Wyman, *DPs*, 135–136; Genizi, *America's Fair Share*, 29.

6. From the Harrison Report, as seen in Dinnerstein, *America and the Survivors*, 300.

7. Benjamin Shwadran, "Zionist and Pro-Palestine Activities," in *American Jewish Year Book, 1946–1947*, vol. 48 (Philadelphia: Jewish Publication Society, 1948), 228–229. On the Anglo-American Committee of Inquiry, see Naomi Cohen, *American Jews and the Zionist Idea* (New York: KTAV, 1975), 73–78; Dinnerstein, *America and the Survivors*, chap. 3; Kochavi, *Post-Holocaust Politics*, 103–113; Peter Grose, *Israel in the Mind of America* (New York: Alfred A. Knopf, 1983), 202–205; Michael Cohen, *Palestine and the Great Powers* (Princeton: Princeton University Press, 1982).

8. Shwadran, "Zionist and Pro-Palestine Activities," 243.

9. On the history of American Zionism during and after World War II, see Berman, *Nazism, Jews, and American Zionism*; Cohen, *American Jews*; Samuel Halperin, *The Political World of American Zionism* (Detroit: Wayne State University Press, 1961); Melvin Urofsky, *American Zionism from Herzl to the Holocaust* (Garden City, NY: Anchor Press, 1976).

10. Halperin, *Political World*, 327.

11. Shwadran, "Zionist and Pro-Palestine Activities," 242.

12. "1948 Destiny Campaign, UJA of Greater Washington," *Washington Post*, 11 April 1948, M19.

13. Ibid.

14. In Melvin Urofsky, *We Are One: American Jewry and Israel* (Garden City, NY: Doubleday, 1978), 107.

15. Ibid., 233–234.

16. Leonard Dinnerstein, *Antisemitism in America* (Oxford: Oxford University Press, 1994), 160–161.

17. Joshua Trachtenberg, "Religious Activities," in *American Jewish Year Book, 1945–1946*, vol. 47 (Philadelphia: Jewish Publication Society, 1945), 225–226.

18. From the Harrison Report, as seen in Gil Loescher and John Scanlan, *Calculated Kindness: Refugees and America's Half-Open Door, 1945 to the Present* (New York: Free Press, 1986), 5.

19. Ibid.

20. As quoted in Dinnerstein, *America and the Survivors*, 113.

21. [American Jewish Committee], "Immigration and Refugee Aid," in *American Jewish Year Book, 1946–1947*, vol. 48 (Philadelphia: Jewish Publication Society, 1949), 219.

22. It gave preference to orphans, many of whom were Jewish. See Chapter 5.

23. *American Jewish Year Book, 1946–1947*, vol. 48 (Philadelphia: Jewish Publication Society, 1948), 218–220.

24. Ibid.

25. Ibid.

26. Sidney Liskofsky, "Jewish Migration," in *American Jewish Yearbook, 1948–1949*, vol. 50 (Philadelphia: Jewish Publication Society, 1949), 751–752.
27. Lyman Cromwell White, *300,000 New Americans* (New York: Harper, 1957).
28. Liskofsky, "Jewish Migration," 751–752.
29. The only precedent to this was the U.S. Committee for the Care of European Children, which was the first agency permitted to grant corporate affidavits during the war years.
30. White, *300,000 New Americans*, 73.
31. Dinnerstein, *America and the Survivors*, 114.
32. Ibid., 101.
33. Leonard Dinnerstein, "America, Britain, and Palestine: The Anglo-American Committee of Inquiry and the Displaced Persons, 1945–1946," *Diplomatic History* 4 (Summer 1980): 283–302.
34. Harry Truman, "Special Message to the Congress on Admission of Displaced Persons," 7 July 1947, Public Papers of the Presidents, available from www.trumanlibrary.org.
35. Maurice Davie, "Immigration and Refugee Aid," *American Jewish Yearbook, 1948–1949*, vol. 50, 232–233.
36. Many Jewish DPs, traveling first to their former homes, arrived in the American zone after the pogroms of summer 1946. Others entered from other zones after that date.
37. Davie, "Immigration and Refugee Aid," 234.
38. Ibid.
39. Ibid., 234–236.
40. Walter Laqueur, ed., *Encyclopedia of the Holocaust* (New Haven: Yale University Press, 2001), 157; Wyman, *DPs*, chap. 6; *Historical Atlas of the Holocaust* (New York: Macmillan, 1996), 217.
41. Dinnerstein, *America and the Survivors*, 288. These figures agree with USNA and NYANA statistics.
42. Maurice Goldblum, "Western Europe," in *American Jewish Yearbook, 1946–1947*, vol. 48, 294, 300, 316.
43. Yehuda Bauer, paper read at the Life Reborn Conference, United States Holocaust Memorial Museum, Washington, DC, January 1999.
44. Heinz Sandelowski, interview by the author, tape recording, Providence, RI, 9 March 2000.
45. Ibid.
46. H. E., Letter to the JDC, 15 July 1948, NYANA Case File 290, NYANA Archive.
47. White, *300,000 New Americans*, 78.
48. Ibid.
49. NYANA Case File 269, NYANA Archive.
50. Amalie Sandelowski, interview by the author, tape recording, Providence, RI, 3 March 2000.
51. Mildred Faulk, "Modern-Day Pilgrims Happy," *New York Daily Sun*, 25 November 1947.
52. White, *300,000 New Americans*, 211.
53. Ibid., 79.

54. Ibid.
55. Davie, "Immigration and Refugee Aid," 227.
56. White, *300,000 New Americans*, 158–159.
57. Ibid., 166–167.
58. "How the Job Is Being Done: Report of the Executive Director to the Annual Meeting," Address by Edwin Rosenberg, President of USNA, Annual Meeting, 10–11 January 1948, New York, YIVO Institute for Jewish Research Archives, RG 246, Roll 1, File 16.
59. Financial Needs of United Service as presented at United Service for New Americans' Annual Meeting, January 1948, New York, YIVO Institute for Jewish Research Archives, RG 246, Roll 1, File 16.
60. USNA survey, quoted in White, *300,000 New Americans*, 83–84.
61. Edwin Rosenberg, USNA Annual Meeting, 8 January 1948, New York, YIVO Institute for Jewish Research Archives, RG 246, MKM 24.1, File 16.
62. White, *300,000 New Americans*, 157.
63. "Demographic Characteristics of the Recent Jewish Immigrant," NYANA Executive Report, 1950, NYANA Executive Meetings, 1950, NYANA Archive.
64. Ibid.
65. Ibid., 2.
66. Ibid.
67. Ibid.
68. S. L. Shneiderman, ed., *Warsaw Ghetto: A Diary by Mary Berg* (New York: Fischer, 1945).
69. Esther Elbaum, "An Interview with Mary Berg," *Hadassah Newsletter*, March–April 1945, 20–25.
70. "Relative Hunted Here by Refugee," *New York Times*, 23 March 1949, 9.
71. "Missing Relative Found Block Away," *New York Times*, 25 March 1949, 6.
72. "Two Young Survivors of Nazidom Wed," *New York Times*, 28 October, 1949, 15.
73. "Blind D.P. and Dog Find a Haven Here," *New York Times*, 25 April 1952, 14.
74. "Nazi Brutality Victims Are Reunited Here," *Washington Post*, 4 May 1953, 25.
75. *Kapelye; On the Air*, produced by Henry Sapoznik Shanachie Entertainment, 1995.
76. In Joyce Antler, "Yesterday's Woman, Today's Moral Guide: Molly Goldberg as Jewish Mother," in *Key Texts in American Jewish Culture*, ed. Jack Kugelmass (New Brunswick: Rutgers University Press, 2003), 139–140.

CHAPTER 2   *Welcome to America!*

1. "813 European DPs Arrive in New York," *Washington Post*, 31 October 1948, M4.
2. Memo to Field Staff from Joseph Beck, Executive Director, USNA, 5 November 1948, American Jewish Joint Distribution Committee (JDC) Archives, JDC Collection, 1945–1964, File 4027.
3. NYANA Executive Report, 27 November 1950, NYANA Archive.
4. Frank Auerbach, *The Admission and Resettlement of Displaced Persons in the United States* (New York: Common Council for American Unity, 1950), 14–18.
5. Conversation with the author, New York City, 6 November 2002.

6. "The Problems of Controlling Immigration to Assure a Reasonable Quota for New York City, and Sound Case-Work Policy," Meeting of Board of NYANA Directors, 6 December 1951, NYANA Executive Meetings, NYANA Archive.

7. Ibid.

8. C. Klein-Polak, RG-50.549.02*0012, 24 February 1998, Postwar Testimonies, United States Holocaust Memorial Museum (USHMM) Archives.

9. Minutes, USNA Staff Meeting, 26 April 1950, in White, *300,000 New Americans*, 147.

10. Rabbi Isaac Trainin, interview by the author, tape recording, New York, 11 April 2002.

11. Ben Seligman and Harvey Swados, "Jewish Population Studies in the United States," *American Jewish Year Book, 1948–1949*, vol. 50 (Philadelphia: Jewish Publication Society, 1948), 667, 683, 717 (based on the 1940 census).

12. Ronald Sanders, *Shores of Refugee: A Hundred Years of Jewish Emigration* (New York: Schocken Books, 1988), 239–240. See also Mark Wischnitzer, *Visas to Freedom: The History of HIAS* (New York: World, 1956), 60–61, 66.

13. Wischnitzer, *Visas to Freedom*, 60.

14. "The Problems of Controlling Immigration to Assure a Reasonable Quota for New York City, and Sound Case-Work Policy," Report to NYANA Board, 6 December 1951, NYANA Archive.

15. Dinnerstein, *America and Survivors of the Holocaust*, 183.

16. Letter to Jewish Organizations from Joseph Beck, Executive Director, USNA, 20 February 1948, JDC Archives, JDC Collection, 1945–1964, File 4027.

17. Memo to Field Staff from Joseph Beck, 5 November 1948, JDC Archives, JDC Collection.

18. *New Neighbors* 2 (May 1949): 1.

19. Ibid.

20. Letter to Emil Saloman, Director, Tulsa Jewish Federation from Al Meyers, USNA Field Representative, 13 July 1949, JDC Archives, JDC Collection, 1945–1964, File 405.

21. "Communities Get Plea to Aid D.P.'s, William Rosenwald Declares Jewish Groups Must Act Now to Help on Jobs, Housing," *New York Times*, 20 November 1949, 9.

22. Settlements of USNA Assisted Arrivals, 31 December 1949, YIVO Institute for Jewish Research Archives, RG 246.1, Folder 1633.

23. *American Jewish Year Book, 1948–1949*, vol. 50 (Philadelphia: Jewish Publication Society, 1948), 671 (1940 census).

24. Based on agreed quota and number of case files in JFCS, Denver's collection.

25. Letter to Arthur Greenleigh, Executive Director, USNA, from A. Neumann, Executive Director, JFCS, Denver, 10 January 1951, YIVO Institute for Jewish Research Archives, RG 246, MKM 24.30.

26. Letter to Beatrice Behrman, Director of Resettlement, USNA, from Alfred Neumann, Executive Director, JFCS, Denver, 20 June 1951, YIVO Institute for Jewish Research Archives, RG 246, MKM 24.30.

27. Ibid.

28. Record Group I-065, Box 21, File 1852, JFCS, Denver, American Jewish Historical Society.

29. Report by R. Ross, Casework Supervisor, Record Group I-065, Box 21, File 1852, JFCS, Denver, American Jewish Historical Society.

30. Letter from R. Ross, Casework Supervisor, JFCS, to B. Behrman, USNA, 31 August 1951, Record Group I-065, Box 21, File 1852, JFCS, Denver, American Jewish Historical Society.

31. Letter from B. Behrman to R. Ross, 18 September 1951, Record Group I-065, Box 21, File 1852, JFCS, Denver, American Jewish Historical Society.

32. Ibid.

33. Letter to Beatrice Behrman, Director of Resettlement, USNA, from Alfred Neumann, Executive Director, JFCS, Denver, 6 December 1951, YIVO Institute for Jewish Research Archives, RG 246, MKM 24.30, File 707.

34. Ibid.

35. Letter from Emil Saloman to AL Meyers, USNA Field Representative, 6 July 1949, JDC Archives, JDC Collection, 1945–1964, File 405.

36. Ibid.

37. Letter to Edwin Rosenberg, USNA President, from E. Saloman, Tulsa, 30 May 1949, JDC Archives, JDC Collection, 1945–1964, File 405.

38. Ibid.

39. Letter to Edwin Rosenberg, USNA President, from E. Saloman, Tulsa, 20 April 1950, JDC Archives, JDC Collection, 1945–1964, File 405.

40. Letter to Walter Bieringer, President, USNA, from Sons of Israel Congregation, Philipsburg, PA, 15 May 1950, YIVO Institute for Jewish Research Archives, RG 246.1, MKM 24.60, File 1455.

41. "A Primer in Resettlement for Small Communities," *New Neighbors* 2 (May 1949): 4–5.

42. Ibid.

43. Columbia Field Reports to USNA, 1950, YIVO Institute for Jewish Research Archives, RG 246, MKM 24.53, File 1333.

44. Letter from Dena Banks to Milton Krochmal, Community Relations Department, USNA, 30 March 1950, YIVO Institute for Jewish Research Archives, RG 246, MKM 24.53, File 1333.

45. Hannah Rubin, telephone conversation with the author, 28 January 2002.

46. Ibid.

47. Ibid.

48. Bluma G., telephone conversation with the author, 30 January 2002.

49. Ibid.

50. Bluma G., "Interview by Survivors of the Shoah Visual History Foundation," Columbia, South Carolina, 18 June 1998, University of Southern California Shoah Foundation Institute for Visual History and Education, 43565, 3:18:05.

51. USNA Field Report, Columbia, South Carolina, by Albert Meyers, 29 September 1949, YIVO Institute for Jewish Research Archives, RG 246, MKM 24.53, File 1332.

52. Bluma G., telephone conversation.

53. Record Group I-065, Box 31, File 745, JFCS, Denver, American Jewish Historical Society.

54. Ibid.

55. Record Group I-065, Box 9, File 1943, JFCS, Denver, American Jewish Historical Society.

56. Record Group I-065, Box 18, File 1467, JFCS, Denver, American Jewish Historical Society.

57. Record Group I-065, Box 31, File 745, JFCS, Denver, American Jewish Historical Society.

58. Record Group I-065, Box 9, File 1943, JFCS, Denver, American Jewish Historical Society.

59. "The Problem of Controlling Immigration to Assure a Reasonable Quota for New York City, and Sound Case-Work Policy," Meeting of Board of Directors, 6 December 1951, NYANA Executive Meetings, NYANA Archive, 2.

60. Ibid.

61. NYANA Case File 389-51, NYANA Archive.

62. NYANA Case File 420-52, NYANA Archive.

63. NYANA Case File 324-49, NYANA Archive.

64. A. Beer, RG-50.091*0005, 7 November 1984, Oral History Project of the National Council of Jewish Women, Cleveland, USHMM Archives.

65. NYANA Case File 419-51, NYANA Archive.

66. NYANA Case File 390-51, NYANA Archive.

67. NYANA Case File 398-51, NYANA Archive.

68. P. K., interview with the author, Bronx, New York, 7 March 2002.

69. N. G., conversation with the author, Washington, DC, 15 March 2005.

70. NYANA Case File 361-50, NYANA Archive.

71. B. Senders, RG 50-549.02*0011, 22 February 1998, Postwar Testimonies, USHMM Archives.

72. C. Klein-Polak, RG-50.549.02*0012, 24 February 1998, Postwar Testimonies, USHMM Archives.

73. Ibid.

74. M. C., conversation with the author, New York, 17 November 2002.

75. Ibid.

76. F. Fritzshall, RG-50.549.02*0020, 22 September 1998, Postwar Testimonies, USHMM Archives.

77. R. Slivka, RG-50.549.02*0026, 22 October 1998, Postwar Testimonies, USHMM Archives.

CHAPTER 3   *Case Closed*

1. "A Summing Up," *New Neighbors* 3 (1950): 4.

2. Ibid.

3. White, *300,000 New Americans*, 21.

4. Address by NYANA President A. Askin, NYANA Second Annual Meeting, 5 April 1951, Executive Board Meetings, NYANA Archive.

5. Press Release, 21 June 1949, NYANA Publicity, 1949, NYANA Archive.

6. Josh Friedland, *The Lamp beside the Golden Door: The Story of NYANA* (New York: NYANA, 1999), 20.

7. Ibid., 46–47.

8. NYANA, Statement of Services and Functions, 17 February 1950, 16, NYANA Administrative Records, NYANA Archive.

9. NYANA Case File 365-50, NYANA Archive.

10. Report to the Executive Board, 21 September 1950, 2, NYANA Board Meetings, 1950, NYANA Archive.

11. Ibid.

12. "The Use of Limits in NYANA Casework Practice," in Executive Report, 8 November 1951, 2, NYANA Board Meetings, 1951, NYANA Archive.

13. "Demographic Characteristics of the Recent Jewish Immigrant," 24 May 1950, Executive Report, NYANA Board Meetings, 1950, NYANA Archive.

14. Report to the Council of Jewish Federations, November 1953, NYANA Administrative Records, 1953, NYANA Archive.

15. NYANA Case File 401-51, NYANA Archive.

16. Ibid.

17. Ibid.

18. NYANA Case File 365-50, 1, NYANA Archive.

19. Ibid.

20. Ibid.

21. According the U.S. Bureau of Labor and Statistics, the national unemployment rate rose from 3.8 percent in 1948 to 5.9 percent in 1949. It remained at more than 5 percent in 1950 and returned to 3.3 percent in 1951. City unemployment records were not recorded at the time, but comments such as those in this case files and numerous others about finding work (and subsequent layoffs) reflect fluctuations in the national statistics.

22. NYANA Case File 430-53, NYANA Archive.

23. Ibid.

24. Monthly Statistical Report to the Board of Directors, January 1951, NYANA Board Meetings, 1951, NYANA Archive.

25. Ibid.

26. Ibid.

27. "VSD Program," 30 March 1950, NYANA Archive, cited in Friedland, *Lamp beside the Golden Door*, 24.

28. *Inside NYANA* 1, no. 6 (28 December 1950): 2, NYANA Internal Publicity, NYANA Archive.

29. Ibid.

30. "From Relief Rolls to Pay Rolls," in Report to the Executive Board, 21 September 1950, 2, NYANA Board Meetings, 1950, NYANA Archive.

31. Monthly Statistical Report to Board of Directors, January 1951, NYANA Archive.

32. "DPs Learn as They Earn," *New Neighbors* 3 (1950): n.p.

33. "The San Francisco Utility Workshop for the Aged and Handicapped," *Jewish Social Service Quarterly* (Winter 1952): 148–151. This paper was prepared by the staff of the San Francisco Committee for Service to Émigrés.

34. "Descriptions of Typical Beginning Jobs for Immigrants," YIVO Institute for Jewish Research Archives, RG 246.1, Folder 1717, 1–9.

35. NYANA Case File BB-49, NYANA Archive.

36. Ibid.

37. *American Jewish Yearbook* 1950, 53, 60.
38. NYANA Case File MN-49, NYANA Archive.
39. Ibid. (Mr. Finkelstein is a pseudonym.)
40. Ibid.
41. Ibid.
42. NYANA Monthly Statistical Report, February 1950, NYANA Archive.
43. Board Meeting Minutes, JFCS, Denver, February 1951, YIVO Institute for Jewish Research Archives, RG 246, MKM 24.53, File 705.
44. Ibid.
45. "Major Job Occupations among Displaced Persons in Relation to Agency Assurances," Problems of Distribution of Refugees, YIVO Institute for Jewish Research Archives, RG 246.1, Folder 1717.
46. Letter from Dr. Alfred Neumann, JFCS, Denver, to Verna Salkind, USNA Migration Services, 16 January 1950, Record Group I-065, Box 39, 1090, JFCS, Denver, American Jewish Historical Society.
47. Ibid.
48. Letter from Alfred Neumann, JFCS, to Migrations Services, USNA, 10 July 1953, Record Group I-065, Box 39, 1090, JFCS, Denver, American Jewish Historical Society.
49. Reports by B. L. and R. R., 16 June 1951–30 April 1955. Record Group I-065, Box 16, (no file number), JFCS, Denver, American Jewish Historical Society.
50. Ibid.
51. Ibid., 3a.
52. Report by S. J., 11 April 1949, Record Group I-065, Box 26, File 897, 2, JFCS, Denver, American Jewish Historical Society.
53. Reports by S. J., A. K., A. N., 3 January 1950–3 October 1951, Record Group I-065, Box 17 (no file number) JFCS, Denver, American Jewish Historical Society.
54. Ibid.
55. Report by S. J., 11 April 1949, Record Group I-065, Box 6, File 2433, JFCS, Denver, American Jewish Historical Society.
56. Ibid.
57. Letter by J. G. to C. R., social worker, 8 June 1948, Box 6, File 2433, JFCS, Denver, American Jewish Historical Society.

CHAPTER 4   *"Bearded Refugees"*

1. Jack Roth, "DP Rabbi, Family Dock, Full of Joy," *New York Times*, 6 April 1949, 16.
2. Ibid.
3. Report by B. G., 5 August 1954, Record Group I-065, JFCS, Denver, Box 20, (Rabbi F., no file number), American Jewish Historical Society.
4. For a discussion of the Vaad Hatzala's postwar work with DPs, see Alex Grobman, *Battling for Souls* (Jersey City, NJ: KTAV, 2004).
5. NYANA, Statement of Services and Functions, 18.
6. When NYANA was created in 1949, the RFD was absorbed by the new agency
7. Gilbert Klaperman, *The Story of Yeshiva University: The First Jewish University in America* (New York: Macmillan, 1969); Deborah Dash Moore, *At Home in*

America (New York: Columbia University Press, 1981), 178–180. For an overview of American Orthodox Judaism, see Jeffrey Gurock, *American Jewish Orthodoxy in Historical Perspective* (Hoboken, NJ: KTAV, 1985).

8. Rabbi Isaac Trainin, interview by the author, tape recording, New York, 11 April 2002.

9. Ibid.

10. "DP Rabbis Studying Here: Teachers Also to Be Prepared for Jobs in Schools in U.S.," *New York Times*, 23 February 1949, 24.

11. Ibid.

12. Rabbi Trainin, interview.

13. Ibid.

14. Ibid.

15. Ibid.

16. "Regarding Refugee Rabbis," *Jewish Morning Journal*, New York, 1 July 1949.

17. Characteristics of the Caseload of the Religious Functionary Division, USNA Division of Research and Statistics, June 1948, YIVO Institute for Jewish Research Archives, RG 246, MKM 24.23, File 1840.

18. Letter to the American Consul in Shanghai, China, from Rabbi Rothenberg, JDC Archives, JDC Collection, 1945–1964, File 4114.

19. Letter to Joseph Beck, Executive Director of USNA, from Harold Silver, Executive Director, Detroit Resettlement Service, 26 August 1946, JDC Archives, JDC Collection, 1945–1964, File 4114.

20. Sylvia Bernice Fleck Abrams, "Searching for a Policy: Attitudes and Policies of Non-governmental Agencies toward the Adjustment of Jewish Immigrants of the Holocaust Era, 1933–1953, as Reflected in Cleveland, Ohio" (unpublished PhD diss., Case Western Reserve University, 1988), 209–232.

21. USNA Executive Committee Meeting Report to JDC and UPA, 30 June 1947, YIVO Institute for Jewish Research Archives, RG 246.1, Box 11, File 1694.

22. Meeting of Policy Committee on Questions Relating to the Religious Functionary Division (emphasis in original), YIVO Institute for Jewish Research Archives, RG 246.1, 1695, p. 29, June 1948.

23. Letter to Charles Jordan, Executive Director, JDC, Paris, 1 July 1949, JDC Archives, JDC Collection, 1945–1964, File 1307.

24. NYANA, *Statement of Purpose*, 21.

25. NYANA Case File 362-50, 1, NYANA Archive.

26. Minutes of the Meeting of the Religious Functionary Committee, 1 December 1949, Executive Minutes, 1, NYANA Archive.

27. Ibid.

28. This policy mandated that able-bodied DPs were entitled to a maximum of one year of relief. See Chapter 3.

29. NYANA Case File 312-49, NYANA Archive.

30. Ibid.

31. NYANA Case File 340-49, NYANA Archive.

32. Ibid., 6.

33. NYANA Case File 312-49, NYANA Archive.

34. Most, but not all, religious functionaries were male. *Bearded refugees* was the term NYANA used euphemistically for Orthodox men.
35. NYANA Case File 320-49, NYANA Archive.
36. Letter to members of United Popular Dress Manufacturers Association from Executive Director, Nat Boriskin, 21 August 1950, NYANA Archive.
37. Report of United Job Finding Campaign, 22 December 1950, 1, NYANA Archive.
38. Ibid., 11.
39. L. L., interview with the author, New York, 12 February 2002.
40. Ibid.
41. NYANA Case File 220-49, NYANA Archive.
42. NYANA Case File 318-49, NYANA Archive
43. NYANA Case File 340-49, NYANA Archive.
44. Rabbi Trainin, interview.
45. Naftali Lis, interview with the author, Sharon, MA, 31 March 2002.
46. From Yiddish—a person from the same hometown or area in Eastern Europe.
47. Ibid. Here he uses the Yiddish word for the Sabbath.
48. Ibid.
49. Rabbi Baruch Goldstein, interview with the author, Providence, RI, 22 July 2004. Literally, *yeshiva bocher* (Yiddish) is a yeshiva student, but the term also, as in this case, connotes one who is a product of an insulated religious life and has little involvement in the secular world.
50. Ibid.
51. "Resettlement of Difficult Cases on a Rotation Basis," Minutes of TAC (Technical Advisory Committee) Meeting, 9 June 1950, YIVO Institute for Jewish Research Archives, RG 240, MKM 24.5, 93.
52. Letter to B. Behrman, Director, Community Service Department, USNA, from A. Neumann, 6 December 1951, YIVO Institute for Jewish Research Archives, RG 246, MKM 24.53, 707.
53. Letter to B. Behrman, USNA, from A. Neumann, 18 December 1951, YIVO Institute for Jewish Research Archives, RG 246, MKM 24.53, 707.
54. Draft for discussion, "Re: Religious Functionaries and Yeshiva Students," 2 June 1948, YIVO Institute for Jewish Research Archives, RG 246.1, 1694.
55. Letter from Esther Einbinder, Settlement Consultant, USNA, to Dr. Neumann, JFCS, Denver, 22 December 1949, Record Group I-065, JFCS, Denver, Box 46, File 1134. American Jewish Historical Society.
56. Letter from Dr. Neumann, JFCS, Denver, to E. Einbinder, USNA, 28 December 1949, Record Group I-065, JFCS, Denver, Box 46, File 1134, American Jewish Historical Society.
57. Letter from E. Einbinder, USNA, to Dr. Neumann, JFCS, 25 April 1950, Record Group I-065, JFCS, Denver, Box 42, File 1345, American Jewish Historical Society.
58. Western Union Telegram from Dr. Neumann to E. Einbinder, USNA, 16 May 1949, Record Group I-065, JFCS, Denver, Box 3, File 715, American Jewish Historical Society.
59. Report by S. J., JFCS, Denver, 5 April 1950, Record Group I-065, JFCS, Denver, Box 23 (G. Family, no file number), American Jewish Historical Society.

60. Letter from Ralph Ross, Casework Supervisor, JFCS, Denver, to Miss Behrman, USNA, 21 January 1953, Record Group I-065, JFCS, Denver, Box 8, File 2308, American Jewish Historical Society.
61. Letter from Rabbi R. to president, JFCS, Denver, 15 March 1952, Record Group I-065, JFCS, Denver, Box 44, File 2061, American Jewish Historical Society.
62. Ibid.
63. Letter from Dr. T. Salzberg, Vocational Counselor, JFCS, to Rabbi R., 24 March 1952, Record Group I-065, JFCS, Denver, Box 44, File 2061, American Jewish Historical Society, Newton Centre, MA, and New York.
64. Memorandum to Henry Levy, Emigration Department, JDC, 27 March 1951, Executive Report, NYANA Archive.

CHAPTER 5   *"Unaccompanied Minors"*

1. "20 War Orphans among 945 on The Ernie Pyle," *Herald-Tribune*, 1 October 1946, 1.
2. Ibid.
3. Ibid.
4. Cornelia Goodhue, "We Gain New Candidates for Citizenship," *The Child* 11 (1946): 2–7.
5. Beatrice Glanz, "Factors in the Adjustment of New American Children in Their First Year in the United States" (master's thesis, Simmons College, 1950), 2–5.
6. Ibid.
7. Loescher and Scanlon, *Calculated Kindness*, 6.
8. Glantz, "Factors in the Adjustment," 3.
9. Statistics indicate that more adult men than women survived the Holocaust. I do not have the global statistics for minors but it appears from several studies that males predominated among those young people who came to the United States.
10. Glantz, "Factors in the Adjustment," 20–21.
11. Goodhue, "We Gain New Candidates," 3.
12. Deborah Portnoy, "The Adolescent Immigrant," *Jewish Social Service Quarterly* 25 (September 1948): 268–273.
13. Ibid., 269.
14. Editha Sterba, "Emotional Problems of Displaced Children," *Journal of Social Casework* 30 (May 1949): 175–181.
15. Report by B. H., 13 November 1947, Record Group I-065, JFCS, Denver, Box 39 (no file number), American Jewish Historical Society.
16. Ibid.
17. U.S. Committee for the Care of European Children Semi-annual Report, June 1950, Record Group I-065, JFCS, Denver, Box 39 (no file number), American Jewish Historical Society.
18. Letter from A. Neumann, Director, JFCS, to Lotte Marcuse, European-Jewish Children's Aid, 19 July 1948, Record Group I-065, JFCS, Denver, Box 39 (no file number), American Jewish Historical Society.
19. Letter from A. Neumann, Director, JFCS, to Lotte Marcuse, European-Jewish Children's Aid, 22 February 1949, Record Group I-065, JFCS, Denver, Box 39 (no file number), American Jewish Historical Society.

20. Ella Zwerdling and Grace Polansky, "Foster Home Placement of Refugee Children," *Journal of Social Case Work* 30 (July 1949): 277–282.
21. NYANA Case File 359-50, NYANA Archive.
22. Ibid.
23. Marion Nachman, interview by the author, tape recording, Darien, CT, 21 January 2002.
24. NYANA Case File 359-50, NYANA Archive.
25. Ibid.
26. Lea W., telephone conversation with the author, Sharon, MA, 3 January 2002.
27. Ibid.
28. Ibid.
29. Ibid.
30. Nachman, interview.
31. Ibid.
32. Michel Jeruchim, telephone conversations with the author, Sharon, MA, 27 December 2001, 2 January 2002.
33. Frances N., "Interview by Survivors of the Shoah Visual History Foundation," Trenton, NJ, 20 November 1996, University of Southern California Shoah Foundation Institute for Visual History and Education, Tape 22187.
34. Ibid.
35. Ibid.
36. Robert Berger, interview by the author, tape recording, Brookline, MA, 5 February 2002.
37. Miriam W., RG-50.091.0133, 1 November 1984, Oral History Project, National Council of Jewish Women, Cleveland, USHMM Archives.
38. Ibid.
39. A. B., Case Material from Reception Center, YIVO Institute for Jewish Research Archives, RG 249, EJCA, Subseries 2.31, Folder 1616.
40. Ibid.
41. As seen in case of the D. family, Box 13, File 424, Record Group I-065, JFCS, Denver, Box 39 (no file number), American Jewish Historical Society.
42. Glanz, "Factors in the Adjustment," 27.
43. Beatrice Carter, "Social Case Work with the Adolescent in a Program of Social Case Work with Displaced Persons," paper read at National Conference of Social Work, Atlantic City, 1950, cited in Glantz, "Factors in the Adjustment," 27.
44. Leonard Serkess, interview by the author, tape recording, Newton, MA, 27 February 2002.
45. Ibid.
46. Berger, interview.
47. Ibid.
48. Robert Graham, "Dachau Victims Transformed into Husky Americans in Maine," *Boston Sunday Herald*, 1 August 1948, 6.
49. Harry Plow, "Why We Put the Play On," in "Twice Born," ed. Joshua Rosenberg, writings from the New Americans Unit, Camp Kingswood, Bridgton, ME, Summer 1948, 21.

50. Berger, interview.

51. Serkess, interview.

52. Berger, interview.

53. Marion Pritchard, interview with the author, tape recording, Worcester, MA, 10 April 2000; Berger, interview; Serkess, interview.

54. Berger, interview.

55. Serkess, interview.

56. Ibid.

57. Berger, interview.

58. Ibid.

59. Boston JFCS's response to the orphans resonates with a similar model in England that historian Martin Gilbert described in *The Boys: The Story of 732 Young Concentration Camp Survivors* (New York: Henry Holt, 1996). There, too, a group of orphans benefited from an environment where they had the companionship of other child survivors within an institutional setting. Many in both the American and British groups remain deeply connected in one another's lives today and express positive feelings about these group arrangements. Whether it was the patience and understanding of the staff, the companionship of other DP orphans, a sense of family, an allowance for a transitional time, or a combination of factors, the efforts to create a nurturing group environment around the particular needs of these children seems to have offered benefits that most foster care did not.

60. Berger, interview.

CHAPTER 6   *The Bumpy Road*

1. H. Faber, *New York Times*, 19 January 1950, 1.

2. Ibid.

3. William Helmreich, *Against All Odds: Holocaust Survivors and the Successful Lives They Made in America* (New Brunswick, NJ: Transaction Press, 1996).

4. Lawrence Langer, "Holocaust and Jewish Memory in the Paintings of Samuel Bak," public lecture, Strassler Family Center for Holocaust and Genocide Studies, Clark University, Worcester, MA, 25 September 2002.

5. Lawrence Langer, *Admitting the Holocaust* (Oxford: Oxford University Press, 1995), 14, 18, 20.

6. UJA Press Release, Community Relations Department, 14 May 1947, YIVO Institute for Jewish Research Archives, RG 246, Box 66, File 2598.

7. Ibid.

8. Jerome Edelberg and Harry Coren, "Pride, Hope Inspire 'I Am an American' Day," *New York Daily Mirror*, 14 May 1948.

9. Ibid.

10. NYANA Case File 425-53, NYANA Archive.

11. NYANA Case File 316-49, 2, NYANA Archive.

12. Ibid., 3.

13. NYANA Case File 329-49, 7, NYANA Archive.

14. Report by D. G., JFCS Caseworker, 15 May 1951, Box 35, File 1004, Record Group I-065, JFCS, Denver, American Jewish Historical Society.

15. Ibid.
16. Report by A. S., JFCS Caseworker, 23 September 1949, 3, Record Group I-065, JFCS, Denver, Box 16, File, 980, p. 1, American Jewish Historical Society.
17. Reports by E. M., JFCS Caseworker, 14–20 July 1952, Box 16, File 2106, Record Group I-065, JFCS, Denver, American Jewish Historical Society.
18. NYANA Case File 331-49, 1, NYANA Archive.
19. NYANA Case File 303-48, 5, NYANA Archive.
20. NYANA Case File 374-50, 1, NYANA Archive.
21. See Gilbert, *The Boys*. Morris referred to this as "Bloomsbury House," as did many child survivors, as recorded by Gilbert. Bloomsbury House was the building where the Central British Fund was located.
22. NYANA Case File 374-50, 2, NYANA Archive.
23. Case File Report, Box 14, File 146, 4, Record Group I-065, JFCS, Denver, American Jewish Historical Society.
24. NYANA Case File 368-50, p. 4, NYANA Archive.
25. Tim Feder, "Life in the DP Camps," in Rosensaft, *Life Reborn*, 44.
26. Case File Report, Box 6, File 2433, 6–7, Record Group I-065, JFCS, Denver, American Jewish Historical Society.
27. Ibid., 12.
28. Ibid., 13.
29. Ibid., 14–28.
30. Case File Report, Box 13, File 424, 1, Record Group I-065, JFCS, Denver, American Jewish Historical Society.
31. Ibid., 3.
32. Ibid. This institution is also mentioned in Chapter 5.
33. Ibid.
34. Case File Report, Box 3, File 1766B, 4, Record Group I-065, JFCS, Denver, American Jewish Historical Society.
35. Ibid., 4–5.
36. Gary Zucker, M.D., interviewed in New York by Liz Jaffee for the NYANA Oral History Project, New York, 4 May 1993. Reproduced with permission of Dr. Zucker.
37. Ibid., 2.
38. Ibid., 4.
39. Ibid., 5.
40. Ibid.
41. Case File Report, Box 16, Mrs. F. (no file number), Record Group I-065, JFCS, Denver, American Jewish Historical Society.
42. NYANA Case File 325-49, NYANA Archive.
43. Letter from Psychiatrist to NYANA Social Worker, 31 January 1950, NYANA Case File 325-49, NYANA Archive.
44. NYANA Case File 324-49, NYANA Archive.
45. Letter to USNA from Dr. S., 2 June 1950, NYANA Case File 324-49, NYANA Archive.
46. Reports by A. N., R. K., and S. J., JFCS Caseworkers, 3 January 1950–10 March 1951, Box 17, F. family (no file number), 10, Record Group I-065, JFCS, Denver, American Jewish Historical Society.

47. Ibid., 12.
48. Ibid., 20.
49. Ibid.
50. Ibid., 21.
51. Examples cited in interviews with Rabbi Trainin and Robert Berger, M.D.
52. Bluma G., "Interview by Survivors of the Shoah Visual History Foundation," Columbia, South Carolina, 18 June 1998, University of Southern California Shoah Foundation Institute for Visual History and Education, 43565, 3:18:05.
53. Case File Reports, Box 36, File 1806, Record Group I-065, JFCS, Denver, American Jewish Historical Society.

CHAPTER 7   *The Helping Process*

1. For early history of social work, see John Ehrenreich, *The Altruistic Imagination: A History of Social Work and Social Policy in the United States* (Ithaca: Cornell University Press, 1985), chaps. 1–2; Carel Germain, "Casework and Science: A Historical Encounter," in *Theories of Social Casework*, ed. R. W. Roberts and R. H. Nee (Chicago: University of Chicago Press, 1970), 5–32; James Leiby, *A History of Social Welfare and Social Work in the United States* (New York: Columbia University Press, 1978), chaps. 1–13; Roy Lubove, *The Professional Altruist: The Emergence of Social Work as a Career, 1870–1930* (Cambridge, MA: Harvard University Press, 1965).
2. Ehrenreich, *Altruistic Imagination*, 64. See also Germain, "Casework and Science," 5.
3. Mary Richmond, *Social Diagnosis* (New York: Russell Sage Foundation, 1917).
4. Mary Richmond, *What Is Social Casework?* (New York: Russell Sage Foundation, 1922).
5. Daniel Walkowitz, *Working with Class: Social Workers and the Politics of Middle Class Identity* (Chapel Hill: University of North Carolina Press, 1999), 200.
6. Bertha Reynolds, *An Uncharted Journey: Fifty Years of Growth in Social Work* (New York: Citadel Press), 54–55. This is a personal account of a woman who was involved in the field from 1914 through the 1960s.
7. For discussion of the early influence of psychoanalysis on social work, see Jacques Quen and Eric Carlson, eds., *American Psychoanalysis: Origins and Developments* (New York: Brunner/Mazel, 1978); Ehrenreich, *Altruistic Imagination*, 66–77; Ethel Ginsberg, "Freud's Contribution to the Philosophy and Practice of Social Work," *American Journal of Orthopsychiatry* 10 (1940): 877; Alfred Kadushin, "The Knowledge Base of Social Work," in *Issues in American Social Work*, ed. Alfred Kahn (New York: Columbia University Press, 1959), 55–58; Leiby, *History of Social Welfare*, 183–186; Lubove, *Professional Altruist*, 86–89.
8. Walkowitz, *Working with Class*, 200.
9. Ruth Smalley, *Theory for Social Work Practice* (New York: Columbia University Press, 1967), 82. There is a tremendous body of literature on this topic. See also Frank Bruno, *Trends in Social Work, 1874–1956* (New York: Columbia University Press, 1957); Ann Garrett, "Historical Survey of the Evolution of

Casework," *Journal of Social Casework* 30 (June 1949): 219–229; Helen Perlman, *Social Casework* (Chicago: University of Chicago Press, 1957); Robert Roberts and Robert Nee, eds., *Theories of Social Casework* (Chicago: University of Chicago Press, 1970).

10. Ruth Smalley, "The Functional Approach to Casework," in Roberts and Nee, *Theories of Social Casework*, 77–128.

11. Avi Kaye, "The Impact of Attitudes toward the Holocaust and Holocaust Survivors in the United States on the Adult Psychological Development of American Holocaust Survivors," paper read at "Beyond Forced Labor and Camps, Current Research on Survivors of Nazi Persecution" conference, London, 29 January 2003.

12. For example, P. Hammond's "The Psychological Impact of Unprecedented Social Catasrophe: An Analysis of Three Topical Autobiographies of Young Displaced Persons"; A. S. Brown's "Analysis of Topical Autobiographies of Displaced Persons of Christian Faith"; and A. Uher's "An Analysis of Four Topical Autobiographies of Mature Displaced Persons" were all unpublished master's theses written from 1951 and 1952 under the guidance of David Boder, Illinois Institute of Technology. Paul Steinfeld wrote a master's thesis in 1947 at Columbia University titled "Problems of Jewish Children Survivors of European Concentration Camps in American Foster Homes: A Preliminary Study of Forty-six Cases." Beatrice Glantz wrote "Factors in the Adjustment of New American Children in Their First Year in the United States" for her master's degree at Simmons College in 1950. No doubt there were others.

13. It appeared in the *American OSE Review*, a journal "devoted to Health and Hygiene among Jews" published by the Organization for the Health and Protection of Jews (OSE). Originally a charitable Russian Jewish organization founded in 1912 to provide wide-ranging care, OSE operated in Nazi-occupied countries during the war and provided postwar care to refugees in Europe. Its journal was geared to the medical world.

14. Eugene Minkowski, M.D., "The Psychology of the Deportees," *American OSE Review* 4 (Summer–Fall 1947): 2–3, 17–22.

15. Ibid., 20–21.

16. Ibid., 21.

17. Minkowski used the term *deportees* to refer to those who had been deported from France and returned, that is, survivors.

18. Ibid.

19. Ibid., 22.

20. Minkowski continued to address these issues in "Les consequences psychologiques et psychopathologiques de la guerre et du Nazism" (The Psychological and Psychopathological Consequences of War and Nazism) *Archives Suisse de Neurologie et de Psychiatrie* 61 (1948), as cited in "Psychological Consequences of War and Nazism," *American OSE Review* 6 (Spring 1949): 3–10.

21. David Boder, *I Did Not Interview the Dead* (Urbana: University of Illinois Press, 1949).

22. Ibid.

23. Paul Friedman, "The Road Back for the D.P.'s," *Commentary* 6 (1948): 502–510.
24. Paul Friedman, "Some Aspects of Concentration Camp Psychology," *American Journal of Psychiatry* 105 (February 1949): 604.
25. Friedman, "The Road Back." 502.
26. Ibid.
27. Ibid.
28. Ibid.
29. Friedman, "Some Aspects," 602.
30. Ibid.
31. Ibid.
32. Ibid., 605.
33. Hilde Bluhm, "How Did They Survive: Mechanisms of Defense in Nazi Concentration Camps," *American Journal of Psychotherapy* 2 (1948): 3–32 is another study through a traditional psychoanalytic lens.
34. Friedman, "Some Aspects," 603.
35. In all his works, Friedman quoted from Freud's *Civilization and Its Discontents*.
36. Bergmann and Jucovy, eds., *Generations of the Holocaust* (New York: Columbia University Press, 1982), 6–7. William Niederland, consulting psychiatrist to USNA, also touches on this briefly in "The Problem of the Survivor," in *Massive Psychic Trauma*, ed. Henry Krystal (New York: International Universities Press), 15.
37. Report by A. S., 23 September 1949, 3, Record Group I-065, JFCS, Denver, Box 16, File, 980, American Jewish Historical Society.
38. NYANA Case File 324-49, NYANA Archive. For additional examples, see Chapter 4, this volume.
39. Telephone interview with the author, 24 June 2005.
40. Conversation with the author, USHMM, Washington, DC, November 2004.
41. Bluma G., "Interview by Survivors of the Shoah Visual History Foundation," Columbia, South Carolina, 18 June 1998, University of Southern California Shoah Foundation Institute for Visual History and Education, 43565, 3:18:05.
42. J. Goldstein, I. F. Lukoff, and H. Strauss, "A Case History of a Concentration Camp Survivor," *American OSE Review* 8 (Fall 1951): 11–28.
43. Ibid., 11.
44. Ibid.
45. Elie Cohen, *Human Behavior in the Concentration Camp* (New York: Norton, 1953), 5.
46. See Henry Krystal, ed., *Massive Psychic Trauma* (New York: International Universities Press). His bibliography reflects the renewed interest in survivors in that decade beginning in 1961 with Niederland's study, "The Problem of the Survivor," *Journal of Hillside Hospital* 10 (1961): 233–247. Attention continued to focus on camp survivors and, eventually, their children.
47. Robert Morris and Michael Freund, *Trends and Issues in Jewish Social Welfare in the United States, 1899–1958* (Philadelphia: Jewish Publication Society, 1966), 456–457.
48. Paul Friedman, "Can Freedom Be Taught?" *Journal of Social Casework* 29 (July 1948): 247–255.

49. Sanford Sherman, "Differentials in Case Work with Newcomers," *Jewish Social Service Quarterly* 25 (September 1948): 274–285.
50. Friedman, "Can Freedom Be Taught?" 50.
51. Ibid., 253.
52. Ibid., 254.
53. Sherman, "Differentials in Case Work," 275.
54. Ibid.
55. Ibid.
56. Ibid., 278.
57. Ibid., 282.
58. Ibid.
59. Ibid., 283.
60. Allen Cowett, "Case Work Elements in Dealing with Job Refusals by Newcomers," *Jewish Social Service Quarterly* 28 (June 1952): 431.
61. Rita Spaulding, "Techniques in Casework with Displaced Persons," *Social Casework* 31 (February 1950): 70–77.
62. Ibid., 71.
63. Ibid.
64. Cowett, "Casework Elements," 428–433.
65. Ibid., 428.
66. Ibid.
67. Wolkowitz, *Working with Class*, 202–203.
68. NYANA, *Statement of Purpose*, 13.
69. NYANA, Statement of Services and Functions, February 1950.
70. Ibid., 6.
71. Ibid., 7.
72. Ibid., 8.
73. Marcel Kovarsky, "Overseas Services as Seen by the Local Agency," *Jewish Social Services Quarterly* 27 (September 1950): 100–104.
74. NYANA, *Statement of Services*, 14.
75. Ibid.
76. White, *300,000 New Americans*, 23.
77. Ibid., 24.
78. Ibid., 14.
79. M. P., NYANA Case File 334a-49, 9, NYANA Archive.
80. Ibid., 14.
81. NYANA Case File 402-51, NYANA Archive.
82. NYANA Case File 393-51, NYANA Archive.
83. Kovarsky, "Overseas Services," 101. It seems that he meant a DP camp.
84. Ibid.
85. NYANA Case File 393-51, NYANA Archive.
86. NYANA Case File 303-48, NYANA Archive.
87. Ibid.
88. Ibid.
89. As quoted in Barbara Burstin, "Holocaust Survivors: Rescue and Resettlement," in *Jewish Women in America: An Historical Encyclopedia*, ed. Paula Hyman and Deborah Dash Moore (New York: Routledge, 1997), 656.

90. Gabi Schiff, interview by the author, tape recording, Queens, NY, 4 March 2002.
91. Ibid.
92. Report by A. S., 23 September 1949, p. 3, Record Group I-065, JFCS, Denver, Box 16, File, 980, American Jewish Historical Society.
93. NYANA Case File 305-49, 21, NYANA Archive.
94. Ibid., 25.
95. Ibid.
96. NYANA Case File 303-48, 5, NYANA Archive.
97. Ibid., 6.
98. Ibid., 57.
99. NYANA Case File 305-49, 25, NYANA Archive.
100. Schiff, interview.
101. L. L., interview by the author, tape recording, New York, 10 April 2002.
102. NYANA Case File 324-49, NYANA Archive.
103. More than 60 percent of survivors describe physical problems and illness in the 350 files I analyzed. This figure is similar, proportionately, to the number of ill survivors that Dr. Friedman noted in his work in Cyprus.
104. NYANA Case File 303-48, 29–30, NYANA Archive.
105. Ibid.
106. Simona Frajndlich, telephone interview with the author, 12 April 2005.
107. Report by A. S., Record Group I-065, JFCS, Denver, Box 16, File, 980, American Jewish Historical Society.

CHAPTER 8   *The Myth of Silence*

1. N. Godin, RG-50.549.01*0009, Postwar Interviews, 14 December 1995, USHMM Archives.
2. N. Salsitz, RG-50.549.02*0052, Postwar Interviews, 5 July 1999, USHMM Archives.
3. H. Taube, interview with the author, tape recording, Rockville, MD, 2 December 2004.
4. H. Liebman, RG-50.407*0086, Postwar Interviews, 10 August 1996, USHMM Archives.
5. A. Salsitz, RG-50.549.02*0054, Postwar Interviews, 8 July 1999, USHMM Archives.
6. Sandelowski, interview.
7. Bernie Sayonne, interview by the author, tape recording, Denver, CO, 19 December 2002.
8. Estelle Beder, RG-50.091*0004, 27 August 1984, National Council of Jewish Women Oral History Project, Cleveland, USHMM Archives.
9. Godin, interview.
10. Ibid.
11. T. R., telephone conversation with author, Sharon, MA, 3 December 2002.
12. Sayonne, interview.
13. Paul Krell, interview by the author, tape recording, Bronx, NY, 7 March 2002.

14. Helen Glassman, *Adjustment in Freedom* (Cleveland: United HIAS Service and Jewish Family Service of Cleveland, Ohio, 1956), 69.

15. Daniel Soyer, in *Jewish Immigrant Associations and American Identity in New York, 1880–1939* (Cambridge, MA: Harvard University Press, 1997), 1, uses the WPA Yiddish Writer's Group study, *Di yidishe landsmanschaftn fun nyu york* (New York: Yiddish Writers Union, 1938), edited by I. Rontsch, for the estimate of three thousand societies with four hundred thousand members in the late 1930s.

16. Studies of *landsmanschaftn* include Soyer's *Jewish Immigrant Associations*, which provides an excellent analysis that examines the societies and their influence on the immigrants' identity and acculturation through 1939; a work produced as a WPA Yiddish writers' project (Yiddish Writer's Group, *Di yidishe landsmanschaftn fun nyu york)*, which is the most comprehensive contemporary description of landsmanschaftn in the 1930s; Hannah Kliger's *Jewish Hometown Associations and Family Circles in New York: The WPA Yiddish Writers' Group Study* (Bloomington: Indiana University Press, 1992), which offers an edited English translation of Rontsch's study with foreword and afterword; and "The Present State of the *Landsmanschaften*," *Jewish Social Service Quarterly* 15 (1939): 360–378, which gives an English synopsis of Rontsch's group's work.

17. Kliger, *Jewish Hometown Associations*, 120.

18. Soyer, *Jewish Immigrant Associations*, 161; and I. Rybal, L. Kronick, and I. Shmulewitz, eds., *The Bialystoker Memorial Book* (Brooklyn, NY: Empire Press, 1982), 171.

19. For early history of the JDC, see Oscar Handlin, *A Continuing Task: The American Joint Jewish Distribution Committee, 1914–1964* (New York: Random House, 1964). Yehuda Bauer, in *My Brother's Keeper: A History of the American Joint Distribution Committee* (Philadelphia: Jewish Publication Society, 1974), and Tom Shachtman et al., in *I Seek My Brethren: Ralph Goldman and "The Joint"—Rescue, Relief, and Reconstruction; the Work of the AJDC* (New York: Newmarket Press, 2001), touch briefly on the JDC's inception.

20. Soyer, *Jewish Immigrant Associations*, 162.

21. Ibid.

22. Theo Richmond, *Konin* (New York: Pantheon, 1995), 142.

23. Certificate of Incorporation, Kamenetz-Podoler Relief Organization, Inc., YIVO Institute for Jewish Research Archives, RG 972, Box 1.

24. J. Mogil, ed., *The Grodner* (New York: United Grodner Relief, Inc.), March 1948, YIVO Institute for Jewish Research Archives, RG 996, Box 1.

25. Ibid.

26. Ibid.

27. J. Mogil, "Grodner Relief Organizations to Raise $100,000 Fund to Build a Grodno Community in Israel," *The Grodner* (New York: United Grodner Relief), March 1949, YIVO Institute for Jewish Research Archives, RG 996, Box 1.

28. Rybal et al., *Bialystoker Memorial Book*, 183.

29. Hiller Bell, telephone conversation with author, Sharon, MA, 12 January 2003.

30. Kliger, *Jewish Hometown Associations*, 120.

31. Bell, telephone conversation.

32. Ibid.

33. Richmond, *Konin*, 142.
34. Rybal et al., *Bialaystoker Memorial Book*, 10; Kliger, in *Jewish Hometown Associations*, 128, also mentions the club.
35. Schwartz and Milamed, *A Guide to YIVO's Landsmanschaftn Archive* (New York: YIVO, 1986), 22.
36. Leon Blatman, ed., *Bulletin, Kamenetz-Poloder Relief Organization*, 1947 (New York: Kamenetz-Poloder Relief Organization, 1947). Translated from the Yiddish by the author.
37. "Demographic Characteristics of the Recent Jewish Immigrant," NYANA Executive Report, NYANA 1950 Executive Meeting, NYANA Archive.
38. Kliger, *Jewish Hometown Associations*, 120.
39. Roman Weingarten, telephone conversation with author, Sharon, MA, 20 January 2003.
40. Edie Druyan, interview by the author, tape recording, New York, 9 January 2003.
41. Druyan, interview.
42. Weingarten, telephone conversation.
43. Weingarten, telephone conversation.
44. NYANA Case File 399-51, NYANA Archive, NYANA Archive.
45. Ibid.
46. Ibid.
47. *To Remember Is to Know* (Los Angeles: Club 1939, 1982). 3.
48. Sayonne, interview.
49. "Around the Nation," *New Neighbors* 3 (May 1950): 7.
50. Ibid.
51. Morris Indik, telephone conversation with author, Sharon, MA, 4 February 2003.
52. Glassman, *Adjustment in Freedom*, 68.
53. Heinz Sandelowski, interview by the author, tape recording, Providence, RI, 9 March 2000.
54. Sidi Natansohn, interview by the author, tape recording, Sharon, MA, 5 December 2000.
55. Krell, interview.
56. Naftali Lis, interview by the author, tape recording, Sharon, MA, 21 March 2002.
57. Sayonne, interview.
58. N. Scherman and M. Zlotowitz, eds., *The Complete Artscroll Siddur* (New York: Mesorah, 2001), 815.
59. Weingarten, telephone conversation.
60. Bell, telephone conversation.
61. Yizkor Flyer, United Grodner Relief, Inc., of New York, N.Y., 1954, YIVO Institute for Jewish Research Archives, RG 996, Box 1, New York.
62. Sayonne, interview.
63. *To Remember Is to Know*, 5.
64. Bell, telephone conversation.
65. For an analytical overview of memorial books, see the introduction and bibliography of yizkor books in Jack Kugelmass and Jonathan Boyarin, *From a Ruined Garden: The Memorial Books of Polish Jewry* (Bloomington: Indiana University Press in association with the United States Holocaust Memorial Museum, 1998).

66. M. Sodarsky and J. Katzenelenbogen, eds. *Lithuania*, vol. 1 (New York: Futuro Press, 1951), 33. Translated from the Yiddish by the author.

67. Literally meaning "burnt sacrifice," this became the Yiddish word to describe Jewish communal tragedies in history after the destruction of the First and Second Temples and eventually included the Holocaust. See David Roskies, *Against the Apocalypse: Responses to Catastrophe in Modern Jewish Culture* (Cambridge, MA: Harvard University Press, 1984), 7, 14, 261.

68. James Young, *The Texture of Memory: Holocaust Memorials and Meaning* (New Haven: Yale University Press, 1993), 7.

69. Kugelmass and Boyarin, *From a Ruined Garden*, 1.

70. Joost Merloo, "Delayed Mourning in Victims of Extermination Camps," in *Massive Psychic Trauma*, ed. Henry Krystal (New York: 1968), 74, as quoted in Young, *The Texture of Memory*, 7.

71. In *Against the Apocalypse*, Roskies situates Jewish response during the Holocaust within the context of the Jews' long history of persecution.

72. Abraham Wein, "Memorial Books as a Source for Research into the History of Jewish Communities in Europe," *Yad Vashem Studies* 9 (1973): 255–272.

73. Ibid., 257.

74. Philip Friedman, in *Di landsmanschaftn in di fahreynikte shtatn in di letzte 10 yohr* (The Landsmanschaftn in the United States in the Last Ten Years), *Jewish Book Annual* 10 (1951): 81–96, surveys the memorial books published in that period.

75. Alter Levite, ed., *A Yizkor Book to Riteve* (Cape Town: Kaplan-Kushlick Foundation, 2000).

76. Kugelmass and Boyarin, *From a Ruined Garden*, 6–7.

77. Rybal et al., *Bialystoker Memorial Book*, 88, 110, 137.

78. *Yizkor* Flyer.

79. Elias Schulman, "A Survey and Evaluation of *Yizkor* Books," *Jewish Book Annual* 25 (1967–1968): 184–191.

80. Weingarten, telephone conversation.

81. Druyan, interview.

82. Bell, telephone conversation.

83. Rybal et al., *Bialystoker Memorial Book*, 161–201.

84. S. L. Schneiderman, ed. *Warsaw Ghetto: A Diary by Mary Berg* (New York: Fischer, 1945).

85. S. L. Schneiderman, interview by the author, tape recording, Ramat-Aviv, Israel, 20 July 1998.

86. Philip Friedman, "One Hundred Yiddish Books on Destruction and Bravery," *Jewish Book Annual* 8 (1949–1950).

87. Jan Schwartz, "A Library of Destruction and Hope: The First One Hundred Volumes of Poylishe Yidntum, 1946–54," paper read at the thirty-fourth annual conference of the Association for Jewish Studies, 15 December 2002, Los Angeles.

88. S. J. Kahn, "Cultural Activities," in *The American Jewish Year Book*, vol. 50, ed. Schneiderman and Fine (Philadelphia: Jewish Publication Society, 1949), 129, 528–530.

Conclusion

1. "Estimates of Needs for 1954," NYANA Executive Report, November 1953, 5, NYANA Archive.
2. White, *300,000 New Americans*, 397.
3. "Estimates of Needs for 1954," NYANA Archive. It had a staff of six hundred at the height of its operation.
4. Langer, *Admitting the Holocaust*, 6.
5. Arlene Fine, "Desperate Hours Again for Aging Holocaust Survivors," www. ClevelandJewishNews.com., 27 May 2005.
6. Ibid.

BIBLIOGRAPHY

Archives and Libraries

American Jewish Historical Society, Newton, MA, and New York
    Case files of Jewish Family and Children's Services, Denver, CO, 150 files of
    refugees who came to Denver from 1946 to 1957
American Jewish Joint Distribution Committee Archives, New York
    JDC Collection, 1945–1964
Brandeis University Library Judaica Collection, Waltham, MA
    Yizkor books
New York Association for New Americans Archives, New York
    Case files of Family Service Department, two hundred randomly selected files,
    1949–1954
    NYANA Papers, 1946–1954
New York Public Library, New York
Rose Library, Strassler Family Center for Holocaust and Genocide Studies, Clark
    University, Worcester, MA
Survivors of the Shoah Visual History Foundation, University of Southern California,
    Los Angeles
    Survivor Testimonies
United States Holocaust Memorial Museum Archives, Washington, DC
    Oral Histories, National Council of Jewish Women, Cleveland Section
    Oral Histories, Postwar Collection
YIVO Institute for Jewish Research Archives, New York
    Archive of United Service for New Americans
    Archive of European-Jewish Children's Aid
    Archive of German-Jewish Children's Aid
    Landsmanschaftn Collection

Books, Periodicals, and Articles

Agar, Herbert. *The Saving Remnant.* London: Rupert Hart-Davis, 1960.
Auerbach, Frank. *The Admission and Resettlement of DPs in the U.S.* New York:
    Common Council for American Unity, 1950.

Avisar, Ilan. *Screening the Holocaust.* Bloomington: Indiana University Press, 1988.

Bachrach, Susan, ed. *Liberation 1945.* Washington, DC: United States Holocaust Memorial Museum, 1995.

Bar-On, Dan. *Between Fear and Hope: Three Generations of the Holocaust.* Cambridge, MA: Harvard University Press, 1999.

Bauer, Yehuda. *American Jewry and the Holocaust: The American Joint Distribution Committee, 1939–1945.* Detroit: Wayne State University Press, 1981.

———. *My Brother's Keeper.* Philadelphia: Jewish Publication Society, 1974.

———. *Out of the Ashes: The Impact of American Jews on Post-Holocaust Jewry.* New York: Oxford University Press, 1988.

———. *Rethinking the Holocaust.* New Haven: Yale University Press, 2001.

Baumel, Judith. *Unfilled Promise: Rescue and Resettlement of Jewish Refugee Children in the United States, 1934–1945.* Juneau, AK: Denali Press, 1990.

Berger, Joseph. *Displaced Persons: Growing Up American after the Holocaust.* New York: Scribner, 2001.

Bergman, Martin S., and Milton E. Jucovy, eds. *Generations of the Holocaust.* New York: Columbia University Press, 1982.

Berl, Fred. "Adjustment of Displaced Persons." *Jewish Social Service Quarterly* 25 (December 1948): 254–263.

———."The Immigrant Situation as Focus of the Helping Process," *Journal of Jewish Communal Service* 26, no. 3 (1950): 377–390.

Berman, Aaron. *Nazism, the Jews, and American Zionism, 1933–1948.* Detroit: Wayne State University Press, 1990.

Berman, I., and S. Shapiro. "Psychological Problems Met in Counseling and Placement of Refugees." *Journal of Jewish Communal Service* 26 (Winter 1949): 277–282.

Berman, R., and C. Rawley. "Case Work Process in Working with American Relatives of Displaced Persons." *Jewish Social Service Quarterly* 24 (June 1948): 264–267.

Bluhm, Hilda. "How Did They Survive? Mechanisms of Defense in Nazi Concentration Camps." *American Journal of Psychotherapy* 2 (1948): 23–28.

Blum, John. *V Was for Victory: Politics and American Culture during World War II.* New York: Harcourt Brace, 1976.

Boder, David. *I Did Not Interview the Dead.* Urbana: University of Illinois Press, 1949.

Brenner, Michael. *After the Holocaust: Rebuilding Jewish Lives in Post-war Germany.* Princeton: Princeton University Press, 1997.

Brink, T. L., ed. *Holocaust Survivors' Mental Health.* Binghamton, NY: Haworth Press, 1994.

Bukiet, Melvin. *After.* New York: St. Martin's Press, 1996.

Burstin, Barbara. *After the Holocaust: The Migration of Polish Jews and Christians to Pittsburgh.* Pittsburgh: University of Pittsburgh Press, 1985.

Close, Kathleen. *Transplanted Children.* New York: United States Committee for the Care of European Children, 1953.

Cohen, Elie. *Human Behavior in the Concentration Camp.* New York: Universal Library, 1953.

Cohen, Naomi. *American Jews and the Zionist Idea.* Hoboken, NJ: KTAV, 1975.

Cohen, Michael. *Palestine and the Great Powers*. Princeton: Princeton University Press, 1982.

Cowett, Allen. "Casework Elements in Dealing with Job Refusals by Newcomers." *Jewish Social Service Quarterly* 28 (June 1952): 428–433.

Davie, Maurice, et al., "Refugees in America: Report of the Committee for the Study of Recent Immigration from Europe." 1947.

Dijour, Ilja. "Changing Emphasis in Jewish Migration," *Journal of Jewish Communal Service* 27 (Fall 1950): 72–79.

Diner, Hasia, et al., eds. *Lower East Side Memory*. Princeton: Princeton University Press, 2000.

Dinnerstein, Leonard. *America and the Survivors of the Holocaust*. New York: Columbia University Press, 1982.

———. *Antisemitism in America*. New York: Columbia University Press, 1994.

Dobkowski, Michael, ed. *Jewish American Voluntary Organizations*. New York: Greenwood Press, 1986.

Dwork, Debórah. *Children with a Star*. New Haven: Yale University Press, 1991.

Dwork, D., and Robert Jan van Pelt. *The Holocaust: A History*. New York: W. W. Norton, 2002.

Ehrenreich, John. *The Altruistic Imagination: A History of Social Work and Social Policy in the United States*. Ithaca: Cornell University Press, 1985.

Eisenberg, S. "Phases in the Resettlement Process and Their Significance for Case Work with New Americans." *Jewish Social Service Quarterly* 29 (September 1950): 86–96.

Farber, Roberta, and Chaim Waxman, eds. *Jews in America: A Contemporary Reader*. Hanover: Brandeis/University Press of New England, 1999.

Feingold, Henry. *Bearing Witness: How America and Its Jews Responded to the Holocaust*. Syracuse: Syracuse University Press, 1995.

———. *The Politics of Rescue: The Roosevelt Administration and the Holocaust, 1938–1945*. New York: Schocken Books, 1970.

———. *A Time for Searching: Entering the Mainstream, 1920–1945*. Baltimore: Johns Hopkins University Press, 1992.

Figley, Charles, ed. *Trauma and Its Wake: The Study and Treatment of Post-traumatic Stress Disorder*. New York: Bruner/Mazel, 1985.

Finklestein, Norman. *The Holocaust Industry*. New York: Verso Books, 2000.

Frankl, Victor. *The Doctor and the Soul*. New York: Knopf, 1955.

Fried, Jacob. *Judaism and the Community: New Directions in Jewish Social Work*. New York: Thomas Yoseloff, 1968.

Friedland, Joshua. *The Lamp beside the Golden Door*. New York: New York Association for New Americans, 1999.

Friedlander, Saul. *No Haven for the Oppressed: United States Policy towards Jewish Refugees, 1938–1945*. Detroit: Wayne State University Press, 1973.

Friedman, Paul. "The Road Back for the DP's." *Commentary* 6 (December 1948): 502–510.

———. "Some Aspects of Concentration Camp Psychology." *American Journal of Psychiatry* 105 (February 1949): 601–605.

Friedman, Philip. "The Landsmanschaftn in the United States in the Last Ten Years." In *Jewish Book Annual*. Philadelphia: Jewish Publication Society of America 10 (1951): 81–96.

Genizi, Haim. *America's Fair Share: The Admission and Resettlement of Displaced Persons, 1945–1952*. Detroit: Wayne State University Press, 1993.

Gilbert, Martin. *The Boys: The Story of 732 Young Concentration Camp Survivors*. New York: Henry Holt, 1996.

Glassman, Helen. *Adjustment in Freedom*. Cleveland: United HIAS Service and Jewish Family Service of Cleveland, Ohio, 1956.

Goodhue, Cornelia. "We Gain New Candidates for Citizenship." *The Child* 11 (1946): 2–7.

Goren, Arthur. *New York Jews and the Quest for Community*. New York: Columbia University Press, 1970.

Greenleigh, Arthur. "The Overseas Program and Its Relation in National Planning." *The Jewish Social Service Quarterly* (September 1950): 80–85.

Greenspan, Henry. *On Listening to Holocaust Survivors*. New York: Praeger, 1998.

Grobman, Alex. *Battling for Souls: The Vaad Hatzala Rescue Committee in Postwar Europe*. Jersey City, NJ: KTAV, 2004.

———. *Rekindling the Flame: American Jewish Chaplains and the Survivors of European Jewry*. Detroit: Wayne State University Press, 1993.

Grodzinsky, Yosef. *In the Shadow of the Holocaust*. Monroe, ME: Common Courage Press, 2004.

Grose, Peter. *Israel in the Mind of America*. New York: Alfred A. Knopf, 1983.

Grossman, Kurt R. *The Jewish DP Problem: Its Origins, Scope, and Liquidation*. New York: Institute of Jewish Affairs, World Jewish Congress, 1951.

Gruber, Ruth. *Haven: The Unknown Story of 1000 World War II Refugees*. New York: New American Library, 1984.

Gurock, Jeffrey. *American Jewish Orthodoxy in Historical Perspective*. Hoboken, NJ: KTAV, 1985.

Halberstam, David. *The Fifties*. New York: Random House, 1993.

Halperin, Samuel. *The Political World of American Zionism*. Detroit: Wayne State University Press, 1961.

Handlin, Oscar. *A Continuing Task: The American Joint Jewish Distribution Committee, 1914–1964*. New York: Random House, 1964.

———. *The Uprooted*. Boston: Little, Brown, 1951.

Hass, Aaron. *The Aftermath: Living with the Holocaust*. Cambridge: Cambridge University Press, 1995.

Helmreich, William. *Against All Odds: Holocaust Survivors and the Successful Lives They Made in America*. New Brunswick, NJ: Transaction, 1996.

Historical Atlas of the Holocaust. New York: Macmillan, 1996.

Horowitz, Rosemary. *Literacy and Cultural Transmission in the Reading, Writing, and Rewriting of Jewish Memorial Books*. San Francisco: Austin and Winfeld, 1998.

Howe, Irving. *World of Our Fathers*. New York: Random House, 1989.

Hyman, Abraham. *The Undefeated*. Hewlett, NY: Gefen, 1992.

Hyman, Paula, and Deborah Dash Moore, eds. *Jewish Women in America: An Historical Encyclopedia*. New York: Routledge, 1997.

Isenstadt, Theodore. "Local Components of Resettlement Planning: Standards of Assistance." *Jewish Social Service Quarterly* 27 (September 1950): 97–99.

Jacobson, Kenneth. *Embattled Selves.* New York: Atlantic Monthly Press, 1994.

Jordan, Charles. "Current European Emigration Problems." *Journal of Jewish Communal Service* 26 (Spring 1950): 354–361.

Kahn, Alfred, ed. *Issues in American Social Work.* New York: Columbia University Press, 1959.

Kahn, Sholom J. "Cultural Activities." In *American Jewish Year Book, 1948–49,* vol. 50, edited by Schneiderman and Fine. Philadelphia: Jewish Publication Society of America, 1949, 178–201.

Karp, William. "The Application of Vocational Services to Supplementary Assistance Cases." *Journal of Jewish Communal Service* 29 (Spring 1953): 45–49.

Kirschmann, Doris, and Sylvia Savin. "Refugee Adjustment: Five Years Later." *Jewish Social Service Quarterly* 30 (December 1953): 197–201.

Kliger, Hannah, ed. *Jewish Hometown Associations and Family Circles in New York.* Bloomington: Indiana University Press, 1992.

———. "Traditions of Grass-Roots Organization and Leadership: The Continuity of *Landsmanschaftn* in New York." *American Jewish History* 6, no. 1 (1986): 25–39.

Kochavi, Arieh. *Post-Holocaust Politics: Britain, the United States, and Jewish Refugees, 1945–1948.* Chapel Hill: University of North Carolina Press, 2001.

Konigseder, Angelika, and Juliane Wetzel. *Waiting for Hope: Jewish Displaced Persons in Post–World War II Germany.* Evanston, IL: Northwestern University Press, 2001.

Kovarsky, Marcel. "Overseas Services as Seen by the Local Agency." *Jewish Social Service Quarterly* 27 (September 1950): 100–104.

Kranzler, David. *Thy Brother's Blood: The Orthodox Jewish Response During the Holocaust.* Brooklyn, NY: Mesorah, 1987.

Kraus, Hertha. "The Newcomer's Orientation to the American Community." *Journal of Social Casework* 30 (January 1949): 9–13.

Krystal, Henry, ed. *Massive Psychic Trauma.* New York: International Universities Press, 1968.

Krystal, Henry, and William G. Niederland, eds. *Psychic Traumatization: Aftereffects in Individuals and Communities.* Boston: Little, Brown, 1971.

Kugelmass, Jack. *Key Texts in American Jewish Culture.* New Brunswick: Rutgers University Press, 2003.

Kugelmass, Jack, and Jonathan Boyarin, eds. *From a Ruined Garden: The Memorial Books of Polish Jewry.* Bloomington: Indiana University Press in association with the United States Holocaust Memorial Museum, 1998.

Kurlansky, Mark. *A Chosen Few: The Resurrection of European Jewry.* New York: Addison-Wesley, 1995.

Kutzik, Alfred. *Social Work and Jewish Values.* Washington, DC: Public Affairs Press, 1959.

Langer, Lawrence. *Admitting the Holocaust.* New Haven: Yale University Press, 1995.

———. *Holocaust Testimonies: The Ruins of Memory.* New Haven: Yale University Press, 1993.

Lappin, Ben. *The Redeemed Children: The Story of the Rescue of War Orphans by the Jewish Community of Canada.* Toronto: University of Toronto Press, 1963.

Lavsky, Hagit. *New Beginnings: Holocaust Survivors in Bergen-Belsen and the British Zone in Germany, 1945–1950.* Detroit: Wayne State University Press, 2002.

Levite, Alter, ed. *A Yizkor Book to Riteve.* Cape Town: Kaplan-Kushlick Foundation, 2000.

Linenthal, Edward. *Preserving Memory.* New York: Columbia University Press, 1995.

Lipstadt, Deborah. *Beyond Belief: The American Press and the Coming of the Holocaust.* New York: Touchstone Books, 1993.

Loescher, Gil, and John Scanlon. *Calculated Kindness: Refugees and America's Half-Open Door, 1945 to the Present.* New York: Free Press, 1986.

Lowenstein, Steven. *Frankfurt on the Hudson: The German-Jewish Community of Washington Heights, 1933–1983.* Detroit: Wayne State University Press, 1985.

Lubove, Roy. *The Professional Altruist: The Emergence of Social Work as a Profession, 1880–1930.* Cambridge, MA: Harvard University Press, 1965.

Marcus, P., and A. Rosenberg. *Healing Their Wounds: Psychotherapy with Holocaust Survivors and Their Families.* New York: Praeger, 1989.

Marrus, Michael. *The Unwanted: European Refugees in the Twentieth Century.* Oxford: Oxford University Press, 1985.

Miller, Judith. *One, by One, by One: Facing the Holocaust.* New York: Simon and Schuster, 1990.

Minkowski, Eugene. "The Psychology of the Deportees." *American OSE Review* 4 (Summer–Fall 1947): 17–22.

Mintz, Alan. *Popular Culture and the Shaping of Holocaust Memory in America.* Seattle: University of Washington Press, 2001.

Moore, Dash Deborah. *At Home in America: Second Generation New York Jews.* New York: Columbia University Press, 1981.

Morris, Robert, and Michael Freund. *Trends and Issues in Jewish Social Welfare in the United States, 1899–1958.* Philadelphia: Jewish Publication Society of America, 1966.

Niewyk, Donald L. *Fresh Wounds: Early Narratives of Holocaust Survivors.* Chapel Hill: University of North Carolina Press, 1998.

Neusner, Jacob. *Strangers at Home: "The Holocaust," Zionism, and American Judaism.* Chicago: University of Chicago Press, 1981.

Novick, Peter. *The Holocaust in American Life.* New York: Houghton Mifflin, 1999.

Ofer, Dalia. *Escaping the Holocaust: Illegal Immigration to the Land of Israel, 1930–44.* Oxford: Oxford University Press, 1999.

Petluck, Ann. "Public Law 414—The McCarran-Walter Act—or the Immigration and Nationality Act of 1952." *Jewish Social Service Quarterly* (May 1953): 421–427.

Poplack, Alvin. *Carved in Granite: Holocaust Memorials in Metropolitan New York Jewish Cemeteries.* New York: Jay Street, 2003.

Portnoy, Deborah. "The Adolescent Immigrant." *Jewish Social Service Quarterly* (September 1948): 268–273.

Proudfoot, M. J. *European Refugees, 1939–1952: A Study in Forced Population Movement.* Evanston: Northwestern University Press, 1956.

Quen, Jacques, and Enc Carlson, eds. *American Psychoanalysis: Origins and Developments.* New York: Brumer/Mazel, 1978.

Rabinowitz, Dorothy. *New Lives: Survivors of the Holocaust Living in America.* New York: Avon, 1977.

Rafael, Mark Lee. *Profiles in American Judaism*. New York: Harpers and Row, 1985.

Rawley, Callman. "The Adjustment of Jewish Displaced Persons." *Journal of Social Casework* (June 1948): 316–321.

Richmond, Mary. *Social Diagnosis*. New York: Russel Sage Foundation, 1917.

———. *What Is Social Casework?* New York: Russel Sage Foundation, 1922.

Richmond, Theo. *Konin*. New York: Pantheon, 1995.

Rischin, Moses. *The Promised City*. Cambridge, MA: Harvard University Press, 1977.

Roberts, Robert W., and Robert H. Nee, eds. *Theories of Social Casework*. Chicago: University of Chicago Press, 1970.

Romalis, Frieda. "Interpreting Current Problems Facing Jews from Overseas." *Jewish Social Service Quarterly* 26 (March 1950): 373–376.

Rontsch, Isaac. "The Present State of the Landsmanschaftn," *Jewish Social Service Quarterly* 15 (March 1939): 360–378.

Rosensaft, Menachem, ed. *Life Reborn: Jewish Displaced Persons, 1945–1951*. Conference proceedings, "Life Reborn" conference, Washington, DC, 14–17 January 2000. Washington, DC: United States Holocaust Memorial Museum, 2001.

Roskies, David. *Against the Apocalypse: Responses to Catastrophe in Modern Jewish Culture*. Cambridge, MA: Harvard University Press, 1984.

Rybal, I., L. Kronick, and I. Shmulewitz, eds. *The Bialystoker Memorial Book*. Brooklyn, NY: Empire Press, 1982.

Sachar, Howard. *The Course of Modern Jewish History*. New York: Vintage. 1990.

Sarna, Jonathan. *The American Jewish Experience*. New York: Holmes and Meier, 1997.

Saunders, Ronald. *Shores of Refuge: A Hundred Years of Jewish Emigration*. New York: Schocken Books, 1988.

Scherman, N., and M. Zlotowitz, eds. *The Complete Artscroll Siddur*. New York: Mesorah, 2001.

Schneiderman, S. L., ed. *Warsaw Ghetto: A Diary by Mary Berg*. New York: Fischer, 1945.

Schulman, Elias. "A Survey and Evaluation of Yizkor Books." In *Jewish Book Annual*, vol. 25. Philadelphia: Jewish Publication Society, 1967–1968.

Schwartz, Jan. "A Library of Destruction and Hope: The First One Hundred Volumes of Poylishe Yidntum, 1946–1954." Paper presented at the Association of Jewish Studies Conference, Los Angeles, 15 December 2002.

Schwartz, Leo W. *The Redeemers: A Saga of the War Years, 1942–1952*. New York: Farrar, Straus and Young, 1953.

Schwartz, Rosaline, and Susan Milamed. *A Guide to YIVO's Landsmanschaftn Archive*. New York: YIVO, 1986.

Sebald, Winfried G. *The Emigrants*. New York: New Directions, 1997.

Shandler, Jeffrey. *While America Watches: Televising the Holocaust*. Oxford: Oxford University Press, 2000.

Shapiro, Edward. *A Time for Healing: American Jewry Since WWII*. Baltimore: Johns Hopkins University Press, 1992.

Sherman, Sanford. "Differentials in Case Work with Newcomers." *Jewish Social Service Quarterly* 24 (March 1948): 274–285.

Siebold, Janet. "Helping New Americans." *Journal of Social Casework* 30 (February 1949): 71–77.

Slatt, Vincent. "Nowhere to Go: Displaced Persons in Post-V-E-Day Germany." *Historian* 66 (Spring 2002): 275–294.

Sodarsky, M., and U. Katzenelenbogen, eds. *Lithuania*. Vol. 1. New York: Futuro Press, 1951.

Soyer, Daniel. *Jewish Immigrant Associations and American Identity in New York, 1880–1939*. Cambridge, MA: Harvard University Press, 1997.

Spaulding, Rita. "Techniques in Casework with Displaced Persons," *Journal of Social Casework* 31 (February 1950): 70–77.

Steinberg, Stephen. *The Ethnic Myth: Race, Ethnicity, and Class in America*. Boston: Beacon Press, 1989.

Stouffer, Samuel. *Measurement and Prediction: Studies in Social Psychology in World War II*. Princeton: Princeton University Press, 1950.

Suedfeld, Peter, ed. *Light from the Ashes: Social Science Careers of Young Holocaust Refugees and Survivors*. Ann Arbor: University of Michigan Press, 2001.

Tartakower, Arieh, and Kurt Grossman. *The Jewish Refugee*. New York: Institute of Jewish Affairs of the American Jewish Congress and World Jewish Congress, 1944.

Tenenbaum, Joseph E. *Legacy and Redemption: A Life Renewed*. Washington, DC: United States Holocaust Memorial Museum, 2005.

Urofsky, Melvin. *American Zionism from Herzl to the Holocaust*. Garden City, NY: Anchor Press, 1976.

Vernant, Jaques. *The Refugee in the Postwar World*. New Haven: Yale University Press, 1951.

Warhaftig, Zorach. *Uprooted: Jewish Refugees and Displaced Persons after Liberation*. New York: Institute of Jewish Affairs, 1946.

Wein, Abraham. "Memorial Books as a Source for Research into the History of Jewish Communities in Europe." *Yad Vashem Studies* (Jerusalem: Yad Vashem), 9 (1973): 255–272.

Weinberg, Werner. *Self-Portrait of a Holocaust Survivor*. Jefferson, NC: McFarland, 1985.

Weisser, Michael. *A Brotherhood of Memory: Jewish Landsmanshaften in the New World*. New York: Basic Books, 1985.

Wenger, Beth. *New York Jews and the Great Depression*. Syracuse: Syracuse University Press, 1998.

White, Lyman Cromwell. *300,000 New Americans: The Epic of a Modern Immigrant-Aid Service*. New York: Harper, 1957.

Wischnitzer, Mark. *Visas to Freedom: The History of HIAS*. New York: World, 1956.

Wyman, David. *The Abandonment of the Jews: America and the Holocaust, 1941–1945*. New York: Random House, 1986.

———. *Paper Walls: America and the Refugee Crisis, 1938–1941*. Amherst: University of Massachusetts Press, 1968.

Wyman, David, and Rafael Medoff. *A Race against Death: Peter Bergson, America, and the Holocaust*. New York: New Press, 2002.

Wyman, Mark. *DPs: Europe's Displaced Persons, 1945–1951*. Ithaca: Cornell University Press, 1989.

Yablonka, Hanna. *Survivors of the Holocaust: Israel after the War*. New York: New York University Press, 2000.

Young, James. *The Texture of Memory: Holocaust Memorials and Meaning.* New Haven: Yale University Press, 1993.

Zertal, Idith. *From Catastrophe to Power: Holocaust Survivors and the Emergence of Israel.* Berkeley and Los Angeles: University of California Press, 1998.

Unpublished Material

Abrams, Sylvia Bernice Fleck. "Searching for a Policy: Attitudes and Policies of Non-governmental Agencies toward the Adjustment of Jewish Immigrants of the Holocaust Era, 1933–1953, as Reflected in Cleveland, Ohio." PhD diss., Case Western Reserve University, 1988.

Glantz, Beatrice. "Factors in the Adjustment of New American Children in Their First Year in the United States." Master's thesis, Simmons College, 1950.

Newman, Roberta. "Delayed Pilgrims: The Radio Programs of the United Service for New Americans, 1947–48." Master's thesis, New York University, 1996.

Rosenberg, Joshua, ed. "Twice Born." Writings from the New Americans Unit, Camp Kingswood, Bridgton, ME, Summer 1948.

Steinfeld, Paul. "Problems of Jewish Children Survivors of European Concentration Camps in American Foster Homes: A Preliminary Study of Forty-six Cases." Master's thesis, Columbia University, 1947.

INDEX

Page numbers in italics indicate illustrations.

ABOUT THE AUTHOR

Beth B. Cohen was one of the first students to receive a Ph.D. in Holocaust history from Clark University's Strassler Family Center for Holocaust and Genocide Studies. Recently she spent six months as a Life Reborn fellow at the U.S. Holocaust Memorial Museum. She currently resides and teaches in Los Angeles, California.